Jackson
UNVEILED

Jackson
UNVEILED

The complete story of the
KING OF POP

By James Fletcher, Jan Disley
and Ros Wynne-Jones

© Haynes Publishing, © Daily Mirror, 2009

The right of James Fletcher, Jan Disley and Ros Wynne-Jones to be identified as the authors of this Work has been asserted by them in accordance with the Copyright, Designs & Patents Act 1988.

First published in 2009. A catalogue record for this book is available from the British Library

ISBN: 978-1-844259-39-7

Published by Haynes Publishing, Sparkford, Yeovil, Somerset BA22 7JJ, UK

Tel: 01963 442030 Fax: 01963 440001 Int. tel: +44 1963 442030 Int. fax: +44 1963 440001

E-mail: sales@haynes.co.uk Website: www.haynes.co.uk

Haynes North America Inc., 861 Lawrence Drive, Newbury Park, California 91320, USA

All images © Mirrorpix

Creative Director: Kevin Gardner

Packaged for Haynes by Green Umbrella Publishing

Printed and bound in by J F Print Ltd., Sparkford, Somerset

The publishers and authors would like to thank the following people for their help in producing Jackson Unveiled.

Richard Havers and Elizabeth Stone for their editorial skills. Kev and Vanessa at Green Umbrella and the team at JF Print for working around the clock to design and print the book.

All at the Daily Mirror and MirrorPix for help in getting the project moving so swiftly and finally all at Haynes Publishing and in particular Marjolein for the support for the project from start to finish.

Contents

The King of Pop is dead

"I'm not like other boys. I mean I'm different..."

Michael Jackson, video for *Thriller*, 1982

Where were you when Michael Jackson died?

On June 25, 2009, in the city at the beating heart of show business, a world icon became a lost legend. Pop's controversial Peter Pan had resisted old age in the most dramatic way – dead of a heart attack at the age of 50.

This was a 21st-century death, catalogued on Twitter, Facebook and Google, news flying around the globe in nanoseconds as cyberspace was swamped with millions of blogs, texts and tweets.

In the United States, fans began gathering at Jackson's rented home in Holmby Hills, and outside UCLA hospital.

In Britain, Glastonbury festival briefly stood still. There were flowers left in tribute outside the Lyric Theatre in London, where *Thriller Live* was showing.

A mass Moonwalk was organized on Facebook to take place at Liverpool Street station. The BBC filmed a special last-minute scene, working in news of Jackson's death to the TV soap *EastEnders*.

Fans, wearing single white gloves gathered at the O2 Arena, the planned venue for his 'This is It!' comeback tour.

Around the world, in sunny Swedish squares and French highrise towers, Michael Jackson's fans began vigils in memory of their idol. Within hours, *Thriller*, the world-class album that has never been outsold, and the song 'Man In The Mirror' were once more at number one.

Michael Jackson's career had begun where it had ended – at the top of the charts.

Ten days later, the worldwide scenes were more appropriate to the deaths of popes and princesses. The extraordinary memorial service caused one billion people to pause in their daily lives, transfixed at the television set and computer screen.

As the legendary poet Maya Angelou wrote for Michael's funeral: "Today in Tokyo, beneath the Eiffel Tower, in Ghana's Blackstar Square, in Johannesburg, and Pittsburgh, in Birmingham, Alabama and Birmingham, England we are missing Michael Jackson. But we do know we had him and we are the world."

Whatever Jackson was accused of, he touched a nerve of grief in millions of people. With the massive outpouring of emotion that flickered across Britain in the wake of Diana's death, psychologists believed people were grieving for their own lost loved ones. With Jackson, it was as if he came to symbolise every tortured talent and every broken child. However frail and faltering, his lost voice still spoke to millions, even in death.

Even without such a dramatic ending, on the verge of a brilliant comeback and a sellout tour, Jackson's story would still be an astonishing modern day fable.

A rollercoaster of soaring highs and crashing lows, it is both the story of stunning, innovative talent, and the corruption of that talent by the abuse he experienced in childhood.

The damage he suffered at the fists of his brutal father, Joseph Jackson is not unique. But combined with extraordinary wealth, power and unparalleled celebrity, it created a man who remained a terrified child all his life – and a monstrous manipulator capable of his own abuses of power.

In the *Thriller* video, acclaimed again and again as the best pop has ever produced, Jackson says: "I'm not like other boys... you see, I'm different..." A split second later, he turns into a werewolf – a misunderstood creature that cannot help what it becomes.

Thriller did transform Jackson – into a global celebrity, entering a stratospheric level of fame inhabited only by legends like the Beatles and Elvis Presley.

But, hailed as the King of Pop, his link to the real world – and his distant subjects – became ever weaker. Slowly, the sweet, gentle-faced Michael Jackson began to disappear behind a mask of plastic surgery.

He became, if not a werewolf, a man whose humanity was slipping away.

"The stage is where I live," Jackson once said. "That's where I was born. That's where I feel safe."

Away from the stage, the headlines over more than four decades tell their own story – a literally off-the-wall private world of chimps treated as children and children treated as toys, of secret operations and oxygen tents, of surrogate mothers and child abuse allegations.

Michael Jackson was becoming "Wacko Jacko", a man standing on the edge of his own sanity, a pair of dark brown eyes looking out from behind his own increasingly bizarre face.

Slowly, the lurid sexual revelations, the court cases, and his increasingly alarming appearance, had begun to eclipse his genius.

But as preparations for the 'This Is It!' comeback tour started, Michaelmania began again in earnest.

After years of turning up with placards to Jackson's court cases, his army of loyal fans once again had something to celebrate – lining the pavement outside London's O2 venue in the sort of dramatic emotional scenes Jackson inspired his whole life.

Suddenly, it was once again all about Jackson's bewitching music – the hard, lean bass line of 'Billie Jean', the howling madness of *Thriller* and the irresistible disco pop of *Off The Wall*.

In the end, the contradictions of his life are the key to Michael Jackson. He was the child star denied a childhood. A black icon who broke through the colour bar of the music charts and television stations, but who bleached his skin until it was badly damaged. A 50-year-old man who refused to grow up.

A man whose music could be as gentle as his falsetto voice or as dark as the horror movies with which he was obsessed.

So perhaps it is not surprising that the world remains divided on the legacy of Michael Jackson. One man's saint is another man's sinner.

But whatever the world's ultimate verdict on the boy from Gary, Indiana, there is no doubt his compelling life story deserves to be told.

The aim of his book is not to judge Michael Jackson but to tell his extraordinary life story warts and all, acknowledging his flaws as well as his genius, his failings and his gifts.

It starts with his first ever live performance at the age of five in September 1963, at Garnett Elementary School in Gary, Indiana. It ends with his final ever live performance on July 7, 2009 at the Staples Center in Los Angeles.

On that day, the reunion his brothers dreamed of for so many years, was given a final ironic twist, with Michael joining them on stage in a gold casket draped with red roses.

Like one of his own Neverland rides, the story between those two performances is horrifying, amusing, captivating and frightening by turns.

The central tragedy is that Jackson's experiences of childhood cruelty literally beat him out of shape and meant he was never able to enjoy his talent or his fame.

His genius is ultimately tarnished by repeated allegations of child abuse. But his personal biography is also a story of modern celebrity, and as such, a fable of our times.

"This is my final curtain call," Jackson said in March of this year. "I'll see you in July. I love you all."

It wasn't to be.

But there is no doubt that Michael Jackson – now finally living in a perpetual Neverland – will go on to outlive his own myth.

The King of Pop is dead. Long live the King.

CHAPTER ONE

Climb Every Mountain

It is 9am on September 1963, at Garnett Elementary in Gary, Indiana. Rows of parents are watching a special school assembly, smiling indulgently as their children sing their favourite songs.

Then five-year-old Michael Jackson takes to the stage dressed in a white shirt and shorts. His song is 'Climb Ev'ry Mountain' from the *Sound of Music*, and as he begins to sing without accompaniment, a hush falls over the assembly hall.

"Climb ev'ry mountain," Michael sings, "ford every stream.... Follow every rainbow, till you find your dream…"

His mother Katherine, and grandfather, Samuel are moved to tears. His class teacher begins to cry into a tissue. The audience and fellow performers get to their feet in a standing ovation.

"The reaction in the auditorium overwhelmed me," Michael remembers in his autobiography, *Moonwalk*. "The applause was thunderous and people were smiling; some of them were standing.... It was such a great feeling."

For the future King of Pop, it was a sweet first taste of live performance and crowd adulation. But perhaps most significantly, it was also the moment the musical Jackson brothers – Tito, Jackie, Jermaine and Marlon – became the Jackson Five.

At five years old, Michael had already spent almost a year begging to join his older brothers in their band, started after his father Joseph Jackson had discovered a broken string on the guitar he kept locked in the wardrobe.

Michael's nine-year-old brother Tito had been badly beaten for breaking the string and the admission that he and his brothers had been playing the guitar while Joseph was out – but had then shown his father how good he was on the instrument.

Joseph, sensing that his sons' talents might take over where his own dreams of musical stardom had failed, had surprised the family days later by bringing home a bright red, electric guitar. But despite the daily after school rehearsals for Tito, aged 11, Jermaine, 10, Jackie, 12 and Marlon, 6, he had so far refused Michael's pleas to join, saying he was too young.

Michael's mother – who had also watched her young son's concentrated imitations of Jermaine singing James Brown – told Joseph: "I think we have another lead singer". And 12-year-old Jackie told the other boys it was now time for Michael to become "the lead guy".

Born on August 29, 1958 in Gary, an industrial suburb of Chicago on the shores of Lake Michigan, Michael Jackson was given the middle name Joseph after the father he would grow to love and hate in almost equal measure.

The eighth of ten children, one of whom died shortly after birth, his mother remembers him having a "funny-looking head, big brown eyes and long hands."

The family of 11 lived, coincidentally, at 2300 Jackson Street, in a tiny, cramped two-bedroom house "no bigger than a garage" – Michael sharing the middle berth of a triple bunk bed with his brother Marlon all of his early life.

Michael's parents Joseph and Katherine Jackson had met in a whirlwind romance. Their first child, Maureen, nicknamed Rebbie, was born on May 29, 1950, Sigmund Esco, nicknamed Jackie followed May 4, 1951 and Tarino Adaryl or Tito followed two years later October 15, 1953. Then, on December 11, 1954, Jermaine LaJuane was born, followed by La Toya Yvonne on May 29, 1956, and then premature twins Marlon David and Brandon – who died within 24 hours of his birth.

After Michael Joseph came Steven Randall on October 29, 1961 and finally Janet Dameta on May 16, 1966.

The air from the nearby factories was thick enough to make the young Jackson children feel sick. Gangs roamed the streets, crime was high and unemployment was even higher.

The three girls shared a sofa in the living room and Randy slept on a second couch. In the winter the family would gather in the kitchen in front of the open oven for warmth.

With so little coming in, and with such a large family, money was desperately short. Joseph Jackson worked an eight hour shift until midnight as a crane operator at Inland Steel in East Chicago and yet seldom made more than $65 a week – even with extra hours working as a welder and at the potato harvest.

Katherine made ends meet by hand-making all the family's clothes, cooking potatoes a dozen ways and by praying to God – becoming a devout Jehovah's Witness in 1963.

There are very few photographs of the young Jackson family as Joseph and Katherine simply couldn't afford to buy them. They had no telephone for their first five years on Jackson Street and when Jermaine contracted the kidney disease nephritis aged just four, and needed hospital treatment for three weeks the family finances were hit hard.

The financial hardship and uncertainty of employment left Joseph bitterly frustrated. He was a man filled with pride and yet felt he was failing if he was unable to even feed his family.

The only good part about Joseph's life – and the only release from poverty – was through music. His rhythm and blues band, The Falcons – formed with his brother Luther and three friends – performed in small clubs and bars and provided a much needed additional source of revenue for the Jackson family.

Yet, Joseph's abilities were never quite equal to the love and passion he had for music, and ultimately the band failed to make the big time. His guitar was locked away in a cupboard for safekeeping and his anger and bitterness grew.

It was Katherine who would quietly take down the guitar from the high shelf inside the cupboard while Joseph worked long, soul-destroying hours at Inland Steel and the day shift at American Foundries, all the time bemoaning his misfortune, his lack of luck.

Mrs Jackson would gather her children in the living room and they would sing together and country songs like 'Wabash Cannonball', 'The Great Speckled Bird' would fill the air and tumble out onto Jackson Street.

The guitar would be fetched down from the high shelf within the bedroom cupboard and the music, the singing, the laughter and love would fill their tiny home, all the time remaining their secret as Joseph toiled in the sweaty steel works.

The Jackson children were rarely allowed out to play as their parents feared for them in their tough neighbourhood. If they wanted to sing they had each other, Katherine decided. Why did they need to leave the house?

When the television broke they made their own entertainment. Their father's guitar became an even more central part of their lives. Jackie, Tito and Jermaine enjoyed their music so much they couldn't always wait for their mother and instead, as soon as Joseph had left for work they would creep into the bedroom and help themselves.

Tito would play the magical instrument and the three brothers would sing their hearts out, learning new songs and creating their own fun until one day Katherine returned home early and caught the boys with her husband's prized possession.

They froze in terror but need not have worried. Katherine was delighted and having spotted their potential encouraged them to continue.

For months the young Jackson children kept playing – and then disaster struck. Tito broke a string on the guitar.

He put the guitar back into the cupboard and waited. And waited. And then it came. Joseph exploded in a fit of rage. Katherine lied in a desperate bid to protect her children from his anger by claiming she had given the boys permission to use the guitar but her pleas fell on deaf ears.

Joseph tore into Tito, Jermaine and Jackie. It was a beating the boys never forgot and yet that the broken string was the beginning of the musical legend that would become the Jackson Five and foster their younger brother's stratospheric career.

Once Joseph's anger had subsided he went into his son's bedroom. Tito was still crying on his bunk bed but somehow summoned enough courage to blurt the words: "You know I can play that thing, I really can."

Stunned at his young son's audacity Joseph challenged him to prove himself. So he did. He grabbed the guitar and started to play, Jermaine and Jackie sang a little and Joseph just stood and stared.

The truth was Joseph was amazed. He had no idea about his son's secret prior to that bedroom audition but what he now knew was that the musical ability he craved so much was there in abundance, not within him but his sons.

He spent that night deep in thought, his mind racing with what he had just witnessed. Was it real potential? Did his son's really possess genuine talent? Could this be his opportunity to open the door to the music industry, could he potentially live out his own personal dream through the lives of his sons?

Maybe, maybe not. But the following day he returned home from work holding something behind his back. He summoned his three oldest sons together – Jackie, nine, Tito, seven and Jermaine, six – and presented them with a parcel.

Inside was their very own red electric guitar. The smiles from the three Jackson boys were wider than Jackson Street and for once, the entire family were united.

Katherine and Joseph passed on tips to the three youngsters and the rehearsals began and in truth, never really ended. The trio were hardly ever seen without that red guitar while Marlon and Michael would sit in the corner and watch.

The incessant rehearsals alienated the Jackson boys from the rest of the neighbourhood. They didn't mix with other children, a combination of their parents' fear of the gangs that roamed the street, their devotion to their religion and their father's desire to escape Gary, Indiana.

Some of their neighbours would mock, saying the Jacksons felt they were "too good" to mix with the other children. They didn't need to join the singing groups that were springing up around the area. They had their own.

Other youngsters would taunt them from the street, hurling abuse and insults through the open window of their house. But the boys didn't care and their father certainly didn't.

For three hours a night, every night, they practised and their sessions now carried an intensity, a focus, a drive. The boys didn't really care or notice, they were having fun making music – but for Joseph the clock was ticking.

With each passing day he became more and more certain that his sons could indeed deliver his dream. He was determined that his boys could make their mark on the music industry. And that meant a passport out of their tiny two bedroom brick and aluminium home on Jackson Street.

Joseph began spending his meagre earnings on guitars, amplifiers, and microphones. It led to heated arguments with Katherine, but Joseph tried to make a joke of the cheap food at the table.

"I used to tell them we were eating soul food in order to be able to play soul music… Black people were used to struggling to make ends meet."

Marlon joined their Jackson 'group' in 1962, playing the bongos, and singing even though it was clear the five-year-old did not possess the same talent. Katherine insisted that he should be allowed to join his brothers.

Then one day, four-year-old Michael began imitating his brother Jermaine as he sang a James Brown song. Joseph was at work and Katherine could barely contain herself. She waited at the door for her husband to return, describing Michael's performance in detail, and telling exactly how strong and pure his voice had sounded.

In truth, Michael had always stood out from his brothers and sisters. Certainly he shared their love of music. He was often caught singing to the rhythm of the washing machine with a hairbrush acting as his microphone.

"I remember seeing marching bands go down the street," he would later tell Jesse Jackson. "I would remember the rhythm of the band and the beats of the drum. And every sound around me seem to record in my head and start making rhythms and dancing.

"I used to dance to the rhythm of the washing machine. My mother went to the corner store to wash the clothes. I would dance to the rhythm and people would crowd around.

"I remember those kind of stories. They would crowd around pretty much and watch me. Those kind of little things. They are reflections really."

Everyone agreed that Michael was the most sensitive of the Jackson children. But he was also the most defiant – and the only one to stand up to his bullying father.

Joseph regularly turned his rage against the unfairness and hardships of life into violence meted out to his children, but little Michael was the only one who refused to be cowed by the ex-boxer's fists.

The same little boy his mother would laugh at for dancing along to the rhythm of the washing machine faced Joseph's beatings with rebellion.

In response, Joseph's behaviour grew more extreme. One day when Michael was five years old, he knocked him to the ground, bloodied, for no apparent reason.

"That's for whatcha did yesterday," he told Michael. "And tomorrow, I'm gonna get you for what you'll do today."

"But I didn't do nothin' yet," Michael sobbed through his tears.

"Oh, but you will, boy," Joseph said. "You will."

Joseph didn't just beat his children. It wasn't unusual for him to push the youngsters into walls, use a belt, electrical cable, anything that he could get his hands on.

The older boys and girls learned to submit to Joseph's rages. Even when he was just three years old, and midway through a beating, Michael took off a shoe and hurled it at his father. He missed but Joseph exploded.

Marlon later told how Joseph grabbed Michael, held him upside down by one leg and beat him over and over, hitting him on his back and his backside. The screams were deafening and Katherine begged her husband to stop – fearing he would actually kill her son if the beating continued.

Eventually, Joseph relented and released a terrified Michael who ran to his room sobbing, screaming his hatred for Joseph. His words merely relit the touch paper and Joseph followed him to the bedroom, slammed the door shut and then continued his assault.

It was not uncommon for Joseph to lock Michael in a closet for hours as a punishment. He would not tolerate his children's inability to succeed and he would certainly not tolerate any backchat or lack of discipline.

He wanted his children to be winners and in his eyes that meant toughening them up. They would not be weak. They were going to succeed. He would not allow them to fail.

If he saw his sons had carelessly left a window open, Marlon remembers, Joseph would force his way in through the bedroom window wearing a Halloween mask and terrify them with shouts and screams. For many years afterwards, Michael suffered nightmares about being kidnapped from his bedroom.

The violence and discipline was particularly tough for Katherine. She could barely believe that her husband, such a kind and loving man when they first met would discipline her children so frequently and with such violence. It didn't make sense to her how someone could be so kind and gentle and romantic and yet then in a second be such a monster to her children, and at times even to her.

Certainly she knew he was a commanding man who liked to take control. With his power and physique there came a sense of safety. He was good looking, oozed charm and charisma and he made her laugh.

Katherine and Joseph were total opposites. She was soft, reasonable, and romantic while he was hard, explosive and pragmatic yet at some level, despite Joseph's rages, their relationship clearly worked.

Katherine was born near to Russell County, Alabama on May 4, 1930. She was christened Kattie B. Scruse after an aunt although her parents, Prince Albert Scruse and Martha Upshaw, always knew her as Katherine, Kate or Katie.

Prince Scruse worked for the Seminole Railroad and as a tenant cotton farmer, just as his father and his father before had done. Her great-grandfather Kendal

Brown had been a slave for an Alabama family named Scruse, and when he was freed, like many other slaves, he adopted their name as his own. Kendal Brown Scruse also possessed a terrific voice – singing every Sunday in a Russell County church.

Katherine almost died at the age of just 18 months. She was stricken with polio and there was no vaccine in those days. It was not uncommon for children to die or be left severely crippled from the virus. She wore a brace or used crutches until she was 16 and would be hampered with a limp for the rest of her life.

The Scruse family moved to East Chicago, Indiana in 1934 searching for work. Prince Scruse was employed in the steel mills before eventually settling as a Pullman porter with Illinois Central Railroad yet within a year his marriage collapsed and the children moved in with their mother Martha.

Katherine was a shy, introverted child, mainly because of the after effects of polio, but her constant hospital visits provided her school friends with the perfect opportunity to taunt her and she failed to graduate from high school though she did external courses in a desperate and ultimately successful attempt to gain her diploma.

Music was the only real joy in her life. She and her sister Hattie grew up listening to country and western on the radio and were members of the high school orchestra, the church junior band and school choir. She dreamed of a career in show business, initially as an actress but then as a singer.

Joseph Walter Jackson, meanwhile, also grew up dreaming of becoming a musician. Born on July 26, 1929 to Samuel and Chrystal Jackson in Fountain Hill, Arkansas, he was the eldest of five children and moved to Oakland, California with his father when his parents divorced.

When his father remarried, the teenager moved back to live with his mother in Indiana. By eleventh grade he had dropped out of school and started boxing.

When Joseph and Katherine met, it was music that united them. As well as being a talented pianist and clarinet player, Katherine had a soft, soothing and beautiful voice that her son Michael would one day inherit. Joseph like many of his contemporaries loved the blues and he also played guitar.

It was love at first sight. Joseph had previously been married but was quickly divorced and the pair dated and were soon engaged. They married just six months later; it was a whirlwind romance.

They were wed on November 5, 1949, in Crown Point, Indiana. Having come from a broken home Katherine vowed privately that once she was married she would make it work whatever happened.

Jackson biographer J. Randy Taraborrelli claimed in his book *Michael Jackson, the Magic and the Madness* that Joseph once hit his wife Katherine in the face.

He claimed that Katherine warned him she would leave if he ever struck her again. The claims were never substantiated or ever surfaced again.

Michael Jackson grew up in terrible fear of his father. He was constantly looking left and right, over his shoulder, surveying the room before he entered. He was always expecting to be hit or tripped or beaten.

The fear and the intimidation meant he was never able to truly bond with his father. In truth, none of the Jackson children ever really trusted Joseph long after they left the family home.

They would enjoy fishing trips and camping weekends and Joseph taught the boys how to box, but there was always the distance created by their father's unpredictable violence.

Instead, Michael grew closer and closer to his mother whom he adored. He felt safe with Katherine and often recalled that even though she had nine children she made them all feel as if they were the only child.

Her attention, her warmth and her love were unconditional. She taught her children crucial life lessons in kindness and consideration. Michael began to crave the approval of other adults who would love him and not beat him – taking items of his mother's jewellery and give it teachers at Garnett Elementary School as tokens of affection.

Meanwhile, the relationship with Joseph worsened.

Now that Michael had joined the band, his father, far from praising and encouraging his little son, would sit in a chair with a belt in his hands and if his sons "didn't do it the right way, he would tear (them) up, really get (them)".

Michael would never really recover from the violence. In 2003, Michael told Martin Bashir in the documentary, 'Living with Michael Jackson', that things were so bad "I used to throw up whenever I would think of him".

It was to be the defining relationship of his life.

CHAPTER TWO

Chitlin'

It was 1964, as the Jackson Brothers performed in the local Roosevelt Talent Contest in Gary, Indiana, that Michael Jackson revealed his next astonishing talent. This time the audience weren't just captivated by the six-year-old boy's singing, but by his dancing too.

The brothers had already performed the Temptations' 'My Girl' to tumultuous applause, but it was during their second number that Michael started dancing around the stage.

Then, he suddenly kicked off his shoes. It wasn't yet a Moonwalk, but it had the crowd in raptures and the Jacksons won first prize. It was a moment that Michael cherished right up until his death.

"Marlon was a good dancer, maybe better than Mike," Jermaine remembers. "But Mike loved it more. You'd always catch him dancing for himself in the mirror. He'd go off alone and practise, and come back and show us this new step…"

Michael had an uncanny ability to watch someone else dance and immediately be able to pull off the steps – learning whole new routines from watching James Brown on television. Despite his tender years, Michael was soon firmly installed as the Jacksons' choreographer.

Jermaine, now 12, and previously the lead singer in the group, increasingly had to take a back seat and let his little brother run the show. It hurt him deeply, and is believed to have been the trigger for the stutter he developed as he desperately struggled for self-confidence.

Despite his private heartache, Jermaine vowed to support the decision. His ego was bruised but even he could see the talent that Michael possessed was pretty inspiring.

Michael, however, felt exposed by his father's favouritism. Joseph would single him out and tell the other brothers they should follow his lead. It was tough for the youngster, particularly as his brothers were so much older. At the same time his father also singled him out for beatings, using physical punishment to force him towards a perfect performance on stage.

Yet, despite his apparent dislike of Joseph as a father there was no doubting in Michael's mind that Joseph was a brilliant manager. He shaped the young Michael, he created the showman, and put in place the foundations for the superstar his young son was to become.

The Jackson boys, and Michael in particular, were always quick to praise the part their father played in honing their career. He knew how to perform and passed on everything he knew to his young protégés – his experiences, observations and instincts, and the all important way to win an audience.

As the boys progressed, Joseph was determined to spend his every last dime on his sons to ensure they had a chance of succeeding where he had failed. He also began devoting more and more time to driving them to talent shows as far away as in Chicago.

Within months the brothers had won dozens of times and were soon performing on a circuit of bars and strip clubs from Gary to Chicago, often getting home at 5am on a Monday morning to sleep for a couple of hours before school.

If Joseph needed any confirmation that his boys were as talented as he thought, it came from their first ever paid for performance at Mr Lucky's, a nightclub in their hometown. The Jacksons made only around $7 (about £5) from the performance but others quickly followed and the boys were showered with coins and notes from the excited audience.

Word spread around the neighbourhood about the talented Jackson kids, and many local boys would follow them, sometimes even accompanying them on stage.

In 1966, Johnny Porter Jackson joined them as a permanent drummer. Even though he was not related his surname meant he was considered a "cousin" and Ronny Rancifer, a keyboard player came on board to accompany Michael, aged eight, on lead vocals, Tito on guitar, Jermaine on bass, Jackie playing maracas and Marlon singing harmony and dancing.

One day a model named Evelyn Leahy approached Joseph in a Gary shopping mall and suggested a name change, pointing out that the "Jackson Brothers" sounded old-fashioned. Her suggestion was "the Jackson Five" and everyone agreed this should be their new name.

The youngsters played around Gary and travelled to gigs further afield in a Volkswagen bus – sometimes for entire weekends. Joseph was proud of his talented children, and at last they were making money. The boys had pockets full of change that enabled them to buy sweets and all the little luxuries their harsh upbringing had so far denied them.

For her part, Katherine was pleased with the family's success, but began to have deep concerns over the direction the children were heading. As a devoted Jehovah's Witness her religion had taught her that it was the value of what her children were doing that was important, not the money they were making from it.

But by now everyone wanted a piece of the Jackson Five. More and more club dates followed as they hit the so-called chitlin' circuit – tough 2,000-seater theatres in downtown inner city areas like Cleveland, Ohio, Baltimore, Maryland and Washington DC.

There was a lot of competition and often the boys would find themselves on the same bill as established artists including the Four Tops, but mostly the groups were unknowns, all vying for attention and hoping for a break.

For Michael, it was an education. He would stand in the wings and watch the other acts, taking mental notes from every performance that he would use to perfect his own routine.

Of all the performers, he was particularly interested in James Brown. He studied Brown's dance moves and vocal performance and incorporated them in his own routines including the famous manoeuvre of dropping the microphone but catching it before it hit the floor. When Brown performed the moves they won applause and admiration – when a seven-year-old boy copied them on stage they brought the house down.

Encouraged and bullied by Joseph, the boys learned from every one of their performances. They won an amateur talent show at the Regal Theatre in Chicago for three weeks running and their performances improved with every week – in every way they were becoming more professional.

Soon their reputation was spreading and they were being invited to open for the Temptations, the O'Jays, and Jackie Wilson.

Then came the big test. The Apollo Theatre in Harlem, New York, was world-renowned. At that time, it was a venue most black entertainers could only dream of playing. If the audience liked you then you had made it. If not, they threw bottles, food, anything they could get their hands on.

In August 1967, as Michael was turning nine, Jackie was 16, Tito was 13, Jermaine was 12 and Marlon was ten, the Jackson Five brought the house down at the Apollo and were crowned winners of the talent contest. At last, they had truly arrived.

Maybe it was a bit of luck, maybe they had a bit of help from the fabled Tree of Hope, maybe they were just brilliant. They certainly took the Tree of Hope seriously.

The tall elm had once stood in Harlem in front of Connie's Inn where Louis Armstrong had performed and Fats Waller's show *Hot Chocolates* had opened before moving to Broadway. Over the years hundreds of performers would stand under the tree for good luck and it became tradition.

When New York City's Seventh Avenue was widened during road works the tree was uprooted. Bill 'Bojangles' Robinson, who had christened the tree arranged for it to be moved but eventually it was cut down. All that remained was a plaque on Seventh Avenue, south of 132nd Street.

A log from the tree was mounted on a pedestal backstage at the Apollo and it became a tradition for first time performances at the theatre to touch it for good luck. The Jacksons followed suit, in fact Michael, just to be sure, ran back to touch it a second time.

If only it could have all been as glamorous as mythical trees and playing Harlem's most legendary venue. The harsh reality was that to make money the Jackson boys also had to play a wide variety of gigs – including seedy strip joints where men leered at women as they took off their clothes.

Michael was encouraged by his father to crawl under tables and lift up women's skirts and look at their panties during a rendition of soul singer Joe Tex's 'Skinny Legs and All'. Ever the showman, Michael carried out the instructions to the letter to the delight of the crowd. But he found these performances upsetting and confusing.

Katherine, had she known, would never have approved – but Joseph was in his element and enjoyed himself immensely.

As the youngest, Michael struggled the most with these harsh environments; he was only ever comfortable once he was on the stage. Away from it he did not know how to handle himself.

When the boys played the Peppermint Lounge in Chicago there was a peephole in their dressing room with a clear view into the ladies bathroom. The older boys took it in turns to spy on women, but Michael simply wasn't interested. He didn't even understand why he should be.

Later, when Michael was 13 and the Jackson Five performed in London, they found themselves in a dressing room next to theatre star Carol Channing. Marlon realized she was naked. He told his brothers who all took a peep including Michael. Alone amongst the boys, he found her nakedness upsetting.

Meanwhile, the vastly different attitudes of his parents towards sex and sexuality became increasingly confusing for the young Michael. While Katherine the devoted Jehovah's Witness remained at home looking after the younger children, Joseph was thoroughly enjoying his sons' success – and all the trappings that came with it. His sons were too young to make much use of the groupies desperate to get a piece of the Jackson Five. Joseph, in contrast, was only too happy to take them back to his room.

He did little to hide his misdemeanours from his children. It affected all the boys, but Michael in particular was sickened by Joseph's behaviour. Not telling their mother made them complicit in their father's actions, but they couldn't bear to hurt her.

Joseph meanwhile felt as though he had earned his right to behave like a big star. After all, he was the boys' mentor, it was his determination and backing that had bought them success – why shouldn't he be allowed to enjoy it?

Katherine, in stark contrast, never once strayed. She remained fiercely loyal even when she began to suspect what her husband might be getting up to on his travels. Her quiet discretion only made the bond between her and the children stronger, while widening the gap between them and their father.

Such was the boys' success at the Apollo that Joseph was convinced that they were maybe even better than he thought. In 1968 he made the brave decision to go part-time at Inland Steel and even though his earnings dropped to $5,100, rather than his usual $8,000-$10,000, he was quickly proved right.

The Jacksons started making $600 per performance and finally Joseph could provide properly for his family. Riches the family could only dream of began arriving in the newly redecorated home – a new colour television, as well as new clothes for his wife.

To keep building on the boys' success there were the daily rehearsals, which became increasingly pressured and intense – so much was now riding on their performances.

The greatest pressure of all rested on Michael as the front man and rising star, and the relationship between Michael and his father quickly took a significant downhill turn. Beatings followed mistakes, and Michael was always the one in the firing line.

Then, one day, Joseph insisted Michael execute a particular dance step and when he refused, he smacked his nine-year-old son across the face with such force he knocked him to the floor.

Michael began to cry but stood his ground. As his father stepped forward and raised his hand to continue the assault the youngster warned him that if he hit him again that would be the last time he ever sang for the Jackson Five. His father lowered his hand.

Despite Michael's threat the beatings resumed; if anything they worsened. If any one of them did something wrong during a rehearsal they would receive a beating via a belt, a switch or even a wire cord from a refrigerator. His father just for turning up late for rehearsal once pushed Michael into a drum kit.

One person who had clearly had enough of the culture of bullying at Jackson Street was Rebbie. She had a fantastic voice and Joseph had hoped she too would consider a career in show business but like her mother she was a devoted Jehovah's Witness and considered her course in life was best served bringing up a family.

In 1968 aged just 18 years old she announced she was marrying Nathaniel Brown, a Jehovah's Witness and they were moving to Kentucky. Her mother Katherine was delighted but Joseph was furious. Despite the arguments Rebbie got her way though Joseph had the final word by refusing to give her away.

While Michael's brothers decided their best course of action was to surrender to their father's beatings Michael fought back. And the more he fought back, the more he was singled out.

"I may be young," Michael would tell the crowds who turned up to watch the Jackson Five, "but I do know what the Blues are all about…"

CHAPTER THREE

Steeltown

Newly signed to Steeltown Records, the Jackson Five took part in their very first photo shoot.

As the family stood around, nine-year-old Michael complained that the shots were going to look more like a family portrait than promotional pictures.

His father Joseph agreed to allow his youngest son to rearrange the line-up, placing himself at the front on one knee

The Steeltown executives had to agree, the new pictures were perfect – and it quickly dawned on the professionals that the exciting, young lead singer of their new band was much more than that.

"It was as if he had been a superstar in another life," one executive said later.

Gordon Keith, Steeltown's owner, had had no hesitation in signing the Jackson Five to a limited record deal after yet another talent show success at Beckman Junior High in Gary.

Steeltown's interest in the boys was the start of their professional career. It might have been a small, local label, but it put the boys into a studio for the first time and gave them the chance of making their first record.

At their first recording session, Michael's headphones covered his small ears and came halfway down his neck but he didn't care. The boys were given back-up singers and even a horn section to accompany them on two singles that were released on Steeltown in 1968 – 'Big Boy' backed with 'You've Changed' and 'We Don't Have To Be Over 21 (to Fall in Love)' backed with 'Jam Session'.

The two records may not have been the smash hits the boys dreamed of but it hardly mattered. The moment the family gathered around the radio to listen to their song being played they knew they were now proper musicians, and on their way to fame, fortune and success.

Meanwhile, Joseph was always looking to get the band to the next level. With this in mind, he met young white lawyer Richard Arons in New York and after a brief meeting appointed him co-manager. Joseph believed it would be beneficial to 'Team Jackson' to have a white lawyer on board and the pair began seeking additional concert bookings.

His next step was to send a tape with songs of the Jackson Five to Berry Gordy, the legendary President of Motown – but there was no reaction. Even after singer Gladys Knight arranged for the label's executives to watch the boys at the Regal Theater in Chicago the interest remained lukewarm.

But when they opened for Bobby Taylor and the Vancouvers at Chicago's High Chaparral Club their luck began to change. Bobby Taylor was mightily impressed. So much so he telephoned Ralph Seltzer, head of Motown's creative department and head of the legal division to tell him of their talent.

Seltzer was unsure. There was a buzz about the Jackson brothers but the boys were so young – would their voices change, would they stick at it?

Finally, he invited them to Detroit for an audition, arranging to film it for Berry Gordy, and promised to personally forward it to the boss in Los Angeles if he thought it was worth it.

The audition was fixed on the same day as the boys were due to be interviewed in New York for a television programme, but to Joseph's mind there was no competition.

Motown Records was music. They had created what they had dubbed, "the Sound of Young America," selling millions upon millions of records. Artists signed to the label read like a who's who of popular music as hit record followed hit record.

The Supremes, the Temptations, the Miracles, the Four Tops, Stevie Wonder, Marvin Gaye and Tammi Terrell were all household names – their songs were anthems for a whole generation. Motown was the home of timeless classics and that was exactly what Joseph Jackson wanted for the Jackson Five.

Berry Gordon Junior was seen as a maverick. Yet his visionary style of leadership had been rewarded again and again as he plucked young black hopefuls from the streets and turned them into superstars. He ensured his talented artists were surrounded by the very best in terms of songwriters, producers and arrangers.

Even though there were rumours about Motown's association with the mob and criticism levelled at Berry's style of leadership – many artists had absolutely no idea how much money they were making for the label – every black singer or band wanted to be signed by the label; signing to Motown put you on the road to international stardom.

So on July 23, 1968 the Jackson family loaded their Volkswagen mini-bus with all of their equipment for the drive to "Hitsville", the Detroit headquarters of Motown. It was the most important day of their lives.

On the way Joseph told the boys to remember there were only winners and losers in this life – and no son of his was going to be a loser.

When they arrived, Joseph was furious to discover that Berry wouldn't personally be at the audition – but Seltzer, a tall white man with an intimidating appearance, assured him that the boss would be sent a tape of the performance.

As the family's equipment was loaded into the studio, Seltzer tried to put the boys at ease. But as eight more Motown executives took their places armed with a notepad and pen, it was hard for them to be anything but nervous. The men in suits appeared bored at the prospect of listening to a band of young boys and it was tough to keep focused.

Michael announced to the silent audience that their first song would be James Brown's 'I Got the Feeling'. Then counted his brothers in – Tito on guitar, Jermaine on bass and Johnny Jackson on drums began to play – before he kicked in with the vocal.

Michael easily commanded the small stage, imitating Brown, dancing across the floor and screaming his heart out. Meanwhile, the Motown executives remained motionless. They didn't even applaud at the end of the performance, frantically making notes instead.

Michael thanked them anyway before introducing the band as he did in their live shows, before launching into their second number, 'Tobacco Road'. Still no reaction.

Michael again thanked the executives as if they were a live audience and then introduced Smokey Robinson's 'Who's Loving You', a Motown song.

Again there was no applause but by now it was obvious that the attitude of the Motown executives in that studio now very different from the way they had felt when they had walked in.

Seltzer thanked the boys for auditioning but gave little else away. He did however insist that the Jacksons stay in a nearby hotel for two days while they waited for a decision. It wasn't a long wait.

Berry was sent the black and white film and having watched it called Seltzer with his orders.

Three days after their audition Joseph met Seltzer at Motown's office and he explained that Berry wanted to sign the boys. He insisted the Jackson Five could be huge with the backing of Motown. He talked of Berry's genius and then produced the label's standard nine-page contract. A real, genuine, record contract with Motown. Joseph could hardly believe his eyes.

Seltzer had barely begun talking Joseph through the contract before the pair clashed on the very first clause. The agreement was for seven years and that was too long for Joseph. He wanted one year even though Seltzer patiently explained they needed seven years to properly develop a new artist.

Joseph stood his ground and Seltzer was left with no option but to telephone Berry in Los Angeles. He explained the problem and then handed the phone to Joseph. Joseph was adamant, seven years was too long and that was that.

Berry insisted he wanted the boys and if that was the deal clincher then so be it. The contract was rewritten, stating the group was only contracted for one year.

The boys who had been waiting out in the corridor for two hours were summoned into the office to be told the news. They had a contract with Motown. They hugged each other and jumped in the air. the Jackson Five had a record deal with Motown Records and they were going to be superstars.

At Michael Jackson's memorial service, Berry would tell the hushed auditorium of the Staples Center: "Michael Jackson was ten years old when he and his brothers auditioned for me in Motown in Detroit that July day in 1968, and blew us all away.

"The Jackson Five were just amazing, and little Michael's performance was way beyond his years. This little kid had an incredible knowingness about him... he sung a Smokey Robinson song called 'Who's Lovin' You'.

"He sang it with the sadness and passion of a man who'd been living the blues and heartbreak his whole life. And as great as Smokey sang it, I thought Michael was better."

In the audience of Michael's memorial, Smokey smiled sadly.

"I went to Smokey and said, 'Hey man I think he got you on that one!'. Smokey said: 'Me too!' That was Motown.

"Motown was built on love and competition and sometimes the competition got in the way of the love but the love always won out." The Motown contract had been explained to Joseph but he hadn't actually read it, and neither had any of his sons. Still, they all signed. Even though their signatures were not legally required as the boys were still minors it was a way of making them feel part of the Motown family. They each signed one by one with Joseph countersigning as their parent.

In fact, even though the deal was only for one year Clause Five stated The Jackson Five would be unable to record for another label "at any time prior to the expiration of five years from the expiration or termination of this agreement". In other words, regardless of the one-year deal the Jacksons were tied up in legal knots for at least six years.

The contract also stated that Motown was under no obligation to record or promote the group for five years, Motown would choose all the songs and they would be recorded until Motown were satisfied.

Neither was Motown under an obligation to release any recording and the group would only be paid $12.50 for every song they released – known as a "master" recording. That meant the boys could potentially record dozens of songs without receiving any payment.

Even when they did get paid it wouldn't be very much. Motown's standard terms meant that artists received a 2.7 per cent royalty rate based on a wholesale price (less all the taxes and packaging) of released records. That was fine for Marvin Gaye as a solo artist, but the Jacksons had to split it five ways, meaning each of the boys would only receive just one-fifth of six per cent of 90 per cent of the wholesale price.

In short, Michael would be paid under half of a penny for any single and about two cents per album released.

There was another clause regarding the costs for recording sessions – whether a song was released or not these expenses would be recouped from the royalties generated by sales of the records that were released.

Given that the Jackson Five recorded hundreds of studio tracks this made it virtually impossible to make any money from the records they released.

Another clause stated that if Michael or any of his brothers left the group they would lose the right to say they had been a member of the Jackson Five. Motown also now owned the name Jackson 5 and Jackson Five.

Had Joseph read and understood or taken advice of the consequences of the contract, or shown them to co-manager and lawyer Richard Arons, most of these issues might have been resolved.

Nevertheless, it was a contract – and not just any contract either. It was a piece of paper signing the Jackson Five to Motown Records, and it meant that as of July 26, 1968 the Jackson Five were truly on their way.

CHAPTER FOUR

Motown

Shortly before Christmas 1968, the Jacksons were invited to perform at a special party hosted by Berry Gordy at his impressive Detroit estate.

If the Jackson boys were overawed by their surroundings – which included a swimming pool, theatre, bowling alley and even a marble ballroom – they were even more overwhelmed by the guest list.

The Jacksons could still barely believe they were signed to the same label as Gladys Knight and the Pips, Smokey Robinson, the Temptations and Diana Ross, but that first Motown party put them among their heroes as equals.

Diana Ross and others watched on as Berry's latest signings performed – and they were impressed. Diana took an instant liking to Michael. Afterwards, the boys were introduced to her and she informed them she would soon be working with them.

But things progressed slowly. The boys still had to attend school all week, recording only at the weekends. They grew ever more impatient to release a record. So did Berry Gordy, as the signing of the Jackson Five had been a far more expensive process than he had envisaged.

Firstly, Motown had had to pay Steeltown Records to release the band from their existing contract. Gordy had been paying for studio time and wanted to start seeing a return, yet Bobby Taylor, Motown's legendary producer still did not believe they were ready. the Jackson Five didn't blow Gordy away, but he remained enthralled by the prospect of developing Michael's talent.

A year after that initial audition, Berry summoned the band to Los Angeles and told them he wanted them to relocate.

A few weeks later, half the Jackson family moved to the Tropicana hotel on Santa Monica Boulevard in Hollywood, leaving Katherine in Gary with Janet, Randy and La Toya.

The Tropicana was hardly the high life the family had dreamed of. But even though the downmarket hotel was frequented by pimps and prostitutes, it was still Hollywood.

Once in Los Angeles, Berry took the Jacksons to meet Diana Ross for a second time – on a special visit to her Hollywood home. She told the boys that from now on it was her mission to turn them into superstars.

She was going to work with them, starting with a performance by the Jacksons for her friends and specially invited members of the media. The Jackson Five show was about to hit the ground running.

That show on August 11, 1969, was the launch pad for a whole family's aspirations and the start of a career that even Joseph Jackson would find staggering. It was also the Jackson's first introduction to the murky world of Public Relations, or "spin".

The invite talked of the "sensational eight-year-old Michael Jackson" and yet Michael had already turned ten.

Not any more. Michael was told that from now on he was eight. In fact all of the group were officially two years younger than their actual age. It would also be known from here on that Diana Ross was responsible for discovering the Jacksons even though that honour officially belonged to Bobby Taylor.

After the concert they were interviewed by members of the media and, even when questioned about their age, the Jacksons quickly learned to play the media game.

These were happy times for the Jackson boys, who found in Berry Gordy a kindly mentor a world away from their father's cruel rages.

"We competed on everything and in California we had a baseball game every week, the Jacksons versus the Gordys," Berry recalled at Michael's funeral.

"Unfortunately for us Tito and Jackie were big home run hitters, they would knock the ball out of the park but then, so was my son little Berry. I am not going to tell you who won most of the games but I will tell you the Gordys cried a lot!

"Even though little Michael was the catcher for the Jacksons and missed a lot of balls we still cried a lot.

"We swam and we joked and we played games and when Michael performed his songs you could feel the happiness in his soul because that is what he loved to do."

In an interview with video channel VH1, Michael told how despite some friendly rivalries, the Motown family welcomed the Jackson brothers into their hearts, and into their lives.

"Marvin Gaye used to come to my house at least twice a week to play basketball with my brothers," he said. "Stevie Wonder would come by for gatherings and parties, and I would go to the Supremes' house and Diana Ross would invite the girls over and it was really sincerely one happy family.

"We would have a baseball team where we played against one another, and I was just really little but they let me bat, and it was really a happy family and I do miss all of them – even the Temptations, they would come over to my house all the time."

Despite this rare sunny chapter in the brothers' young lives, they were still struggling to find the hit record they needed to showcase their undoubted talent.

Bobby Taylor produced track after track and the music was definitely good. It was just that it was missing that little something. Berry decided it was time to bring in Deke Richards.

Deke was part of the Motown writing team known as the Clan. He had a close relationship with Berry, even having a special telephone number for his exclusive use. He had been working on a record for Gladys Knight and the Pips with two talented writers, Freddie Perren and Fonce Mizell.

They cut an instrumental version of a song and when he played it for Berry the boss suggested he give it to the Jacksons. They tweaked with the record and then discussed the idea with the youngsters, who immediately loved it.

The Motown team spent hours working on the record with the band recording and re-recording while they worked tirelessly to develop Michael's vocals. Such was the length of time it took to record,

Berry wondered if it would end up being the most expensive record Motown ever produced.

On October 2, 1969, the final mix of their song was completed. It was worth the wait.

While the initial impact of 'I Want You Back' was modest, entering the Billboard's Top 100 at just No. 90, Motown's radio pluggers were determined to get it a decent airing on local radio.

Ten weeks later, the work behind the scenes paid off as the track shot to No. 1.

The record went on to sell more than 2 million copies in America and 4 million overseas – including reaching No. 2 in the UK, remaining on the charts for 13 weeks.

Michael was clearly the star of the show and already he was receiving preferential treatment. On October 1, 1969 he moved into Diana Ross's home while his brothers and father remained in Hollywood hotels.

It was hoped Michael would benefit from Diana's incredible talent. He would study her music, the way she moved, monitor her incredible work ethic and during their time together develop an interest in art and culture. It was all a million miles away from his life in Gary, Indiana.

The rest of the Jacksons were also treated to a makeover with new clothes and serious attention to their Afro hairstyles. Even though some of their outfits were wild and colourful, it certainly made them stand out.

Their new image was introduced to the world on October 18, 1969, when they made their first ever appearance on national television, as guests on the Hollywood Palace hosted by Diana Ross.

Ironically, given their new make-over, the clothes they wore for that appearance were actually bought by Joseph and Katherine Jackson back in Gary,

Indiana, rather than the flash Hollywood boutiques, but it didn't matter. They were singing on television.

But when Diana Ross introduced the band, it was as "Michael Jackson and the Jackson Five" infuriating Joseph as he watched from the wings.

He was adamant that all of his boys were stars and he certainly did not want Michael being singled out. Suddenly it was too late.

In truth, Diana was almost as obsessed with Michael as he was with her. With Katherine hundreds of miles away, she became his surrogate mother, encouraging him before every performance and showering him with praise afterwards.

Meanwhile, even the Motown producers were stunned by Michael's maturity. This was an 11-year-old boy adapting his style to sing about heartbreak, love, and emotions it should have been impossible for him to understand.

Michael has said he had no idea what he was doing in those early days. He claimed it just came from within and if it worked, it worked. Certainly the influences of Diana Ross and the performances of his idol James Brown were rubbing off, but he had also suffered so much at the hands of his father that there was a genuine emotion to his music that was far beyond his years.

"At ten years old he had passion," Berry Gordy said at Michael's funeral. "He had passion to be the greatest entertainer in the world and he was willing to work so hard to do whatever it needed to become the undisputed 'King of Pop', the world over.

"Off stage he was shy, soft spoken and childlike. But when he took the stage in front of his screaming fans he turned into another person. He became a master, a take no prisoners show man. It was like kill or be killed."

To the Jacksons' relief, the family now relocated to a house in Los Angeles. Katherine, La Toya, Janet and Randy left Jackson Street and flew for the very first time to their new home at 1601 Queens Road, a little way north of West Sunset Boulevard. Michael left Diana Ross's home to rejoin his family and was waiting for his mother when she arrived. It was an emotional reunion.

Katherine had never seen anything like their new home; neither did she believe they needed such a mansion to live in, and found their new lifestyle hard to accept at first. In the end, she realized that the only thing that really mattered was that she had her boys back. The family were reunited.

When Motown released the boys' first album *Diana Ross Presents The Jackson Five* it was a massive hit. But, increasingly, not everyone in the family was pleased with the direction in which the band was heading.

In particular, Tito and Jermaine were furious that they were pictured on the front cover holding their instruments but had not actually played on the record. The slick machine that was Motown had decided they were simply not yet good enough to record and instead used their own accomplished musicians. In truth this was nothing unusual but for the teenagers it felt like a slap in the face.

With all the half-truths that were starting to surround the band, the sleeve note for "Diana Ross presents…." makes for particularly hollow reading.

"Honesty has always been a special word for me – a special idea," it says. "But when I think of my own personal idea of honest, I think of something being straight out, all there, on the table – the way it is…

"That's how I feel about The Jackson Five – five brothers by the name of Jackson whom I discovered in Gary, Indiana. They've got great talent. And above all they are honest.'"

The line between outright lies and public relations was growing more blurred by the moment. But that was the Motown way.

And the Motown way was paying dividends. By December 1969, the boys were guests on the high profile *Ed Sullivan Show* – his was the show on which the Beatles first appeared on American TV. The Jacksons were similarly a smash hit. Motown also knew they needed a smash hit as a follow-up to 'I Want You Back'.

ABC was born out of the same chords used in the chorus of 'I Want You Back' and was also a collaboration between Deke Richards, Fonce Mizell and Freddie Perren.

Michael in particular loved the track and it shot straight to the top of the *Billboard* charts, knocking the Beatles' 'Let It Be' off the number one spot by selling more than 2 million copies.

They followed it with 'The Love You Save', giving the Jackson Five three No. 1 singles with their first three releases – the first time that had ever happened in musical history.

In five months the Jackson Five had become a phenomenon. Arriving one day at Philadelphia airport, the boys were mobbed by 3,500 screaming girls.

Their second album *ABC* was a massive hit selling 867,756 copies. The Jacksons were selling out record-breaking concerts, and even released their first ballad, 'I'll Be There', which stayed at No. 1 for five weeks in America, reaching No. 4 in the UK and selling more than 2.5 million copies worldwide.

On January 31, 1971 Joseph and his family achieved possibly their proudest moment so far when they were invited to return home to Gary, Indiana and perform two concerts at Westside High School. Once shunned and taunted by their own neighbours, their former community now welcomed them home as heroes.

More than 15,000 fans came to watch the Jackson Five perform and then Mayor Hatcher took them to their former home on Jackson Street where a special sign had been erected – then onto the city hall where the boys were each presented with individual keys to the city.

Four months later, back in California, Katherine and Joseph bought a large estate at 4641 Hayvenhurst Avenue in the Encino area of Los Angeles, which was home to many other celebrities. They paid $250,000 for the property and still live there today. Joseph also held onto the family home in Gary, Indiana, which remains part of the Jackson property portfolio.

In the days after Michael's death in June 2009 both homes became a focal point for Jackson fans to pay their respects to the King of Pop.

To buy the place in Encino, Joseph had to borrow $100,000 as a down payment against his sons' future earnings. Then, the entire family moved into the two-acre plot in the exclusive community in Southern California.

This house was a world away from Jackson Street. The grounds were filled with citrus trees and exotic plants; there were servants and even a guesthouse. There was an Olympic-sized swimming pool to swim and relax in, a badminton court, and the drive was lined with flash cars.

Joseph and Katherine moved the entire band in. Even with six bedrooms and five bathrooms it was still a busy place but it was at least a fun house to live in. This was the life that Joseph had always dreamed about for his family.

Katherine was not as happy. She appreciated her new home but she missed her real home back in Gary and she missed her friends. The sheer size of the property also left some of the boys unhappy, noticeably Michael. They had spent all of their lives living on top of one another, now they had huge rooms and space. Too much space.

Meanwhile, even his favourite space – the stage – was becoming unsafe. As the Jacksons' career continued its meteoric rise, the boys hardly ever made it to the end of a concert as fans raced on to the stage in a desperate bid to get close to their heroes.

When the audience stormed the stage at Madison Square Garden in August 1971 a terrified Michael was still just 12 years old.

Away from the stage the Jackson boys were still exactly that. Boys. They made their own fun during the hours spent touring America playing games and practical jokes. It was their only real chance to be children, and then only when their minder or security guards were sleeping.

Michael was feeling even more pressured than usual – but there was even more pressure to come.

Joseph Jackson had become fascinated by Donny Osmond. He was the youngest member of the Osmond Brothers and his 1971 single 'Sweet and Innocent' secured his status as a teen idol. His face was on the front cover of magazines and Joseph realized Michael had the potential to follow in his footsteps.

Always seeking a way to make even more money, Joseph also saw that a parallel solo career for Michael could be highly lucrative, attacking the singles and album charts on two fronts.

Michael Jackson's 'Got To Be There' was released in October of that year breaking into the top five in both America and the UK, and selling more than 1.5 million copies.

This success was followed in the winter of 1972 with the release of two more solo singles, 'Rockin' Robin' which peaked at No. 2 in the charts and then 'Ben', a song which still defines Michael Jackson to this day.

'Ben' was a song about boy who befriends a pet rat. It accompanied a film of the same name produced in part by Bing Crosby and it sold a staggering 1.7 million copies. It was also Oscar nominated. Michael's loneliness seemed to ooze from every line. Its sincerity broke the hearts of children around the world, and endeared Michael to their parents.

Michael was now not only recording solo material but he was also singled out in his career as a Jackson Five member. Motown insisted he lay down the lead vocal to the Jackson Five tracks separately from his brothers. His siblings were beginning to resent him.

Increasingly alone, Michael felt he was being isolated, singled out. He didn't want to cause problems with his brothers and yet the Jackson Five were no long the hit they had been overseas.

In the UK their *Maybe Tomorrow* album failed to make the Top 50 and Motown began to have concerns about the longevity of the group. Increasingly, their achievements were becoming dwarfed by Michael's spectacular record sales. Michael Jackson as a solo artist was becoming bigger and bigger.

But when the boys touched down at London's Heathrow Airport it was chaos. It was like the Beatles all over again except this was Jacksonmania.

And these scenes were repeated throughout Europe.

Yet while concert sales remained sold out, record sales for the Jackson Five were falling, and the April release of 'Little Bitty Pretty One' in 1972 was a huge disappointment. The follow-up 'Lookin' Through The Windows' fared even worse, and then 'Corner of the Sky' flopped, selling just 381,426 copies and barely making the US Top 20 and failing to make the UK charts at all.

Joseph Jackson was furious. He felt his boys were not being given the attention they deserved. Berry Gordy was now devoting all his time to Diana Ross' emerging film career.

Ewart Abner who now looked after the Jacksons had little faith in the band. He put the blame for poor sales firmly on the shoulders of the Jacksons, while Joseph insisted it was down to poor promotion and a lack of effort on the part of Motown.

When the Jackson Five album *Skywriter* was released in March it sold just

115,045 copies. It was a disaster. They had a brief reprieve with 'Get It Together' that sold more than 700,000 copies in August 1973 but Joseph was still seething.

Berry and Joseph clashed several times over the need for the band to change their style, their image and choice of music. The boys were growing older; Michael's voice was also changing.

The relationship between the two men was strained further when Jermaine Jackson began dating Berry's daughter Hazel. Initially, the wily Joseph had been in favour, but now he felt he was losing his son to Berry.

Jermaine was tall, good looking and he was a member of the Jackson Five. It was a terrific calling card and Jermaine made the most of it.

Hazel was one of millions of girls who fell for his charms, and at first he was too busy having fun for a relationship.

But Hazel was the boss's daughter. Her father was a driven man. He had not established Motown Records as the label by being soft and she had inherited a lot of her father's drive and determination.

She fell completely in love with Jermaine and had easy access to him as the band rehearsed and recorded at the studio.

By 1973 the pair began spending more and more time together, to the point where she began trying to influence the make-up of the band, to ensure her boyfriend had more of a significant role.

Hazel was mistrustful of relationships – her father had been divorced three times and she had witnessed his seduction of Diana Ross at close hand. She craved stability and was delighted when Jermaine asked to marry her.

Berry liked Jermaine and gave his blessing to the marriage. Joseph was uncertain at first but quickly saw the potential of being related by marriage to the boss of Motown Records. He also realized it could be the beginning of another solo career for one of his boys. The couple were wed on December 15, 1973 in a lavish, over-the-top ceremony that drew comparisons to a marriage involving royalty.

Almost a year later, the Jacksons' fortunes lifted again as they jumped onto the emerging disco scene with 'Dancing Machine'. The record climbed to No. 2 in the American charts, selling more than 2 million copies; it failed to do anything at all in Britain.

In the same year, Joseph and Motown had a major difference of opinion. All his life, Joseph had dreamed of playing Las Vegas. The history of the place seemed to almost overwhelm him and he was determined that his famous family could join the list of show business legends that have played there.

Berry and Motown thought it a suicide mission. They were adamant the Jackson Five were not ready for Vegas. They didn't have the experience or the material and they made it clear to Joseph that if they went, they went alone.

Joseph was furious. They were his boys and he was certain he knew what was best – and that was a trip to Vegas.

He knew what was required and put together a set list that was very different from the Jackson Five's usual stage performances. He enlisted the rest of the family, La Toya, 17, Randy, 12 and Janet, seven and carefully put together a show that clearly drew from the Osmonds.

The Jackson family were sensational. They worked the crowd on April 7, 1974 at the MGM Grand to such an uproar that the entire audience rose to their feet. It was stunning. So much so that Berry and Motown now felt the urge to be seen to be part of their success, issuing press releases and attempting to take the praise, all of which only infuriated Joseph further.

While the shows in Las Vegas were proving incredibly popular the Jackson Five's recording careers were suffering. Two singles from the *Dancing Machine* album, 'Whatever You Got I Want' and 'I Am The Love' did not do well and a solo Michael Jackson song 'Doggin' Around' was cancelled.

Problems continued, as Motown seemed content to sit back rather than push the brothers as they had done previously.

Michael's fourth solo album *Forever Michael* released in January 1975 was a flop, charting at 101, lower even than 'Music and Me' and also failed to chart in the UK. For Joseph, this was the final straw.

Furious, he demanded showdown talks with Berry. The Jackson Five would be leaving Motown. Instead, he would establish a family owned publishing company and ensure that his sons would not be forgotten.

Michael had deep concerns. He agreed with his father and brothers that the relationship with Motown was now not right but he felt fiercely loyal to Berry. After all, Berry was the man who had given the Jacksons their break. He had personally backed them and made superstars of the group – and of Michael as a solo artist.

Even though he was just 16-years-of-age, Michael felt he needed to meet with Berry directly. It had never been done before. Joseph conducted all negotiations for the Jackson family. The boys were simply told what to do and when to do it.

Michael met Berry on May 14, 1975. He made it clear that the Jacksons were not happy and wanted more creative freedom. They wanted to write. They wanted a say in their musical direction.

News of Michael's meeting with Berry soon leaked and Joseph and his brothers were waiting for him when he returned to the family home. They were furious that he had gone behind their back.

The Jackson family had always voted on matters affecting the group and even though Joseph always got his way, at least it appeared that everyone had a say.

This meeting implied that Michael felt he was special and the family were not impressed. They gathered for a family meeting to discuss their next move and voted unanimously – including Michael – to leave Motown.

Only Jermaine missed the meeting. He was on holiday with his wife – since his marriage to Gordy's daughter the Jacksons were no longer sure whether his loyalties lay with them or his new family.

Joseph insisted he would talk Jermaine around. His message to his sons was clear: stay at Motown and die or move elsewhere and become bigger, richer, than you can possibly imagine.

Motown was history.

CHAPTER FIVE

Epic

The Jackson Five were on the move. While it wasn't yet official, Joseph Jackson let it be known he was hunting for a new home and his focus was set on CBS Records.

CBS was a company with a terrific reputation. They were slick, smooth professionals and among the labels they worked with was Philadelphia International Records whose artists included the O'Jays and the Three Degrees. They had benefitted from their commitment and from being distributed by Epic Records, a CBS label.

Joseph had also expected rival label Atlantic Records to be interested in his sons. They specialized in rhythm and blues and yet chairman Ahmet Ertegun was not impressed. Falling record sales had led him to believe that the Jackson Five's moment had been and gone.

Fortunately, Ron Alexenburg, president of Epic, who looked after most of the black artists, told CBS President Walter Yetnikoff that he believed the Jackson Five were far from finished.

Alexenburg believed the band had untapped potential and warned the label they could not afford to miss out on their exciting talent.

Epic put together a package that was worth a staggering 500 times more than the deal they had signed to at Motown. It was breathtaking.

Under the new deal the Jacksons would receive a signing bonus of $750,000, and they would be given a $500,000 recording fund, $35,000 per album. The advance would be recouped from record sales but the group would receive 27 per cent in royalties – compared to the 2.7 per cent at Motown. If an album made more than $500,000 from sales their royalty rate would increase to 30 per cent.

This time, Joseph read the contract carefully. The only sticking point during talks was the group's desire to write their own material. CBS felt they were untried and this was a gamble too far but a compromise was reached and a deal was struck that allowed them to choose at least three songs for each album. They also agreed that if they wrote a song that was deemed good enough it would be considered by the label's executives.

Even Michael acknowledged later that Joseph had negotiated an incredible deal. But he continued to have issues over the loyalty aspect. Motown had been good to the Jacksons and Berry Gordy had been a visionary for him personally.

Still, the Jackson Five had decided they were leaving and so that was it.

All except Jermaine. Jermaine had been excluded from the original meeting. The whole family knew he was in a difficult position, caught between loyalty to his brothers and father – or his wife and father-in-law.

Jermaine believed deep down that Motown held the key to his own personal future. Berry had already marked him out as a solo artist and, in the long term, as a future president of the label.

Jermaine was very close to Berry and his wife Hazel was also very strong-minded. Meanwhile, Jermaine was also bitterly dismayed at not being included in the original family vote. Since his marriage he had felt increasingly like an outcast – as if his own family were withholding information from him in case he betrayed them to his "other" Motown family.

Joseph was in no doubt that ultimately his son would realize he was a Jackson first and foremost. He summoned him to the family home and led him to a bedroom.

There on the table were five contracts. Four of them contained the signatures of his brothers. His was the only one that remained. He was ordered in no uncertain terms to sign it.

His father hammered on and on about the incredible sums of money being offered by Epic but Jermaine was adamant. He was Motown and Motown was his future and he stormed out of the house and reported back to Berry.

The weeks that followed placed an incredible strain on Jermaine and the entire family. They still had gigs to perform and regardless of their future that meant rehearsing and performing together with the arguments over the future constantly raging.

Jermaine finally snapped at the Westbury Music Fair on New York's Long Island. With the rows continuing and Jermaine tired of being trapped in the middle, he received a telephone call from Berry moments before the group was due on stage.

He replaced the receiver and turned to his brothers, tears standing brightly in his eyes, and told them he had to leave. It was over. He would not be leaving Motown.

He had chosen his wife Hazel, Berry and his future at Motown over his brothers and was quitting the group this very moment. Then he ran out, packed his bags and left for Los Angeles leaving the Jacksons stunned.

Ever the professionals, the Jacksons insisted the show must go on and the four brothers took to the stage, led by Michael. They announced Jermaine had flu and promptly bought the house down with a flawless performance. But afterwards, the boys could not hide their hurt and Joseph could not control his burning anger.

For his part, Berry Gordy appeared untroubled by the Jackson Five's decision to quit. Jermaine would remain with him and his daughter and in any case he was focusing on the film world now.

As it happened Motown had the last laugh when Michael Roshkind, Vice-President of the label informed Joseph Jackson that his boys could leave Motown but they would not be taking their name with them.

Still, what's in a name? Michael Jackson remained very pragmatic about the news. They were still the Jacksons. Why not call themselves the Jacksons, the Jackson Family?

So on June 30, 1975, Joseph Jackson and his entire family held a press conference at the Rainbow Grill at the Rockefeller Centre in Manhattan to announce that the Jacksons were signing for Epic as soon as their Motown contract expired on March 10, 1976. Jermaine was not at the press conference.

Berry was furious. The Jackson Five had eight months of their contract still to run and they owed him serious money. He issued a lawsuit claiming $5 million for signing with CBS before their contract with Motown had expired.

Joseph attempted to fight fire with fire by responding with a lawsuit of his own. He believed the Jackson Five were the ones who were owed money but he turned out to be completely wrong.

Under the terms of the contract he signed without reading he had agreed that the Jacksons were liable for the costs of all the songs they recorded for Motown, including the ones that were never released. In total, the Jacksons recorded a staggering 469 songs during the six years they were with the label. Only 174 were ever released leaving the $500,000 shortfall.

Berry also reminded CBS and the public in general that Jermaine would remain with him – as would the Jackson Five name. He was not a man to be beaten and this was now a very serious obstacle to the Epic deal.

The Jackson brothers and Michael in particular were deeply dismayed. They were upset about the split with Jermaine and with Berry – and they were beginning to seriously question their father's leadership. Would an established manager have agreed to the terms of the Motown deal?

Eight frustrating months followed during which time the Jacksons were not allowed into a studio to record for Epic until their Motown deal had expired; instead they filled their time performing in a summer television variety show.

Behind the scenes Michael feared the family was falling apart. Then, Katherine Jackson filed for divorce.

Katherine had been aware of Joseph's philandering lifestyle for many years and had largely turned a blind eye to it despite the deep embarrassment his behaviour caused her. But now, one of Joseph's anonymous string of mistresses had fallen pregnant, ultimately suffering a miscarriage.

This was the final straw for Katherine. Girls had called at their house taunting her, she felt a fool and now all her friends were well aware of Joseph's outrageous behaviour.

The devout Jehovah's Witness had stood by her husband all their life, despite spending many lonely hours at home when Joseph was away with her boys.

The children instantly sided with their mother, without exception. They hated the way their father had treated Katherine. They hated the scenes they had witnessed during the years of touring, and they loved Katherine completely.

There was no doubting Joseph had been entirely responsible for driving the Jackson Five's career all the way to Motown and beyond, but it had come at a terrible price for Katherine. Finally the family saw a way of distancing themselves from his behaviour.

Katherine filed for divorce in Los Angeles on March 9, 1973. She had vowed all her life to make her marriage work, come what may. Now, she decided enough was enough and God would understand.

Joseph was completely stunned by his wife's actions. He had been the controlling factor in the Jackson family life and now all of a sudden, he was anything but in control. And he was devastated. Despite his behaviour he still loved Katherine – she was his rock, however many meaningless lovers he had.

Fearing a public scandal, Motown Records tried everything they could to talk Katherine around but she was adamant. Her mind was made up.

The pair stayed together in the family house without speaking to one another. Joseph promised repeatedly to change. Then two months later, Katherine suddenly withdrew her divorce petition. Her children were devastated.

In fact, around this time, Joseph had got a second Jackson fan pregnant. News of the pregnancy spread during the summer of 1974 – that same summer that the Jackson Five were taking Las Vegas by storm – and Joseph's sons tried everything to keep the news from their mother.

The woman, Cheryl Terrelle, a 26-year-old from Kansas, was a fan who had first singled out Jackie, before meeting Joseph.

For six years they would have no way of knowing whether the rumours were true. In fact, Joh'Vonnie Jackson, Michael's half-sister, was born on August 30, 1974.

Katharine was devastated when the rumours were eventually confirmed, but also typically generous. Despite her own private grief she was determined to do the right thing, insisting Joseph purchase a decent house for Cheryl and Joh'Vonnie, and ensuring they were financially sound.

For Michael and his brothers this was the most uncertain time they had ever known. They were leaving Motown and all those who had nurtured their career since they were small boys. Their parents' marriage was faltering. The rumours about their half-sibling were taking hold. Meanwhile Michael's older brothers were growing up and demanding their own independence, no longer content to be imprisoned under Joseph's stranglehold.

Jermaine had already effectively chosen to leave the family, and Tito had also fallen in love. He had met Delores – who was known as Dee Dee – long before the group became famous but both Joseph and Katherine were concerned about her motives, insisting she sign a pre-nuptial agreement.

Michael had also tried to talk Tito out of his decision to get married, feeling it sent out the wrong message to their army of fans.

As his sense of reality got even more distorted, he felt that the Jackson Five had a duty to deliver whatever the fans wanted. Personal happiness had ceased to matter to Michael.

In the end Tito refused to listen to Michael or his parents. He and Dee Dee were married in June 1972 at a small chapel in Inglewood, California.

Next, it was Jackie's turn to shock the family by suddenly announcing his plans to marry Enid Spann in 1974. Unlike Delores, Enid refused to sign a pre-nuptial agreement – and despite Joseph's furious objections the couple were married without the agreement being signed, in a small chapel at the MGM Grand in Las Vegas in the winter of 1974. But at least Jackie and Tito had stayed with the band.

Jermaine, on the other hand, was in exile. He visited the family home when his father was not present and it was good to see him, but his brothers couldn't shake off the feeling he had betrayed them. The younger family members including Michael, Janet and La Toya spent more and more time studying their faith as Jehovah's Witnesses. The Bible became their solace.

Against this backdrop of family angst and disharmony, the legal arguments continued between Motown, Joseph and Epic. Michael couldn't even take his usual comfort from his work, even hating taking part in the television show, *the Jacksons* being aired on CBS-TV. He made his feelings known but was outvoted. He felt the family was underprepared for the show.

In fact, the television show made the family's legal situation catastrophically worse when an old picture of the Jackson Five, featuring Jermaine, was accidentally used to promote the show.

Despite the publication of an immediate apology, Jermaine was not part of the new Jacksons and his picture should not have been used. The mistake was music to Berry Gordy's ears. The original lawsuit of $5 million was now increased to $20 million.

In truth, Joseph was struggling to cope. Eventually he was forced to admit that he had not read the terms and conditions of the contract or the Parental Agreement he had signed in Detroit and Motown were eventually awarded

$600,000 in damages. The Jacksons were also ordered to pay compensation for songs that were not released.

In the end it cost the Jacksons $2 million to leave Motown. They also surrendered any royalties from future releases of any of their recordings. Freedom turned out to be bittersweet.

Their first album on the Epic label, *The Jacksons*, was released in 1977.

For the first time, the record contained a song written by Michael – called 'Blues Away' – and another written by the group, called 'Style of Life'. The whole family was enjoying being allowed to learn from the Epic song-writing team.

The album reached No. 36 in the American charts and the single 'Enjoy Yourself' peaked at No. 6 but they were now in the surreal position of battling against their own music in the charts.

Motown had issued a Jackson Five album using previously unreleased material at the same time. Meanwhile, their old label was also promoting Jermaine's first album, *My Name is Jermaine*. With mixed emotions, the brothers watched his album reach No. 164 while his single 'Let's Be Young Tonight' only made No. 55 on the charts. It seemed leaving Motown had been the right decision after all.

The music press turned viciously on Jermaine, and his brothers found it hard to take. Despite everything, he was still their brother and they didn't want to see him suffer. They could see that he still wasn't being given the backing or marketing he needed to be a solo success. Certainly he was far more talented than those sales suggested.

For Jermaine's brothers record sales with Epic had got off to a shaky start, but they remained a box office draw playing sell-out concerts. Marlon had now stepped into the shoes vacated by Jermaine and Randy had joined the group to take the numbers back up to five.

Their 1977 Epic follow-up album, *Goin' Places* was another flop – charting at No. 63 in the charts with the single of the same name doing slightly better, peaking at No. 52. Meanwhile, Jermaine also continued to struggle, reaching No. 174 in the US charts with his second album, *Feel the Fire*.

Their poor chart placings and disappointing sales meant the Jacksons faced a new crisis. CBS President Walter Yetnikoff was determined to have Epic drop them from the label, and Joseph – unaware how close the family was to be jettisoned – demanded showdown talks with Epic's Ron Alexenberg, the man who had signed them.

Joseph asked Michael to attend the meeting, the first admission he had ever made of his son's power to persuade. In front of the executives, the two Jacksons argued that the only way Epic would have a hit record with their band was if they allowed them to write their own songs.

It was a close call. In the end, Bobby Colomby, Epic's Head of West Coast Artist Relations, persuaded Alexenberg to give them one more chance.

CHAPTER SIX

Man in the Mirror

By 1977, Michael Jackson may have been the boy who never wanted to grow up, but he was also no longer a child. He was 18 years old, and lost for a means of escape from the Jackson family.

His older brothers had sought their own independence by marrying women and creating their own families. But Michael had little interest in women.

As a boy, on the thousands of nights the family spent on tour, girls would be ushered upstairs into the room that Jermaine usually shared with Marlon and Michael and the younger boys had to pretend to be asleep while their older brother had sex. Marlon developed an interest in women as he got older but Michael didn't understand it.

But Michael was horrified by base ideas of sexuality. Given his early experiences, the sordid antics of his father and the venues he was exposed to during his most formative years, he just wanted nothing to do with it.

He also suffered from cripplingly low self-esteem. All his life his father and brothers had teased him about his bad skin, and called him Big Nose. He felt unloved and unattractive. He also hated the way his face looked like his father's. When he looked at the man in the Mirror he saw his father's nose and eyes staring back. He was dogged by severe acne during his teenage years and only truly felt confident when his face was covered with make-up for stage shows or video shoots.

But if Michael didn't understand why he needed sex in his life, he did still enjoy the company of women. He liked to spend time with them, just talking. Surrounded by boys and men since childhood, and missing the company of his mother for so much of his early life, he took every opportunity to talk to women.

Of all the women he knew, he most loved Diana Ross, his mentor, surrogate mother, and one of the only people to have been truly kind to him in his childhood.

He once told biographer J. Randy Taraborrelli: "I do have one other friend. A very, very close friend that I can tell my deepest, darkest secrets to because I know she won't tell anyone else. Her name is…. Miss Diana Ross".

Taraborrelli questioned him: "You have deep, dark secrets Michael?"

Jackson replied: "Everybody has deep, dark secrets."

Around this time, as an attractive and successful young man who was yet to be associated with any girlfriends, rumours began to circulate that Michael

Jackson was gay.

If he had been it would have been a bitterly difficult situation for the young Michael, as homosexuality is forbidden in the Jehovah's Witness faith, and he believed passionately in his religion.

When *Jet*, an American magazine, ran a story that he was planning a sex change to enable him to marry actor Clifton Davis, the writer of 'Never Can Say Goodbye', Michael was devastated. He had recorded the song when he was just 12 years old and knew Davis, but he now became paranoid that the press would doctor pictures of the two of them if he ever saw the man again.

As the rumours grew ever louder, Michael began to keep a lower and lower profile. He could not handle the pressure, the jibes, and the constant accusations.

In fact, Michael claimed in a documentary with Martin Bashir in 2003 that the only relationship he had had at this time was with the actress Tatum O'Neal.

The child prodigy had won an Oscar aged just nine for her role in *Paper Moon* and was the daughter of Hollywood stars Ryan O'Neal and Joanna Moore. They split when she was just three and she lived with her mother.

Like Michael's, Tatum's was a mixed childhood of extraordinary blessings and personal pain. She struggled to cope with the divorce of her parents and went to live with her father after her mother admitted she could not cope. Deciding she would become an actress, O'Neal secured his daughter's role in *Paper Moon*.

Tatum first met Michael in 1977. She was 13; Michael was due to turn 19 in August. They met at Paul McCartney's party on board the *Queen Mary*, the former liner moored in the port of Long Beach, California, to which he had invited a host of stars. The pair didn't see each other again until two years later. Michael spotted her and her father at a club in Los Angeles.

The way Michael told the story, he was with executives from CBS when Tatum approached him and grabbed his hand. They spent some time together and the following day she invited Michael to dinner at a mansion owned by *Playboy* publisher Hugh Hefner.

They watched television at the Holmby Hills mansion before Tatum suggested they enjoy a dip in the hot tub. Michael was very shy and refused without a bathing suit even though Tatum appeared more than comfortable to enjoy a naked soak.

Michael claimed in his autobiography that Tatum was his first love, but in her autobiography, *A Paper Life*, Tatum remembered their shy meetings very differently.

"I met him at the On the Rox, the club Lou Adler & Jack Nicholson opened upstairs from the Roxy on the Sunset Strip," she writes. "Michael was around

17 at the time, about 5 years older than me, and he seemed very sheltered and fearful and lonely – not at all what you'd expect a world-renowned performer to be. As I recall, he didn't even know how to drive a car.

"He gave me his number, and we started talking every day – long drawn-out conversations that sometimes got so boring I would hand over the receiver to my friend Esme Gray.

"Michael would just keep on, thinking he was talking to me. His usual subject was sex. At 12 I didn't have much to say about sex – all I knew was that it went on, pretty steadily, in my father's room next to mine. But Michael was intensely curious about anything – everything sexual, though in an incredibly sweet and innocent way.

"He was a huge star, but it seemed he barely even dated and knew little about life. He once came to my house and asked to come upstairs because he'd never been in a girl's bedroom before. He sat on the bed, and we kissed very briefly, but it was terribly awkward.

"For all my passionate crushes on people like Dustin Hoffman, I was just 12 and not at all ready for a real-life encounter. So I said, 'I can't.' Michael, who was sweating profusely, seemed as intimidated as I was. He jumped up nervously and said, 'Uh, gotta go'."

Tatum wrote that she believed Michael had fallen in love with her, but she added: "At the time of the supposed seduction, I was barely pubescent, and what I'd seen of sex so far was unappealing and gross.

"It may have been Michael's fantasy that I'd seduce him – and it's a little sad that he cast himself as failing, even in his dream – but it just didn't happen."

In the same autobiography Michael claims to have had romances with Diana Ross and Brooke Shields though they later also denied any such relationship.

Sarah Jackson, an actress and friend of Tatum told J. Randy Taraborrelli that O'Neal had remarked that she believed Michael was uninterested in sex.

"How can any girl have a relationship with him?" Tatum had told her. "When we're together, he hardly says two words. I know he's a virgin. Someone needs to have a talk with him about it. I wonder if he's afraid to have sex. He doesn't seem very interested."

CHAPTER SEVEN

The Wiz

Around this time in Michael's life, Diana Ross had become involved with a film called *The Wiz*.

A musical adaptation of L. Frank Baum's classic *The Wonderful World of Oz*, the idea had been bought by Berry Gordon's Motown Productions.

First aired on Broadway in 1975, the musical had gone on to win seven Tony awards. Now through a deal with Universal the production was to become a film with talented actress Stephanie Mills earmarked for the lead role as Dorothy.

Hearing of the film, Diana Ross had other ideas. She wanted the role for herself and as a Motown artist she was eventually able to persuade Berry to give her the part.

Privately Motown bosses were certain that at 33 years of age Diana Ross was too old to play Dorothy, but they had little choice.

Rob Cohen, the talented head of Motown Productions, set about finding the rest of the cast and he had only one choice for the role of the Scarecrow – Michael Jackson.

Michael Jackson could sing, he could dance and had massive appeal.

The only obstacle lay in the simmering feud between Motown, Berry and the Jackson family, which was showing no signs of subsiding.

Motown approached Michael with Diana Ross acting as the middleman. Joseph ordered his son not to take the part.

Michael stood his ground. He insisted that he could make this a success. Joseph feared the movie would fail and take his son down with it. He also warned that he it would further alienate him from the family and that was the only thing that mattered.

In the end, Joseph was forced to concede. He could see that he was pushing his son further and further away, and could not afford to lose the Jacksons' main attraction.

For Michael, the film would mean something completely new and different away from the claustrophobic stranglehold of his family. It also meant moving to New York, thousands of miles from Joseph. At 19 years old, he would finally be free.

That summer, July 1977, Joseph sent La Toya to share Michael's $2,000 a month apartment in New York. She hated being away from her family and spent most of the time inside their luxurious home eating chocolate, gaining 20 pounds in weight by the time she returned to California.

Michael, for his part, was having a ball – working tirelessly in the day and then partying every single night.

The film cost $24 million to make with work starting on October 3, 1977 at Astoria Studios. The working day began at 4am and would continue for most of the day until it was eventually completed on December 30 the same year.

Michael was learning new dance routines, dressing each day in his spectacular makeup and costume to become the Scarecrow – sometimes even leaving it on to go out partying at night in disguise. It hid the nose he hated, and the makeup covered his acne.

It was the start of his experimentation with costumes, and he loved the freedom he found being dressed as someone else.

Away from his family, Michael's confidence blossomed, and he almost found himself a girlfriend.

Theresa Gonsalves had first met Michael in 1974 at a concert in Las Vegas and the two 16-year-olds struck up a friendship. When Michael was living in Manhattan, he invited Theresa over to visit.

She told J. Randy Taraborrelli; "When I got to the apartment building, he told the doorman to send me up. Toya answered the door. She was irritated. 'Michael didn't tell me that you two had made plans' as though he was supposed to check with her before he made plans and he hadn't".

"So I asked Toya where he was and she said that he was in the kitchen baking chocolate chip cookies.

"After Michael and I talked and ate the cookies I took a look around. The suite had a balcony. Michael used to hang over it like he was going to jump. He loved acting the fool to upset his sister.

"Toya had the most wonderful room, a real showpiece with a huge bed and a mirror above it, a penthouse bedroom befitting a star. Michael had a small simple bedroom with a twin-sized bed in it and a desk. I asked myself, why does she have such a great room and he's stuck with this?"

Theresa told Taraborrelli how days later Michael had returned from the studio excited about a new development on the set. He took her to his bedroom and started showing her his scrapbook of pictures from the film.

She adored Michael and was genuinely excited for him. She claims the pair gazed into each other's eyes and Michael tilted his head and leaned over to her. As they neared each other's lips La Toya burst into the room demanding to know what was going on.

Theresa said: "I wanted to kiss him so badly. And I know he would have if Toya hadn't surprised us."

The Wiz gave Michael the freedom he craved spiritually and creatively, but when it was released in October 1978 it was a critical flop and fared dismally at the box office. Even a single released from the movie failed to bolster interest in the project.

The Motown bosses were bitterly disappointed. Epic were similarly devastated as they had hoped the film could be a launch pad for their new signing. Michael was heartbroken that his first real project away from the family was a failure.

For once the Jackson family rallied around the teenage Michael, telling him that if nothing else it proved that he had the ability and potential to become a much bigger star.

And if his film career was suffering a stuttering start, at least *Destiny*, the group's third album with CBS was doing well. Written entirely by the Jackson brothers, the critics were wildly excited.

No matter that the first single, 'Blame It On The Boogie' failed to make the US Top 40 – a fact that seems staggering given the song's later popularity, although it did make No. 8 in Britain.

After the title song from the album flopped the third single, 'Shake Your Body (Down To The Ground)' was an immediate success, flying to No. 7 in America and No. 4 in the UK, and selling more than 2 million copies.

The executives at Epic – and even their former employees at Motown – now had to admit the Jacksons really could write their own material.

Meanwhile, Michael had returned to the Jackson family a very different young man following his stint in New York. He now had real thoughts and ambitions about his own solo career despite agreeing to dedicate his time and energy to a third Jackson album with CBS.

Deep down, he felt as if he had stagnated. The energy he had shown on stage during his career was ebbing away. Touring was becoming more and more repetitive and he wanted to learn new things and grow as a performer.

Even when the Jacksons' third Epic album sold more than a million copies, Michael still couldn't calm his own restlessness. He was set on finding new horizons that would take him far from his family.

CHAPTER EIGHT

Off The Wall

Whatever *The Wiz's* failings, it did bring Michael Jackson one of his life's most important friendships. The partnership between Michael Jackson and Quincy Jones helped to define his music as a solo performer.

Quincy was a former trumpet player with the Dizzy Gillespie band who went on to write film scores, and compose and arrange music for huge stars like Duke Ellington, Ray Charles and Dinah Washington.

When they met on the set of *The Wiz*, Quincy gave Michael his telephone number and told him if he ever needed help to call. An increasingly frustrated Michael knew it was time to call the number.

In 1979 the two men met up in Los Angeles and began their search for songs, experimenting with beats and melodies and exchanging ideas until they were ready to record.

With Quincy's support, Michael wrote three songs: 'Don't Stop 'Till You Get Enough', 'Working Day And Night' and 'Get On The Floor' – which was co-written with Louis Johnson, the bass player with the Brothers Johnson, whom Quincy had been producing for years.

Quincy was keen to bring a balance to the forthcoming album and pressed for the softer songs 'She's Out Of My Life', 'It's The Falling in Love', 'Rock With You', 'Burn This Disco Out' and 'Off The Wall'. The last three songs were written by his protégé, Rob Temperton, a British composer born in Cleethorpes and former member of the hit group Heatwave who had reached No. 2 in Britain with 'Boogie Nights'.

Session players were drafted in to record the album and 'Don't Stop' was released as the first single on July 28, 1979.

It was immediately obvious to anyone who heard the record, that this was a new Michael Jackson. His voice was different, the sound was completely changed, and he was back on top of the charts. His first solo No. 1 for seven years even crossed the Atlantic, reaching No. 3 in the UK charts. As well as being massively popular, the album was also an overwhelming critical success.

Off The Wall also provided Michael with his first opportunity to record a pop video. It was pretty basic compared with the videos Michael Jackson would later make. But the experience was yet another new beginning – the start of a whole new creative era for Michael Jackson.

The album *Off The Wall* was released in August 1979 featuring Michael on the cover, an iconic image now – a boy on the cusp of manhood, and before the surgery began to destroy his face, dressed in a white tuxedo with sparkling socks.

His nose was new, the result of a bad fall during rehearsals, but otherwise he appears untroubled.

Off The Wall sold more than 3 million copies, reaching No. 3 in America and No. 5 in the UK. 'Rock With You', 'Off The Wall' and 'She's Out of My Life' all followed as singles and soared to the top of the charts making Michael the first solo artist to have four Top Ten singles from one album.

The record also earned Michael a Grammy. He should have been over the moon with his successes, but Michael was disappointed. He'd wanted more than one Grammy and now vowed to do even better with his second album.

His father, Joseph, might have been pleased with his son's success but he was now harbouring grave concerns about the future of the Jacksons and he tried to convince his son to return to the studio.

In truth, he had every reason to be worried. Michael Jackson was now 21 years old. He had more than $1 million in his account thanks to the success of *Off The Wall* and he was finally on the verge of the independence he had begun to dream of as far back as Jackson Street.

Michael dreamed of becoming the biggest name in pop. And he wasn't the sort of person who just dreamed. He was determined to actually achieve his ambition, to follow in the footsteps of his heroes Walt Disney, Fred Astaire and Charlie Chaplin.

To do so meant shaping his own destiny – and that meant leaving Joseph. So far, Michael's father had controlled every aspect of his sons' lives. He negotiated contracts, collected the money, made the decisions over records, touring and rehearsing. That was going to change.

Michael asked his accountant Michael Mesnick to find him a lawyer. Mesnick suggested John Branca, a 31-year-old New Yorker who had negotiated for the Beach Boys, Neil Diamond and Bob Dylan – and didn't know a great deal about Michael Jackson, other than he was tipped for big things.

They immediately got on and Michael hired him, refusing to even meet any other lawyers.

Branca's first task was to renegotiate Michael's contract with Epic. Instead of being part of a collective Jacksons deal, he wanted a separate contract as a solo artist and the pair negotiated the biggest royalty deal in the music business.

Michael would now earn 37 per cent from all record sales, the same deal as Bob Dylan and Neil Diamond. Branca also negotiated a clause that allowed Michael to leave the Jacksons at any time and yet ensure that Epic were still obliged to record Jackson material without him.

Michael hoped that would placate his other brothers who were growing increasingly frustrated and jealous of the success and attention he was receiving. Joseph was furious but he knew he was no longer able to control his son.

Michael's brother Randy was so impressed with the new deal he tried to hire Branca himself but Michael put a stop to it. This was his deal, Branca was his lawyer and they would not copy him. Branca was banned from representing any other members of Michael's family.

CHAPTER NINE

Alone

As Michael reached the end of his teenage years, he was becoming more and more isolated – and even more disconnected from normal life.

In 1979, he admitted in one interview that he didn't even realize Gerald Ford was President of the United States.

He had no interest in politics or current affairs, preferring the magical worlds of Walt Disney and cartoons to hard, cold reality. Disneyland and the Magic Kingdom were the places he preferred to inhabit.

As he retreated further and further into unreality, he also became obsessed with a fantasy idea of himself.

He wanted to remake his own face and get rid of the nose and the acne that upset him so much. But at the point he was considering surgery the decision was taken out of his hands when he tripped and fell badly during a dance routine in early 1979.

Michael flew to Los Angeles for an operation to reset his nose and he loved the results, which feature on the cover shot for the album *Off The Wall*.

Meanwhile, Michael's skin was also clearing up. His brother Jermaine had also suffered with acne and found that switching away from greasy foods and turning vegetarian had helped to clear his skin. Michael always had problems with his skin. His friend of more than 35 years David Gest remembers that at 13 years old, the oils he used to tend his Afro were giving him spots on his forehead.

"We both had huge Afros and were constantly comparing them," he said. "Michael used oil to keep his hair in good condition but that caused bad spots on his forehead.

"So at night he wore a pair of underpants around his hair to keep the oil from seeping on to his skin. I almost peed my pants laughing when he stayed at my house.

"Unfortunately, we both had acne. We'd smear whole bottles of Clearasil spot cream on our faces, point at each other and laugh hysterically."

Now, Michael followed Jermaine's diet and it worked. It also led to dramatic weight loss.

Unfortunately, the nose operation hadn't been entirely successful. Michael now had issues with his breathing that were affecting his singing ability, so Dr Steven Hoefflin suggested a second operation.

Though both operations were medically necessary, there were signs that

Michael was beginning to obsess about his surgeries.

When he confided in his close friend, actress Jane Fonda, she was immediately concerned. She knew Michael was desperately unhappy. He was lonely, unhappy with his body and too shy to meet people. She saw he was becoming badly isolated in an ivory tower built by fortune and fame.

Michael's loneliness was growing ever deeper. Even though he was by now an international superstar, his inner emptiness seemed only to get bigger.

On stage he was a flamboyant entertainer, a bit of a show-off. In the studio he was gaining a reputation as an accomplished producer, learning from Quincy Jones and working with Paul McCartney.

He had also enjoyed working with Steven Spielberg on a storytelling record book of his blockbuster film, ET, with which Michael was obsessed. He was enjoying his solo success, but had less and less inclination to work with his brothers.

Yet now he was committed to a 39-city concert tour of the United States, promoting the Jacksons' new album, *Triumph*. During the hugely successful tour that finished with four sold out shows in Los Angeles he told his brothers it would be his last. He'd had enough being constantly on the road and wanted to commit himself to work in the studio.

Increasingly, he was also tortured by the private family events going on – as ever – in the background of his life. Once again, they concerned his beloved mother and his father's lying and cheating behaviour. And once again, they made him ashamed to be a Jackson.

Katherine had long harboured deep concerns about Joseph's relationship with his PA, Gina Sprague. And according to J. Randy Taraborrelli, the following incident took place, but it was denied by Katherine, Janet and Randy.

Gina – who worked behind the scenes at Joseph Jackson Productions, in Suite 1001 at 6255 Sunset Boulevard – was completely trusted by Joseph. She was the first person he confided in over his secret love child.

Their trusting relationship inevitable created office gossip and word spread they were having an affair. Some time in the run up to October 16, 1980, Katherine decided she had heard enough.

Gina claims that in the days before she received anonymous threatening telephone calls warning her to quit her job. She had no idea who was making the calls.

Then on the afternoon of October 16, she received a visit from Randy Jackson, who was approaching his 20th birthday. There was nothing unusual in the visit, but Randy suddenly ordered all other staff members to leave the office.

Once Gina was alone, Katherine swung into the room with 14-year-old Janet, and proceeded to deliver a verbal roasting to Gina over her alleged relationship.

The verbal assault is then alleged to have become physical. Security staff rushed to the office but were ordered to leave. This was a family affair – and every one of them was an employee of the family.

When Joseph returned from a meeting he discovered Gina collapsed on the floor. Paramedics and police officers were on the way to the scene. She was taken to hospital and treated for cuts, bruises and a minor head injury.

Joseph was distraught. He visited Gina at home the next day and begged her not to press charges against his wife and daughter. He feared that he could lose his family because of the incident and that was something he could not afford.

He even offered her a cheque in an attempt to soothe her, but that merely enraged her further and he was ordered to leave her house with his cheque.

She was furious; especially given that she had been telling lies to Katherine in a bid to cover Joseph's secret visits to his love child.

It was alleged that Katherine became so suspicious of her husband Joseph's relationship with Gina that she confronted her at the office with other members of the family.

Gina was later taken to hospital for treatment for cuts and bruises. The Jackson family insisted they knew nothing of her injuries and police charges were dropped. Gina did file a $21 million lawsuit which was settled out of court. The full extent of the settlement was to remain a secret.

The incident rocked Michael. He could not believe that his kind, gentle mother could possibly have been involved in such a violent incident.

He was so hurt by the story that he simply refused to believe it had happened. He erased that day from his memory.

He also became paranoid that a journalist would ask him about his father's love child and his mother's alleged attack, withdrawing more and more into a private world.

Biographer J. Randy Taraborrelli describes a bizarre incident in his book: *Michael Jackson, The Magic and the Madness*, which shows how much the strain affected Michael.

However much he didn't want to speak to journalists, feeling deeply exposed by his family's behaviour, the executives at Epic insisted he continued with his media duties. They needed him to promote the Jacksons' upcoming tour.

Taraborrelli was a reporter who had spent years covering the Jacksons and had developed a close relationship with the entire family. But this interview was like nothing he had experienced before.

Michael insisted he would only answer questions put to him by his sister Janet. Taraborrelli was put in the ridiculous position of having to ask Janet to ask Michael, and then listen as Michael replied to Janet who in turn passed the answers onto the reporter.

The three of them were all sat within yards of one another in the same room.

As the interview descended into total farce, Taraborrelli decided to end it. The interview never appeared in print.

Around the same time, January 1980, music journalist John Pidgeon went to interview Michael for the *Daily Mirror*.

"30 years ago, I was granted an audience with Michael Jackson to ask him anything I liked – as long as the questions were relayed via his 13-year-old sister Janet," he recalls.

Pidgeon wondered whether the 21-year-old future King of Pop was trying to buy extra time for his answers, or simply didn't want to be addressed directly by a white man.

His conclusion was that the boy star was just "chronically, cripplingly shy – and Janet's re-expression of my words just meant he could respond to a familiar voice with which he was comfortable instead of that of a stranger."

It was Michael's PR woman who made the request, as Pidgeon was ushered into 4641 Hayvenhurst Avenue, the interior of which was decorated as an elfin grotto.

JANET JACKSON: Michael, how did you fit into the Motown setup?

MICHAEL JACKSON: We were doing a show in Chicago and it was like a talent show sort of thing and we won. And Gladys Knight was there as well as a guy called Bobby Taylor and they told Motown about us. And Motown was interested.

So we went to Berry Gordy's mansion estate in Detroit and all the Motown stars were there, from the Supremes to the Temptations, the Marvelettes, the Miracles, and we auditioned and they loved it.

And Diana Ross came after us, special, you know after the concert, and she kissed us all and said we were marvelous. And she said she wanted to play a special part in our career. And that's how it started.

We did our first single 'I Want You Back'.

It was gold, as well as 'ABC', 'The Love You Save'... and that's how it started.

JANET: Was Berry Gordy particularly looking after you guys?

MICHAEL: Berry was the overseer of the Jacksons... head of our whole career at Motown. Berry Gordy, as the world knows, owns Motown Records and he only managed two people in the whole history of Motown – the Supremes and The Jackson Five. So he was the main force behind us as well as my father and mother.

JANET: If it Motown was a school, what things did you learn?

MICHAEL: I learned about producing, I learned how to, erm, to cut a track as well as producing. I learned about writing and just the whole overall thing.

Being with Stevie Wonder, being in his sessions... just sitting in and learning was incredible. Just the way a producer dictates to me. Just the greatest learning point, wonderful. It was the best school.

JANET: Was Motown like a big family?

MICHAEL: Er, yes, that's very true. They were. Everybody worked together.

You'd be doing a session and Berry Gordy would just walk in and change things around and nobody would get mad.

He was like the Disney studios. Walt Disney would go from one studio to the other and just stimulate everybody, like a bee, you know, and pollen, just going from one place to another and stimulating people, keeping them on the right track.

Berry was wonderful at taking a song and leading it to the right direction to make it a hit. He knew just what it takes. And everybody can't do that. He's something.

JANET: Since a lot of people were telling you how to do your songs and things, was it frustrating to you?

MICHAEL: Yes. A lot of times. I've had, um, a couple of disputes with a couple of, um, producers at Motown. And it became a major thing. BG came down to the studio and, er, it kinda got out of hand.

But we finally solved it and I was right.

The producer wanted me to pronounce words a certain way. I told him you pronounce the words so precisely it takes away from the feeling of the song and we got into a little thing with that. But it was over and I was right and I won.

But it was a good learning point, because I knew what he wanted but what he wanted took away so much. He really did.

JANET: When you left Motown, where so many decisions were made, was it is difficult, you know, to adjust?

MICHAEL: Yeah... because at Motown, it's a much smaller company. You know every face that's there. You even know the secretaries by name. And when you have a problem about anything you can call Berry Gordy right up and he'll come down.

Now CBS, it has millions of employees all over the world – and God, it was hard to adjust to such a big family of people.

JANET: Was it to do with *The Wiz* that you got to work with Quincy (Jones)?

MICHAEL: Yes, I met Quincy before at Sammy Davis's house a long time ago. And Sammy told him: "This guy's really gonna..." I wasn't really paying attention.

I met Quincy there; I think he was doing soundtracks, television shows, as well as movies, 12 Angry Men scores and stuff.

But the real meeting with Quincy, the real marriage was *The Wiz* project. And we really got to know one another and we worked beautifully together. Ah, so well. I call Quincy up one day, and I say Quincy I'm ready to do an album, a solo album. I've written the songs I wanna do. But I wanna real good producer to work with me. Can you recommend somebody? And he said:" Smelly (he calls me Smelly), Smelly why don't you let me do it?" I said:" That's' a great idea." And I start giggling. And he said: "Why don't we start?" And next week we got together. And that's how *Off The Wall* came about.

JANET: When you're in the studio, do you go for the vocal straightaway?

MICHAEL: I do vocals pretty quick. Sometimes you do have to get into the song and have the right mood. But, for instance, Ben I did in one take. I went right in.

And I said: "Wanna do another one?" And the guy said:" No! No! It was great!" And I was like:" Was it?" And that's how that came about. I'll never forget a little apple box I stood on 'cos I couldn't reach the microphone. My name was written on it.

JANET: Which do you enjoy most, Michael? The studio or being on stage?

MICHAEL: That is kind of a difficult question because I'm crazy about both... I just enjoy entertaining. It's the best, really.

JANET: Do you work hard on dancing?

MICHAEL: No. I should but I don't! I really should. Like once we get in the room and throw around a couple of ideas. But I don't.

Whatever you see me do is spontaneous reactions on the stage. It's nothing planned. It just happens, through feeling.

JANET: How do you feel about people calling it disco... and saying it's on the way out. How do you feel about that?

MICHAEL: Um, like I told you before, I hate labels because it should be just music. People worked all week, they wanna party and have a good time and they wanna dance. You have to dance to a rhythm, to a beat. You can't dance to da-da-da-da.

You have to take it easy and call it disco, call it anything. I don't know. It's music and whatever they want to label it, it's fine.

But would you call 'Never Can Say Goodbye' disco? Would you call 'Ben' disco? Would you call 'She's Out Of My Life' disco? Off The Wall? 'Rock With You'? I dunno, it's music to me. It's beautiful to the ear and that's what counts. It's like you hear a bird chirping. You don't say that's a bluejay, this one is a crow. It's a beautiful sound. That's all that counts. It's beautiful, you listen to it.

You watch them soar in the sky. It's just beautiful and that's the ugly thing about man.

They categorize too much. You get a little bit too racial about things. It should all be together. That's why you hear us talking about the peacock a lot... the only bird that integrates every colour into one.

That's our main goal in music, just to integrate every race into one through music – and we're doing that.

Michael added: "You see the kids out there dancing, the grown-ups and grandparents. All colours, that's what's great. That's what will keep me going."

CHAPTER TEN

Divorce

The Gina Sprague affair had a dramatic effect not just on Michael, but also on the whole family. For Katherine most of all, the strain was almost unbearable and in the summer of 1982 she snapped after a string of telephone calls to the family home.

Every time Katherine picked up the receiver the line went dead. It had to be another woman and proved yet again that Joseph's promise to reform was yet another in a lifetime of lies.

Katherine decided that this time she didn't even want to hear Joseph's side of the story. She told her husband she was leaving him. Joseph pretended to be unconcerned. He kissed her goodbye and let her walk out of the house. Moments later the telephone rang again and this time he answered and spoke to the woman on the other end.

Unbeknown to Joseph and his lover, Katherine had been listening from the other line in the guesthouse and what she heard broke her already crumbling heart.

She returned to the house and flew into a rage with Joseph, hurling objects at him and ordering him to leave the house. The next day, August 19, 1982, she filed for divorce, detailing what she wanted from the settlement.

Joseph however insisted he was going nowhere and that they would not be getting divorced regardless of her wishes. It was a ridiculous situation that lasted ten stubborn months.

Katherine and Joseph barely spoke. Joseph slept on the couch and remained adamant that he would not leave and would not go along with the divorce.

The children all vowed to stand with their mother and Michael suggested she should have Joseph removed by the police. He even suggested a restraining order.

Katherine would not have that. She could not face the pain and suffering that she would effectively inflict on her son's musical career through the bad press.

Michael was by now desperate to leave home and to create a space where his mother could live and get away from Joseph. He decided they should buy a home together.

He paid $210,000 in cash – which included a $35,000 payment from Katherine – for a three bedroom, three bathroom home at 5420 Lindley Avenue in Encino, not too far from the family home.

But when it came to moving, Michael found it impossible to cut himself off from the family home. Terrified of being lonely away from his brothers, in the end he simply stayed where he was. Just like Katherine he could never quite bringing himself to leave.

In 1983, when Michael decided to axe his father as his manager, it had the ironic effect of bring Katherine to Joseph's rescue – the last thing their son would have wanted.

Joseph was left a broken man by the decision. It had been his entire life and now he had nothing. Even Katherine felt sorry for her husband and she finally withdrew her divorce petition.

CHAPTER 11

Thriller

One of the greatest pop albums ever made almost didn't make it out of the recording studio. Michael Jackson pulled the plug on *Thriller*, insisting it would never see the light of day.

After the incredible success of *Off The Wall* he could not face producing a failure.

When Michael had first finished *Thriller* he was ecstatic, believing it was brilliant. But listening to the album, made in Los Angeles' Westland Studios, Quincy Jones and his manager Ron Weisner did not agree.

Michael was devastated and insisted that the entire album be remixed. It was a time-consuming process.

He was right because once it was remixed it sounded phenomenal. Michael loved it and so did Quincy and Ron, yet both men remained pessimistic about the record's chances of success. The market was changing, they reasoned – and *Off The Wall* had been such an incredible success it was going to be hard to live up to. They wanted to manage their young protégé's expectations.

Michael was furious at the older men's negativity. He only wanted to hear positives and flew into a mood, attacking the pair and insisting the project was shelved. He even ordered lawyer John Branca to instruct Epic that the album would never see the light of day.

When CBS President Walter Yetnikoff heard about the row he was concerned and attempted to placate Michael. He insisted he trusted the singer and promised to back him. If Michael Jackson believed *Thriller* had what it took then that was all he needed to know.

It did the trick. The boost to Michael's ego calmed him down. From now on it would be Michael Jackson who was running the show.

The album was released on December 1, 1982 and the release of the first single, 'The Girl Is Mine' with Paul McCartney was not a hit with the critics, although it did make No. 2 in the American charts.

But the critics could not have been more wrong. The album's next single was 'Billie Jean', Michael's poignant vocals floating over a sharp lean bass line that would go on to become one of the most recognizable in pop.

'Billie Jean' was a stunning success. It shot to No. 1 in the US in March 1983, staying at the top of the charts for seven weeks; in Britain it also topped the singles chart for a week. Michael sang the lyric with real passion and conviction as if he felt every word – and in many ways he did.

Michael had written 'Billie Jean' after a female fan wrote to him claiming he had fathered her child. He had never met the woman and it was not unusual to read such claims. Yet this woman persisted. She sent more letters, pictures of herself, and of her child. Michael began to find her persistence disturbing.

Then the woman sent a package, which contained a gun and a note instructing Michael to kill himself on a particular date. She claimed she would shoot her child and then herself at the same time so they could all be united in the next world.

The package terrified Michael. The woman later ended up in an asylum, but he still feared her and what she might do. That a fan could become so obsessed with him was frightening, but it was the sudden invasion into his private, carefully protected, fortified world that upset him most.

Quincy Jones originally didn't believe that 'Billie Jean' was right for the *Thriller* album but Michael was adamant – and, after all, he was now running the show.

The single was a huge success; meanwhile the album was selling a staggering 500,000 copies a week. Everyone in the world seemed to own a copy of *Thriller*. From the catchy pop of 'Wanna Be Startin' Something' to the theatricality of the title track itself – another Rod Temperton composition – it was a classic from the moment it was released.

By the end of 1983 *Thriller* had sold an astonishing 22 million copies worldwide. It was simultaneously No. 1 in America and the UK – something that had never happened before. Seven of the tracks were top ten hits as singles; an unprecedented success.

Thriller went onto sell more than 50 million copies worldwide and spend more than 37 weeks at No. 1 – even before Michael's death when it was re-released – and it was estimated the record generated more than $60 million for Epic Records.

Thriller also earned Michael an estimated $32 million from US sales and a further $15 million from overseas sales. These figures did not include royalties from the four songs he had written for the album.

The success of Michael Jackson's *Thriller* album was not just down to its musical brilliance. It was also promoted by one of the best pop videos of all time.

Videos were becoming more and more popular and Michael was keen to showcase his talents. He wanted to show his fans another side of him and it gave him an opportunity to show off. Unlike tours and performances they also offered the chance of a lasting legacy.

The new television music station MTV, launched in 1981, barely played black artists up until the Michael Jackson phenomenon. *Thriller* was so extraordinary; it broke through every barrier of prejudice, playing almost constantly for months.

Michael was at the forefront of the video revolution where simple visual versions of songs became elaborate mini-blockbusters costing millions of dollars. The elation he had felt on the set of *The Wiz* now translated to making pop videos instead.

'Billie Jean' and 'Beat It' showcased Michael's incredible dance skills, but gave his fans a glimpse of the man behind the songs – a tantalizing vision of their hero.

For 'Beat It' the producers hired 100 members of a Los Angeles street gang. *Thriller* was its own movie, a shock horror with monsters, zombies and its own voice over by the legendary Vincent Price. This was Michael's big screen and he loved it.

MTV were initially reluctant to take the videos. They had no doubt the records were huge hits, but they worried how the broadcast of black artists would play with Middle America.

The position drew accusations that the channel was racist. CBS Records made MTV an ultimatum: show the videos or they would pull all of their artists from the channel.

It wasn't long before 'Billie Jean' and 'Beat It' were aired throughout the day. Yet again, Michael Jackson had broken the mould.

On television, on the radio, on the airwaves, everywhere anyone could possibly look or listen, Michael Jackson was now scorching hot property. The *Thriller* album and its videos had catapulted him into a whole new stratosphere.

But not everyone was happy. The *Thriller* video, inspired by the cult film *An American Werewolf in London*, did not thrill the Jehovah's Witnesses at the head of Michael's family religion.

The video was a mini-movie, which tells the story of how Michael and his date Ola Ray, a former Playboy centrefold, run out of petrol on a road deep in dark woods.

Michael then turns into a werewolf and chases his date through the woods. In the next scene, Michael and Ola are members of the audience watching the video from a cinema, but on their way home they are chased by ghouls and monsters that emerge from a graveyard.

The film ends with Michael and Ola at his home seemingly waking from a dream but as the camera focuses in on his frightening yellow werewolf eyes Michael flashes an ominous smile suggesting he may be a beast after all.

Halfway through filming the video, Michael was summoned by church elders to a meeting at the Encino Kingdom Hall and warned they believed the video promoted Satanism and the occult. He would be thrown out of the church if

'Thriller' ever screened.

Michael was distraught and ordered the film be scrapped. He was fiercely loyal to the church and was still regularly evangelizing door-to-door for the Jehovah's Witness faith, despite his superstardom.

Only quick thinking from lawyer John Branca saved the day, as he suggested a disclaimer be shown ahead of the video stating that Michael Jackson did not endorse the occult. It did the trick and *Thriller* was released in late 1983.

There can be few people in the western world, or indeed on the planet who have access to a television, who have not seen the *Thriller* video.

The 14-minute video cost a staggering $600,000 to make – at a time when videos could be made for a mere $25,000. To help finance the video, Michael's lawyer John Branca sold the rights to *The Making of Thriller* to a production company and MTV agreed to contribute in exchange for its first screening. In the end the entire project cost more than $1 million.

But *Thriller* was a cinematic masterpiece. If Michael's earlier efforts had made artists and MTV really consider the way they approached music videos, this changed it forever.

CHAPTER 12

Motown 25

For his father, his family, his brothers and even his old bosses at Motown, the Jacksons' 1963 song 'I Want You Back' could hardly have been more relevant.

The family finally got their wish in March 1983, courtesy of *Motown 25: Yesterday, Today and Forever*, a television special to commemorate a quarter of a century of music from the famous record label.

It was also a tribute to Berry Gordy, the founder, the visionary and the person responsible for launching so many careers – including those of Michael Jackson and the Jackson Five.

Yet although Berry's myriad of stars recognized his undoubted genius, many had also come to see how he had also taken advantage of his star names. Signing them might have been a gamble, but the carefully written Motown contracts meant he went on to make vast sums of money from every one of them.

Had Michael Jackson remained with Motown he would never have achieved the riches his CBS contract had brought him. Most importantly for Michael, neither would he have been given the creative freedom he now enjoyed.

As a result there was initial scepticism about *Motown 25*, not just from Michael but also from other former Motown stars including Diana Ross and Marvin Gaye. These artists, however, eventually agreed to perform. Only Michael stood firm.

Michael was uncomfortable with the way things had worked out with Berry and Motown. He also did not particularly want to perform with his brothers. In his mind the Jacksons as a group were history. He was now a very successful solo artist and he did not want to return to his past.

Michael was also a perfectionist. The idea of recording a "live" television show filled him with dread. He was now a complete control freak – and yet this was "live" and could not be controlled.

Berry was distraught. Michael Jackson was a jewel in the Motown crown – a huge star he needed to be on the bill. He paid Michael a surprise visit at his Detroit studio, where he was working on a remix of 'Billie Jean'.

Their meeting prompted a change of heart from Michael, but with conditions. He would appear providing he could perform 'Billie Jean' – even though that was a hit for Epic not Motown – and on the basis that he could have the final edit on the material broadcast.

In exchange Michael would reluctantly appear with the Jackson Five and

Motown would have their show. Berry agreed to anything Michael wanted.

The show itself was a brilliant success. Most importantly, it brought the world what many commentators believe is Michael Jackson's greatest ever performance.

Michael appeared with the Jackson Five and, despite his misgivings, clearly enjoyed the family's performance at the Pasadena Civic Auditorium in California. Performing with Jermaine again proved to be an emotional experience for Michael and the crowd loved it.

Then, as the Jackson brothers shuffled off stage Michael turned and thanked the audience. He was dressed in what had already become his own unique look – a smart black, glittering tuxedo, silver sequined shirt, white glitter socks, shiny shoes and white left handed glove that was to become his trademark.

Michael spoke of his love for the Jackson Five days, but explained that now Michael Jackson was looking forward.

Then he produced a fedora from the sidelines and exploded into 'Billie Jean'. It is a performance that has been endlessly discussed and analysed as the live birth of a global megastar.

Michael began his usual robotic moves, borrowed from the body-popping electro scene, a series of joined up jerky movements, combing his hair, shuffling his feet, hand in pocket, dropping almost to his knees, sliding his feet across the stage.

Then three minutes and 39 seconds into 'Billie Jean', during an instrumental break, Michael Jackson moonwalked – a moment that did for pop what Buzz Aldrin and Neil Armstrong did for mankind.

As Berry Gordy said at Michael's funeral: "Michael Jackson went into orbit and never came down."

Michael's family watched from the sidelines spellbound. He had always had energy and enjoyed dancing but this was something different – their brother had just glided his way into megastardom.

His performance was the talk of America. Even his idol Fred Astraire tracked him down to congratulate him, praise that Michael often said was his greatest ever accolade. Gene Kelly visited his home. The area was swamped with fans, journalists and wellwishers.

The Moonwalk dance was actually improvised from an American television show called *Soul Train* – where dancer Geron 'Caspar' Candidate, a 16-year-old, had invented a move he called the 'Backslide'.

Caspar taught the move to Michael at a rehearsal studio in Los Angeles, practicing the move to Shalamar's hit 'Pop Along Kid'.

Casper claims Michael grasped the concept but couldn't repeat it perfectly for some time. In fact he wondered if his famous client would ever get it –

until he too, like millions of others, watched him perform it on the *Motown 25* television show.

The move wasn't technically the Moonwalk. It was technically the backslide. The moonwalk, according to its young inventor, was actually a similar move but made in a complete circle to create the 'moon' shape.

Regardless, Michael Jackson's signature move became known as the Moonwalk. And Caspar was delighted all the same.

CHAPTER 13

Don King

Jackie Onassis Kennedy – or Jackie O – had been an early obsession of Michael Jackson. His sister La Toya tells how she found a naked picture of Jackie in his chest of drawers – a paparazzi picture snatched without her permission.

In 1978, Michael briefly dated her daughter Caroline, taking her ice skating and then for dinner in the hope of meeting her mother.

Michael was 25 years old before he finally met the object of his desires in 1983, when Jackie accepted his invitation to lunch at his Encino family home.

When her limousine pulled up at the door the house was empty apart from Michael. He had asked all his staff to leave, because he wanted the former wife of the assassinated US President J F Kennedy all to himself.

Later, he took her to Disneyland where the pair made an instantly noticeable couple in their dark sunglasses and chic jackets.

Afterwards Michael told La Toya he admired Jackie's strength and ability to survive. She was someone he should have in his life as a mother figure, he said.

His own Katherine had enough to deal with, looking after her errant husband Joseph, he said. Jackie O could take care of them instead.

Having confirmed live on stage with his performance of 'Billie Jean' that he had now left his family career far behind, Michael now set about making it clear on paper.

His father had managed him with Joseph originally adding Richard Arons to the Jackson team, and then later bringing in Ron Weisner and Freddy DeMann as co-managers.

The pair were experienced, Weisner as a business manager and DeMann as a promoter and they had great contacts within the 'white' sections of the industry.

By the time *Motown 25* had happened, Michael had distanced Joseph further and further from his own affairs. In June 1983, he finally made the break. John Branca was left to tell Joseph, Ron and Freddy that their services were no longer required.

Michael decided they would not be replaced, saying that Branca would now manage him. In truth Michael Jackson planned to manage Michael Jackson.

Friends were concerned. Quincy Jones insisted Michael was creating potentially huge problems but he would not listen to his friend.

Joseph reacted to the news with complete horror. Even Katherine who had been hurt so badly by her husband and his womanizing ways felt the decision was unfair to Joseph. He had, after all, been the person responsible for setting the Jacksons off on the path to stardom and riches beyond their wildest possible dreams.

Michael hadn't even had the courtesy to tell Joseph directly. Instead he ordered Branca to instruct him in writing. Michael ensured he was out when the documents arrived.

Joseph was devastated and tried to talk Michael around but it was not to be. The scenes that followed at their Hayvenhurst home were bitter and made Michael miserable.

Michael was still living at home but had fired his father, a father who slept downstairs because Michael's mother had filed for divorce. For Janet and La Toya who also lived there the scenes were unbearable.

The only light relief came at weekends when their father travelled to spend time with his illegitimate child Joh'Vonnie. At these times, the Jacksons, now in their early twenties, would invite local children to the house to play in their video arcade or with the animals that were by now roaming around the estate grounds.

Michael's career was going from strength to strength, but the rest of the Jacksons were now struggling. His performance with his brothers at the Motown Special, however, had meant a potential revival for their careers.

Michael had reluctantly agreed to appear on, write and sing on two tracks for their new *Victory* album. He would also write a third song for them – but the brothers wanted more.

A tour to promote the *Victory* album would command vast sums of money. Michael Jackson and the Jackson Five would be box office gold dust and it would ensure that their forthcoming album stormed to the top of the charts.

The brothers knew it, and Joseph certainly saw the potential. Michael saw it but was not interested until his father pulled a masterstroke, appointing his wife Katherine as co-promoter.

None of the Jacksons could say no to Katherine and Michael eventually relented and agreed to appear.

Having decided to ditch their former management team, including their father Joseph, the Jacksons now turned to the flamboyant Don King. He was best known for promoting boxing contests involving Muhammad Ali and Sugar Ray Leonard, but the Jacksons knew he was the man who could bring in the most cash – and the most publicity – for their tour.

Don King was known for his flashy, showbusiness style – and it was often remarked that he thought he was the biggest star of whichever show he was involved with. He also had a questionable past, having been jailed in 1966 for manslaughter after killing a man in a street fight.

But whatever the Jacksons' private misgivings about King, he knew how to produce the goods, and in flamboyant style.

King paid the brothers $500,000 each as an advance against concert earnings –$3 million in total and put together a plan for 40 live shows that he believed would gross a staggering $33 million.

He also signed Pepsi-Cola as a sponsor for the tour, pulling in a further $5 million.

For the financially struggling Jacksons this was big money, but it was different for Michael. He was already rich beyond his wildest dreams and couldn't help thinking that he would easily have commanded all of that money personally had he been touring as a solo artist.

When King opened the Jacksons' *Victory* press conference in November 30, 1983 at the Tavern on the Green restaurant in New York City, he spent more than 45 minutes talking about himself, his greatness and even showing a documentary about himself.

By the time he introduced the Jacksons they were deeply unimpressed. This was supposed to be their show and yet they had been relegated to the sidelines.

CHAPTER 14

Fireworks

Fireworks had been expected during the Don King era but not literally.

Michael Jackson had reluctantly agreed to join his brothers for the much hyped 'Victory' tour and album and even more reluctantly agreed to allow Pepsi-Cola to sponsor their performances.

He was not happy. He didn't actually believe in the product and he believed even less in Don King after his incredible start to their partnership.

As part of the Pepsi sponsorship deal Michael Jackson was to appear in two commercials on the basis that he would have complete quality control – even though they were paying more than $5 million for the two adverts.

Michael, ever the perfectionist, decided that if he was going to be involved in the commercials they would be the best in the world, informing Pepsi President Roger Enrico that he would "make Coke wish they were Pepsi."

The first commercial was scheduled for January 27, 1984 and 3000 people were drafted into the Shrine Auditorium in Los Angeles to simulate a live concert. The Jacksons would sing 'You're a Whole New Generation' to the tune of Michael Jackson's smash hit 'Billie Jean.'

The Jacksons had been rehearsing since 9am although Michael didn't arrive on set until much later. As ever, he learned the moves almost instantly, and they began filming at 6.30pm.

As the music started, Michael descended from a podium and came down a staircase towards his brothers who were performing on the stage. Pyrotechnics exploded, smoke filled the stage, a dramatic moment that was pure showbiz.

Michael struck his now trademark pose, then a flash bomb exploded overhead.

Michael started to dance, spinning around and around but there was smoke and he began to feel a burning sensation close to his face.

As he turned towards the mock audience a huge gasp filled the air – Michael Jackson's hair was on fire. Smoke billowed upwards and suddenly he could feel the pain.

Michael collapsed onto the floor as his brothers and technicians rushed onto the stage. Mike Brando – head of Michael's security staff and Marlon Brando's son – burned his fingers trying to put out the flames.

The stunned crowd looked on in horror, fearing in the confusion that they had just witnessed the assassination of Michael Jackson, shot live on stage.

Jackson wanted to reassure his fans that he was still alive and he also realized this was a PR moment beyond comparison. The arena was sprawling with journalists and photographers, inside and out, so he suggested he be loaded into an ambulance in full view of the public.

As he was carried out on a stretcher, bandaged and covered in blankets, Michael raised a lonely sequined-gloved hand to the audience – a gesture bizarrely reminiscent of E.T., the alien created by Steven Spielberg for the blockbuster movie of the same name.

Jackson loved the resulting shots. He called it his moment, "that famous shot of me."

He was taken to the Cedars-Sinai Medical Centre and treated with antiseptic cream and bandages while his family joined him at the Brotman Memorial Hospital in Culver City. He escaped reasonably lightly, with a small area of skin suffering second-degree burns and an even smaller spot that experienced third degree. He was told his hair would grow back.

Pepsi would not get off so lightly.

Ironically, Michael had visited that very same hospital on New Year's Day – and spent time in the burns unit talking to victims. Now, he did so again before leaving the following day signing autographs and posing for pictures with other victims.

That night, he checked into the Sheraton Universal hotel and gathered his team of advisors including Steve Hoefflin, the chief plastic surgeon at Brotman Memorial Hospital and his lawyer John Branca as they watched footage from the commercial.

When Michael saw the film he was enraged. It looked as though his entire head was on fire. Pepsi had set him on fire and now he was determined they would burn.

His team seized the tapes from the cameraman and Michael ordered that they be released to the press. He wanted his fans to see what Pepsi had done to him.

Pepsi President Roger Enrico heard of his plan and was terrified. He knew only too well that if that advert was shown Jackson fans would desert his brand. Pepsi would be in serious trouble.

A photograph was leaked to the Associated Press that made the front pages of newspapers around the world. In truth, the publicity he received personally was far bigger than he would have received for the commercial alone.

The whole world seemed to be reeling from the story. Thousands sent cards and messages to the Brotman Memorial Hospital, even President Ronald Regan, the most powerful man in the world, wanted to pass on his best wishes sending a letter on February 1, 1984.

"I was pleased to learn that you were not seriously hurt in your recent accident," wrote the former film actor. "I know from experience that these things can happen on the set – no matter how much caution is exercised."

Michael's team of advisors begged with him to reconsider his decision to release the footage. They feared it would be too much for some of his young fans.

He agreed but remained determined Pepsi would suffer the consequences, instructing John Branca to seek a financial settlement. Pepsi paid $1.5 million to ensure the matter was never taken to court.

The money was immediately donated by Jackson to the Brotman Hospital, to help finance the Michael Jackson Burn Centre that had been established in the wake of his stay there.

That kind-hearted gesture would prove to be the start of one of Michael Jackson's lasting legacies. Michael would go on to raise countless millions for charity.

CHAPTER 15

King of Pop

Michael Jackson cried when *Off The Wall*, his 1979 album only received one Grammy in the R&B section – despite making recording history at the time with five hit singles and more than 6 million copies sold around the world.

He took the failure personally and refused to consider the political game that had always surrounded the awards as the major record labels appeared more interested in congratulating one another than truly recognizing talented work.

Elvis Presley never received a Grammy, neither had James Brown, the Rolling Stones or Diana Ross.

Michael didn't care. His work was brilliant and it deserved the acclaim and he was determined that he could break the mould.

Since childhood, Michael had been driven by a burning desire to be the best. He was a perfectionist and he would not rest until he had reached the summit of whichever particular mountain he was trying to conquer.

He had spent his childhood being warned by his father Joseph that in life there were winners and losers in life and his boys would be winners. It was not open to debate.

Even after all these years, Michael's desire to prove himself to his father and his family still burned strong. Coupled with his fear of failure was a cripplingly low sense of self-esteem that required constant adulation and confirmation that Michael was truly one of the greatest artists in the world.

It didn't matter that the public, the industry and family clearly loved his work – or that he was astonishingly rich and his records were selling by the millions across the globe. Michael wanted critical acclaim – and to be recognized by the industry.

With *Thriller*, that dream finally came true. The album won him a staggering 12 nominations – the highest number ever for a single performer.

While he waited for the night of the Grammies itself, Michael was inducted into the *Guinness Book of Records* on February 7, 1984, in recognition of *Thriller* having broken all records for album sales, with more than 25 million copies sold.

The Grammy awards were held at the Shrine Auditorium in Los Angeles on February 28, 1984, the venue from which he had been rushed to hospital only a month before – after being burned during filming for Pepsi. With heavy irony, the completed adverts were premiered at the show.

His actress friend Brooke Shields accompanied Michael to the awards after she had begged him to take her with him for the most important night of his life.

At Michael's funeral where Shields gave a long and emotional speech she remembered how the two had met when she was just 13.

"I'm thinking back to when we met and the many times that we spent together and whenever we were out together and there was a picture taken there would be a caption of some kind and the caption would read 'an odd couple' or an 'unlikely pair' but to us it was the most natural and easiest of friendships," she recalled.

"Maybe it was because we both understood what it was like to be in the spotlight from a very early age.

"I used to tease him and I'd say, 'You know, I started when I was 11 months old – you're a slacker'. You were what? Five?

"Both of us needed to be adults very early. But when we were together we were two little kids having fun.

"We never collaborated together, we never performed together or danced on the same stage, although he did try, in vain one night, to, unsuccessfully, to teach me the Moonwalk and he basically just shook his head and crossed his arms at my attempt.

"We never filmed a video or recorded a song but what we did do was laugh.

"It was always a competition to see who could make the other one laugh more or be sillier. Michael loved to laugh. His heart would burst out of him when he was laughing.

"His sense of humour was delightful and he was very mischievous."

She also remembered a hilarious and surreal incident that had occurred when she was Michael's guest at Elizabeth Taylor's wedding.

"I remember the night before Elizabeth Taylor's wedding and he called me prior and asked me to join him – he didn't want to be alone for all the festivities. It was the night before the big day and we tried to sneak in to get the first peek at the dress.

"We were giggling like crazy and almost passed out when we realized that Elizabeth was actually asleep in the bed, we thought she was in an entirely different room and we had to laugh and sneak out.

"Then at the point of the wedding when there was the first dance we had to joke that we were the mother and father of the bride. Yes, it may have seemed very odd to the outside but we made it fun and we made it real."

She also revealed she used to tease Michael about his glove-wearing.

"When he started wearing the glove I was like, 'What's with the glove?' I told him; 'If you're gonna hold my hand it better be the non-glove because sequins hurt me! They would dig in'.

"He would just shake his head and smile. He loved to be teased. Seeing him smile made you feel like everything was going to be alright."

At that year's Grammies, Michael was expected to do well. But even he could not have dreamed of winning an astonishing eight awards out of a possible ten. He was nominated three times in one single category.

It was effectively the music industry officially acknowledging the genius already recognized by millions of people – Michael Jackson had been officially crowned King of Pop.

Michael accepted each award acknowledging his family, his showbiz friends like Katharine Hepburn who was watching from the gallery, and paying tribute to Jackie Wilson, a legend of rhythm and blues who had recently died and was a his personal hero.

Confirmed as one of the most famous and powerful men on the planet Michael now had access to anyone and anywhere he wanted, and invites to A-list parties flowed like water. Everybody wanted Michael Jackson at their party.

Legends of stage and screen would queue up to get their picture with Michael, by now usually dressed in dark sunglasses, a military style jacket, and the outfit completed with white sequined glove. In truth, Michael was often more star struck than they were.

Liza Minnelli became a firm friend and mentor. Michael felt he could trust her and also that after years in showbusiness she understood how things worked and could advise him wisely. The pair became virtually inseparable and he was best man when she eventually wed David Guest in March 2002 along with Elizabeth Taylor who stood as matron of honour.

Meanwhile, Michael Jackson remained committed to the 'Victory' tour with the Jackson five. As his concerns about the 40 concert dates and the involvement of Don King grew, Michael decided to appoint Frank Dileo as his new manager.

He had met Frank in the months leading up to the release of *Thriller*. Head of promotion at Epic Records, he had a reputation for getting things done. He was loud, brash, the diametric opposite of Michael Jackson – but most importantly he was someone who always delivered.

Meanwhile, Michael ordered his lawyer John Branca to draw up a list of demands he believed would protect himself and his finances from King, the former boxing promoter.

The Jackson brothers felt they too needed a new manager and appointed Jack Nance, the groups' former road manager at Motown.

More experts were added to the backroom team. Chuck Sullivan, head of Stadium Management Corporation from Foxboro, Massachusetts would organize concerts, and Irving Azoff, head of MCA, would act as tour consultant. Joseph and Katherine Jackson were there always in the shadows and of course there was King.

Michael was becoming obsessed with the recognition and power that came hand in glove with his newly found fame. As a result it seemed to those around him that the line between fantasy and fact – a line that had barely existed in any case during his fairytale life – was now being completely erased.

When Michael was approached by the US Government about possibly using his track 'Beat It' for a radio commercial highlighting the dangers of drink driving he thought nothing of insisting that he be invited to the White House to meet the President.

President Ronald Reagan, the most powerful man on the planet, had quite a few things to worry about at the time, in particular the Cold War and ensuring that nuclear war was not about to break out, but he was still happy to invite Michael to Washington.

At the White House, he was given a plaque. President Regan told Michael he was "proof of what a person could accomplish through a lifestyle free of alcohol or drug abuse."

"If Americans can follow his example," Reagan said, "then we can face up to the problem of drinking and driving, and we can, in Michael's words, beat it…"

The reception that followed proved to be a bizarre affair. According to friends Michael was invited to tour the White House and meet a few children of staff members. The Diplomatic Reception Room, which had been set aside for this intimate meeting, was packed with adults.

Michael panicked. Unable to deal with the pressure, he fled the room, locking himself in the toilet of the Presidential Library. Soon, his entourage of eight security men, manager Frank Dielo, lawyer John Branca and publicist Normal Winter and a young man in his twenties, unknown to everyone expect Michael, were outside pleading with him to open the door.

Michael insisted he would not come out unless the adults were ordered out and children, as promised, were bought into the room.

President Reagan's staff quickly cleared the room and found the promised children. Frank Dielo assured Michael the coast was clear and then ordered his new client out.

Michael shuffled into the room to find just a few officials and their children, including Elizabeth Dole who was the first to approach, holding out her copy of *Thriller* and asking him if he would sign it.

President Regan and First Lady Nancy joined their guest and were heard speculating about the possibility that Michael Jackson had undergone cosmetic surgery. They both agreed he was a very good-looking man. Or maybe a good-looking man who looked like a girl.

Soon, the whole of America was talking about Michael Jackson, but in a negative way, as one of Don King's stunts backfired badly.

Don King, Joseph Jackson and Chuck Sullivan decided that tickets for the 'Victory' Tour would be sold in lots of four, they would be $30 each and fans would have to pay in advance. This would not guarantee them their ticket. Instead it would buy them in a draw. Those selected, at random by a computer, would receive their tickets, the unlucky ones would have their money returned.

The promoters estimated that more than 12 million fans would mail in around $1.5 BILLION in money orders but only one in ten would receive tickets. This meant the Jacksons would make around $8 million in interest alone from the fans' cash held in the bank as it would take four to six weeks before tickets would be processed and then posted.

Coupons would be printed in newspapers and the Jacksons would insist that those media partners would not charge for the advertising space using the argument that they were performing a public duty.

Michael's brothers thought the scheme was brilliant. It would make them rich again. If this was to be their last payday from their Jackson fame it would be a big one at least.

Outside of their little entourage, the proposal provoked utter outrage. In the real world, Michael Jackson fans could not afford to pay $30 per ticket – especially given that they were being forced to buy four.

The media attacked the Jacksons and Michael as the figurehead for being shamelessly greedy and exploiting their fan base.

Worse still, Michael was criticized by his own loyal supporters. His young fans wanted to see their idol but had no chance.

Even fellow artists were appalled at the apparent flagrant betrayal to their fans. James Brown, Michael's absolute idol, shunned an invite to appear with him at Madison Square Garden in New York because of the incident.

Michael ordered the policy be scrapped, saying he would not perform or be part of the tour unless the system was completely changed. A new over-the-counter scheme was agreed in time for the third date of the 'Victory' tour and Michael Jackson announced at a press conference he would be donating his personal income from the tour to charity. He would also be giving away 2000 tickets for each date to disadvantaged children in each city they visited.

The financial loss was a tiny ripple in the Michael Jackson money pool. He was now worth an estimated $75 million and his income from the tour was estimated at three to $5 million. It was small fry compared with the lasting damage the tour might have done to his reputation had he not forced the change.

Meanwhile, there was worse to come for the Jacksons' PR machine. There were allegations that the band's management had asked for free stadium rent in the cities they were visiting and a share in the profits from food, drink and parking charges – all which would have cost the local tax payers around $5 million.

The album was released and the show hit the road on July 6, 1984 in Kansas City, Missouri. The pressure was immense and it was very soon apparent that the fans were only there to see Michael

His brothers had effectively been reduced to being his backing singers and they didn't like it. They were happy to be taking the cash but a rivalry was emerging and the brothers began sniping at each other, not just privately but to the media.

They were also receiving criticism for the actual show. The concerts, supposedly to promote their *Victory* album, didn't in fact feature any songs from that record. It seemed a bizarre way to celebrate the promotion of a new album,

During this time Michael was becomingly increasing distant from his brothers. He travelled separately in a private jet when they flew with commercial airlines, he invited his friends to concerts when the family had voted none should be allowed and when the Jacksons were approached about a deal to film their show he vowed to walk away if they agreed to it, even though it could earn millions of dollars – only to arrange for his own filming to begin three days later. The brothers were furious and ultimately blocked the film's release.

Family members stayed on separate floors at hotels and refused to talk, and band meetings now included lawyers for each respective Jackson. The 'Victory' tour was anything but. It was ripping the family apart and Michael Jackson perhaps saw it as a fitting final act of destruction. The Jackson Five were already dead in his eyes. The 'Victory' tour was the death throes of the band, and the tearing apart of the final ties to the rest of his family.

As if the perils of the tour weren't enough for Michael to deal with, there came the sudden news that Janet, the sister he referred to as his twin, had eloped and married James DeBarge.

Not unusually for them, the Jackson family did not approve of Janet and James' relationship. DeBarge, part of a family group having a string of hits including the future 'Rhythm of the Night', had a drink and drug problem and the family were worried about Janet. Michael, whose closeness to Janet extended back to childhood, was distraught. Suddenly, he felt completely alone.

Stress, combined with his strict vegetarian diet, was taking its toll on Michael physically. He had lost an incredible amount of weight and was losing interest in anything except fantasy.

The only company he kept was with the children he invited to the palatial Hayvenhurst home he had rebuilt to include a $2 million amusement arcade. Even there he would remain inside his bedroom watching videos or riding alone around the estate on the electric golf buggy he had made to copy Mr Toad's Wilde Ride at Disneyland.

Even when he was in company Michael Jackson felt alone.

CHAPTER 16

Rumours

By 1984, Michael Jackson decided he had had enough of the rumours he was gay. Constant speculation about his homosexuality had reached a fever pitch, and he decided it was time to put a stop to it once and for all.

"I am not a homo," he said. "I'm not going to have a nervous breakdown because people think I like having sex with men. But I don't and that's that."

He lined up Frank Dileo to deliver his message to the world. A carefully worded two page statement that gave a clear warning that Michael Jackson would not tolerate any more speculation.

Frank was a tough talker, a powerful figure and the Michael hoped media would quickly realize they had pushed him too far.

On September 5, 1984, Frank Dileo addressed a major news conference held at a West Hollywood sound studio from behind dark sunglasses, as the smoke curled upwards from a fat cigar.

He read: "For some time now, I have been searching my conscience as to whether or not I should publicly react to the many falsehoods that have been spread about me. I have decided to make this statement based on the injustice of these allegations and the far-reaching trauma those who feel close to me are suffering.

"I feel very fortunate to have been blessed with recognition for my efforts. This recognition also brings with it a responsibility to one's admirers throughout the world. Performers should always serve as role models who set an example for young people.

"It saddens me that many may actually believe the present flurry of accusations.

"To this end, and I do mean END: NO! I've never taken hormones to maintain my high voice; NO! I've never had my cheekbones altered in any way; NO! I've never had cosmetic surgery on my eyes. YES! One day in the future I plan to get married and have a family. Any statements to the contrary are simply untrue.

"Henceforth, as new fantasies are printed, I have advised my attorneys of my willingness to institute legal actions and subsequently prosecute all guilty to the fullest extent of the law.

"As noted earlier, I love children. We all know that kids are very impressionable and therefore susceptible to such stories.

"I'm certain that some have already been hurt by this terrible slander. In addition to their admiration, I would like to keep their respect."

Frank Dileo would not be taking questions. That was the end of the matter. Michael Jackson was not gay.

Except he didn't actually say that in his statement.

In fact, Dileo didn't actually dispel any specific allegation and whilst the statement denied that Michael had had surgery on his eyes it willfully omitted the fact that he had already undergone three operations to his nose. It was a string of half-truths address to a closed press conference without any dialogue with the media or the public.

Far from putting an end to the rumours, the Dileo statement merely prompted more questions.

The constant media speculation was prompted by the absence of a leading lady. Michael Jackson was one of the richest, most powerful men on the planet. He could have any woman he liked, and such was the height of his fame he could probably have slept with every woman on the planet at the same time if he had wanted.

He was photographed with virtually every leading lady, he was the most sought-after guest, organizers wanted him at every 'A' list party and yet he didn't have a girlfriend.

But then Michael Jackson's upbringing hadn't prepared him for adulthood and its relationships. As a child he simply had not had the time to mix with "real" girls. From his earliest years his brothers were part of a family group and the moment he joined them they had began working. His days were full of schooling and then singing.

He had also been brought up as a devoted Jehovah's Witness and so already had very strong feelings on sex, marriage and what was right or wrong.

His religion was also very clear that homosexuality was wrong – so even if Michael had felt he might have been gay it was impossible for him to explore his feelings.

His thoughts on sex, women and relationships were further blurred and twisted by the adult scenes he had witnessed as a young boy. On the road with the Jacksons, he had played at strip clubs while still a child, watching women take their clothes off for men.

Even if that hadn't affected him, the sights, sounds and actions of his father Joseph, paying a blatant disregard for his marriage to Michael's mother as he slept with groupies behind Katherine's back, had hurt him deeply.

Many of Michael's friends believed that his upbringing had left him feeling that sex, in its physical sense, was a dirty, disgusting thing. And his view of relationships was even more jaundiced. After witnessing the failure of his parents' marriage, he had watched as his brothers' relationships had hit the rocks and gradually began to disintegrate, and seen his beloved sister elope and marry a man who was addicted to drink and drugs.

Michael also feared that even if he met someone he would never be able to fully trust them. He had seen the pain and suffering inflicted on his wonderful mother and he was too sensitive to endure that himself.

Of course he could invite any woman in the world to meet him, but how could he meet a real person, someone who would love and trust him as a person, not because he was Michael Jackson?

Deep down, Michael was envious of the fact that his brothers and sister, mother and father all had someone. For all the bad times they were put through they did at least have a soul mate, someone to talk too, to discuss their inner secrets with, to shower them with the intimacy and affection Michael craved.

Michael, in contrast, might have been the most successful in his family, but he had no one. He felt alone. Isolated.

Around this time, Michael began surrounding himself with children. Children, at least, appeared to present no danger to him. They just wanted to have fun, to play; they had no ulterior motive, no interest in exploiting Michael Jackson. And with children he was always in control.

In the adult world, everyone wanted a piece of Michael Jackson. Even his own family had proven through the 'Victory' Tour that they saw him as a chance to make money.

A child himself in so many ways, Michael's home had been lavishly rebuilt to include a mini zoo and more things to play with than inside a toy factory. For the children invited there, hanging around with Michael Jackson was a lot of fun.

Michael could not see, or refused to see the potential risks in spending so much time with younger men and boys.

His relationship with young actor Emmanuel Lewis had already been questioned. Lewis was 12 years old when he met the pop star. He stood just three feet, four inches tall and Michael would carry him as though he were a toddler.

They met after Michael had seen him on television and he contacted the boy's parents and invited the family to his California home. The pair quickly became friends and constantly played together. Michael was by now 25 years old.

Lewis's parents halted their relationship when the pair allegedly booked into the Four Seasons hotel in Los Angeles as father and son.

Ten-year-old Jonathan Spence had become a constant companion; and there was the good-looking unknown teenager who had accompanied him to the White House. Just what was going on with Michael Jackson?

There had been speculation about his apparent obsession with his look – was he trying to look like Diana Ross? Did he want to be a woman? How did his voice remain so high? Was he having hormone injections?

The final straw that prompted Michael's decision to issue the statement was a story in August 1984 that he was having a gay affair with British pop star Boy George. It was not true.

Michael's management team insisted the best way to deal with the innuendo and accusations was to ignore it. Respond and it would merely add substance to the rumour.

Michael refused to listen to the advice, saying his fans deserved the truth.

In fact, his entire career had already been crammed with half-truths, from the Jacksons' very discovery. Michael had been happy to go along with the claims that Diana Ross "discovered" him and the Jacksons in Gary, Indiana, knowing that simply wasn't true.

Meanwhile, he appeared to be developing an uncanny ability for blocking out certain things from his memory. For example, the Gina Sprague incident with his mother simply never happened in his mind. He denied it until the day he died. He had already set a mental precedent that it was okay to gloss over certain events.

This was a short leap to the dishonesty in the statement – which gave the impression that he hadn't had any surgery yet he had already endured three operations to his nose.

Michael Jackson had proved he was the king of spin. On the dance floor and now off it.

During this time, Michael also showed himself to be an untrustworthy friend to the former Beatle Paul McCartney, previously a personal hero.

McCartney had been a friend of Michael's for years. During their time together Paul had revealed how he earned a fortune thanks to other people's songs, more than $40 million a year.

He had purchased the publishing rights to a huge catalogue of songs including those of Buddy Holly which meant every time that particular piece of music was played, on the radio, on the television, in a film, in a commercial, he was paid. It was brilliant.

Ironically, his string of deals didn't include his own music. Paul McCartney and John Lennon had sold the rights to 251 Beatles' records, written between 1964 and 1971, to Dick James publishing.

James later sold the collection, called 'Northern Songs' to ATV Music Group that was in turn purchased by Robert Holmes å Court's Bell Group.

The collection included the Beatles' biggest hits, 'All You Need Is Love',

'Yesterday', 'Help', 'Hey Jude' and 'Let It Be'. Michael had suggested he might buy. McCartney congratulated him on his joke.

Michael had been so taken by Paul's lesson that he immediately began collecting music himself, purchasing the Sly Stone catalogue and other artists.

When John Branca told him in 1984 that the Beatles' collection 'Northern Songs' was available he had no doubts. He wanted it. Whatever the cost.

McCartney had attempted to buy back the music he had so famously written. He had been told a few years earlier he could purchase the collection for $20 million and invited Yoko Ono, John Lennon's widow, to partner him and buy a 50 per cent share but she felt it was too expensive.

There was a fierce bidding war for the collection but Michael Jackson eventually secured the catalogue for $47.5 million. Paul McCartney was furious.

It meant that every time a Beatles' record was played Michael Jackson would receive 50 per cent of the royalties while McCartney and Yoko Ono would split the remaining 50 per cent.

Worst still, every time Paul McCartney performed one of his own songs, he would have to pay Jackson. He was absolutely livid.

He was further enraged with Michael's use of his songs. He sold 'All You Need Is Love' to Panasonic for $240,000, 'Revolution' to Nike and even hired staff to develop films based around song titles.

McCartney believed his actions were cheapening his songs. He was certain John Lennon would have been turning in his grave. He felt betrayed by Michael. How could he have treated him this way?

Michael remained completely ambivalent. He didn't believe he had done anything wrong. This was business and if Paul McCartney, the richest man in music did not want to stump up the cash himself that was not his problem.

For her part, Yoko Ono was quite happy. She felt that it would not have been right if either her estate or McCartney's owned the music.

Michael Jackson was proving himself to be a hard-nosed businessman who was not afraid to make tough decisions. Ironically, Joseph Jackson must have been proud.

CHAPTER 17

"Wacko Jacko"

In an attempt to make up for the ticket fiasco from the 'Victory' tour Jackson had promised to donate all of his earnings from the concerts to charity.

He was as good as his word and handed over $5 million to the T.J Matell Foundation For Cancer Research, The United Negro College Fund and the Ronald McDonald Camp For Good Times.

Then, he was asked to take part in a musical project called 'We Are The World'.

The proposed charity single was a major event, inspired by the British hit single 'Do They Know It's Christmas'. Recorded by a specially-created supergroup of heavyweight record artists including Bono of U2, George Michael and Boy George, the UK song went on to raise millions for starving children in Africa after its launch on November 29, 1984.

Harry Belafonte had witnessed the incredible impact of the 'Band Aid' record and wanted to do something similar in America. He suggested a collaboration of their top stars and asked showbiz manager Ken Kragen if his clients Lionel Richie and Kenny Rogers would help. They enlisted Stevie Wonder and then approached Michael Jackson.

Michael thought the idea was brilliant. He had never been interested in politics. He preferred cartoons and music and old films to anything serious – but also he considered himself to be a child and hated seeing any youngster miserable.

Michael already spent hours after concerts meeting sick children. J. Randy Taraborrelli describes in his biography of Jackson, *The Magic and The Madness* how "a boy with spinal cancer was bought to Michael on a stretcher one night after a show. When the boy reached up to Michael, Michael grabbed his hand and held tight. The child smiled."

Frank Dileo turned away and broke into tears. "He's not afraid to look into the worst suffering and find the smallest part that's positive and beautiful," Frank told Taraborrelli.

Jackson had seen individual cases of children suffering through ill health but he had little, if any, idea of the pain and suffering endured by the victims of famine. The fact that some little boys and girls did not even access to fresh water was too horrendous for Michael to even consider.

He immediately agreed to join 'USA For Africa', the name of the supergroup assembling for the charity single, and he offered to help Lionel Richie write the single that the group would record.

They spent a week at Michael's Hayvenhurst home writing 'We Are The World', finally completing the piece on January 21, 1985.

Michael and Richie then set about assembling an all-star cast of 44-stars including Billy Joel, Ray Charles, Diana Ross, Bob Dylan, Bruce Springsteen, Tina Turner and of course the Jacksons along with producer Quincy Jones.

Few of the assembled stars really understood the exact cause being supported by the record, but they were told it was a worthwhile venture, it was all about helping children and they knew it was a sure fire PR winner.

But thoughts of personal glory were quickly forgotten within a few minutes of a visit from Bob Geldof, lead singer of British band the Boomtown Rats, and the man responsible for Band Aid and the British hit 'Feed The World'.

Geldof told the group of musical stars of his time visiting Ethiopia. The mood instantly changed. He introduced them to two women from the famine-stricken country and the studio at A&M in Hollywood, full of some of the biggest egos in pop, was suddenly silent with emotion.

Michael Jackson taught the cast the melody and their lyrics and 'We Are The World' was laid down as a recording. Only Michael recorded his section separately, adding it later along with the video featuring his section.

The team of egos united for what was to become a magical night and finally completed their record at seven 30 the following morning. It was released on March 7, 1985 and sold out in three days. It went on to become No. 1 in American for a month, No. 1 in the UK and raised more than $8 million for the USA for Africa fund.

At the Grammies that year, 1986, Michael and the 'USA For Africa' team were odds on to win 'Record Of The Year'.

Michael, increasingly detached from reality, had a bizarre publicity idea for the Grammies. He arranged for a female fan to storm the stage and attempt to jump onto him. His security staff would save the day and the event would achieve worldwide publicity. Fortunately, the girl didn't make it through the huge throng of press and other staff backstage.

But stunts like that were making the friends and advisors around Michael concerned. They knew he was eccentric; they ignored his love of children and their games. They ignored the garish clothes that were now part of being Michael Jackson and the lavish spending sprees that were in truth, becoming ridiculous.

Shops would deliberately increase prices when Michael Jackson popped in knowing he was an obsessive spender with little idea as to the real value of things. He knew what was happening but didn't care. Perhaps he thought he was being generous. But shopkeepers simply saw it as an opportunity to make huge sums of money from their eccentric customer.

But Michael's behaviour was moving from eccentric to alarmingly bizarre.

In Michael's eyes, it was perfectly normal to wear a hairy gorilla mask in public, or a surgical facemask, or a huge black fedora. He claimed it was to hide his identity but in fact it attracted enormous attention – and once word spread it was pretty easy to spot Michael Jackson in a crowd.

Behind the mask, Michael's own face was now changing shape so that he was becoming unrecognizable as the handsome young man on the front of the *Thriller* album, of the confident African American teenager in the tuxedo on the cover of *Off The Wall*.

Michael had always been obsessed with achieving perfection. His music, his music videos, and his publicity machine were all the subject of absolute personal scrutiny.

Now his face, body and general personal appearance were receiving more and scrutiny from the man in the mirror. Every day Michael looked at himself and every day he found something he could improve.

Haunted by his father's cruel taunts about his nose and his skin, and the teasing of his brothers, he had a third nose operation and then a cleft added to his chin. He craved a dancer's body and described himself as a work in progress.

He also began bleaching his skin with a product available over the counter called Porcelana. He started to use lots of it. For a black icon, he appeared less and less comfortable not just in his own skin but also with the colour of his skin. What may have started as a way to rid himself of his teenage acne stars began to appear a quest to turn himself into a white man.

Around this time, Michael leaked a story that he now slept at night in an oxygen tank, or hyperbaric chamber. There were so many strange things about him that were now true, yet this was a pure hoax.

Michael planned the story of the oxygen chamber as a brilliant PR stunt. His new project, *Captain EO*, a 3-D, 17-minute film directed by legend Francis Ford Coppola and executively produced by George Lucas, was about to preview at the Epcot Centre in Orlando, Florida and Disneyland in Anaheim, California.

The firm had an astonishing $20 million budget, included stars like Anjelica Huston and the soundtrack was pure Michael Jackson.

Michael had seen the hyperbaric chamber during his treatment for burns after his accident filming the Pepsi commercial. The unit is used to help patients recover. By exposing them to conditions of increased air pressure it floods body tissue with oxygen.

He was fascinated and did seriously consider buying one. He insisted on travelling to see the device properly and asked for a photograph of him inside it.

News of this bizarre incident leaked to the tabloid *National Enquirer* and reporter Charles Montgomery. He tried to confirm the story, but Jackson's manager Frank Dileo flatly denied it.

But when Michael was told of the media interest, he loved it. He decided that the story should be published. He wanted Dileo to tell Montgomery that Michael had bought the chamber to ensure he lived to 150 years of age, and from now on he would sleep in it every night, even taking it with him on tour.

His managers clearly thought it was nonsense. Yet, it didn't harm anyone and if Michael wanted it then who were they to argue.

Charles Montgomery received an amazing phone call. He was drip fed the story, even promised a sensational picture of the superstar sleeping in the chamber – on the basis that it made the front cover.

The Jackson team recruited showbiz publicist Michael Levine to tout the story around the rest of the media on the basis that he never revealed that he was working from them. He was ordered to give the impression that he was effectively exposing the singer. All the time he was on the payroll.

Manager Frank Dileo was also to play his part. When he would be inevitably be contacted by the press he was to confirm the story by telling the media how he banned Jackson from buying the device, citing concerns over his welfare.

When the *National Enquirer* splashed the story on September 16, 1986, it created a media furore. The entire western world was suddenly familiar with the words 'hyperbaric chamber'. Even Michael's family began searching their home for a glimpse of the incredible life-extending device.

Michael loved this new game. He had always appreciated the need for clever public relations but now he was acting as puppet master, exacting revenge on a media that had poured scorn on his personal life, tortured him with slanders and lied about him. Now they were dancing to his tune. And he had a whole back catalogue of tunes he intended to play to them.

Ideas like the 'Elephant Man bones' story. It was a clever concoction: Michael Jackson, mega star, mega rich, wanted to buy the 97-year-old skeleton of John Merrick, a man whose body was so deformed he had become a Victorian sideshow.

The bones were housed in a glass case at the Royal London Hospital. He didn't intend to buy them of course but only he knew that.

Word leaked to the press in May 1987 that he would pay $500,000 for the bones and he would display them at his California home. He was suddenly becoming a headline writer's dream.

The media thought they had fashioned "Wacko Jacko", but he was always Michael's own creation. Like the masks that he wore and the surgery that altered him, his Wacko alter ego was part of an elaborate disguise.

Jackson did actually bid for the bones of Merrick. He didn't want them but felt obliged to go through the motions to ensure that when journalists checked the story it would be confirmed. After all, he was dealing with a world renowned and respected Royal London Hospital, not simply a publicist. They would receive calls and the story would be denied because it clearly wasn't true.

So Jackson offered a million dollars to ensure the story stood up. He reasoned that if the bid was accepted he could afford to blow the money. The bid wasn't accepted, and his plan worked. By making the offer he had at least tried to buy them, making his own claim 100 per cent true.

It was a confusing time for his management team. What was he trying to do?

In 1987 the theatre director Trevor Nunn was privy to a surreal event that was probably truth rather than one of Michael's fictions.

Dileo contacted Nunn while he was in Australia to try and set up a meeting between him and the singer. It emerged Michael yearned to be able to do something really spectacular in his concerts – like fly over the audience.

"Oh I know just how to do that," said Nunn. "I had people flying all over the audience when I did Peter Pan."

"Something seismic happened," says Nunn. "He reacted as if an electric current had just passed through him. He sat up on the edge of his chair, clutching the arms with splayed hands, one of which was gloved."

"You did Peter Pan," he whispered?

"Yeah in London," I said.

"Oh my God, I don't believe it," he said, then kneeling down, his eyes full of tears he placed his hands on Nunn's knees.

"Could I play Peter Pan? Is it too late? Will you let me play Peter? All I ever want to do is play Peter Pan."

Michael knew every line from the text, every incident from the story, said Nunn.

He didn't really want to play Peter Pan, the character. He wanted to be Peter Pan, the person, the real "lost boy".

Michael was going to so much trouble to create crazy stories, when in fact the truth was more fantastic than the fiction.

Visiting Michael's home was now like going to a menagerie or a zoo.

Michael had a huge collection of pets at his California home. There were lamas, snakes, ostriches. Even a chimpanzee called Bubbles.

Bubbles was a three-year-old chimp rescued by Jackson from a cancer research clinic in Texas in 1985. Michael quickly became inseparable from his new primate friend, taking him to public appearances, shopping, and media interviews.

Bubbles accompanied the singer to the studio for the recording of the *Bad* album, made a cameo appearance in the 'Liberian Girl' video, shared hotel suites on tour and even appeared in Kenny Rogers's book, *Your Friends and Mine* at Michael's request.

"Bubbles was so human it was almost frightening," Rogers recalls. "He would take Christopher (Roger's son) by the hand, walk over to the refrigerator, open it, take out a banana and hand it to him. Christopher was amazed. We all were."

Bubbles wore the same clothes as Michael and there were tales of him cleaning the Jackson home, sharing Michael's private bathroom, and any number of truths and fictions as the line between the two became more and more blurred.

The chimpanzee appeared in a later release of Michael Jackson's video game 'Moonwalker' and was the star of 'Michael's Pets', a range of soft toys based on the animals owned by Jackson.

Sculptor Jeff Koons would later be commissioned to make three identical porcelain sculptures of Bubbles and Jackson, worth $250,000 each. One was sold in 2001 auction for a staggering $5.6 million to an anonymous bidder.

In the media, it was now open season. Michael Jackson sold magazines, newspapers and television programmes, and the stories just kept coming, as journalists realized there was huge money to be made from Michael Jackson stories.

Michael had encouraged them. He had baited them. He had rolled the first snowball and pushed it over the mountainside, and now it was rolling down hill at such an incredible speed, gaining a size and momentum even Michael could never have anticipated.

Michael Jackson's PR machine was now totally out of control. Like Frankenstein, he had created his own monster and it was now freely rampaging around the world – a fact he would later concede and bitterly regret.

According to the magazines Michael had seen Jesus in a puff of smoke, met John Lennon's ghost, convinced Elizabeth Taylor to sleep with him in his hyperbaric chamber, fallen in love with Princess Diana and enjoyed a series of love affairs with model Tatiana Thumbtzen.

He was alleged to have accused the pop star Prince of trying to turn Bubbles mad by using powers of "ESP" on the chimpanzee, apparently telling the *National Enquirer*; "What kind of sicko would mess with a monkey? This is the final straw. Poor, poor Bubbles."

Given Michael had started all this himself, how could he possibly complain? How could he ever follow up his earlier threat to the press and sue? Michael's life was out of control, the thing in life he most hated. Surrounded by chimps and lamas, lies and half-truths, yes-men and dysfunctional family members. "Wacko Jacko" might have been his own creation, but slowly it was coming more and more to represent the state of his own mind.

CHAPTER 18

Faith

Throughout his career, even after the spectacular success of *Thriller*, Michael would join his family members at the Kingdom Hall in California two or three times a week as a practising Jehovah's Witness.

Incredibly, however famous he got, he wasn't deterred from continuing to knock on doors in his own neighbourhood or in towns were he was on tour, offering a copy of *The Watchtower*.

By now arguably the most famous man in the world, Michael would wear hats, scarves, fake wigs, moustaches and beards, but even in disguise he was still committed to attracting more followers to his family's faith.

Sometimes his disguise would not work. Where many Jehovah's Witnesses in California simply experienced doors slamming shut, Michael would often be invited in.

Many simply wanted to spend time with Michael Jackson. He could have been selling washing machines, second hand cars or the *Encyclopedia Britannica*. Michael Jackson was in their home. But he also brought in converts, who thought if his religion was good enough to bring him knocking doors while a global superstar there must be something to it.

Michael became a Jehovah's Witness when he was just five years old. His mother Katherine was converted after being visited by a follower in 1963 at their home on Jackson Street in Gary, Indiana.

She insisted that her entire family follow her and every week they would walk to the Kingdom Hall to worship, and even Joseph attended services for a short time.

It was tough for her hardworking children who already had little enough to celebrate. Jehovah's Witnesses do not recognise birthdays, Christmas or Easter – although eventually Joseph and Katherine relaxed that rule.

Michael, La Toya and Rebbie were very serious about their religion, but as Michael's career developed at stratospheric speed it increasingly began to bring him into conflict with his faith.

Jehovah's Witnesses are judged on good deeds, not materialistic possessions and are positively discouraged from spending large sums, and certainly not wasting money.

By the mid-1980s Michael Jackson was spending money like it was going out of fashion. He was making it at an even quicker rate but that was hardly the point.

Even his acts of generosity were looked down upon by the elders. Jehovah's Witnesses were only supposed to donate to the church. Then there was the issue of Michael's alleged homosexuality. Whilst there was no firm evidence as to Michael Jackson's sexual habits or indeed his actual sexuality these rumours persisted, even after his denial that he was gay, and he was continually photographed or witnessed with young boys.

Homosexuality was banned in the faith. It was as simple as that. His mother Katherine had already made it clear that her son was not gay because it was banned by their religion.

It was considered by their faith that Armageddon would one day occur and the world would destruct. When it did, only a few would survive and God would only consider the pure. That meant no homosexual behaviour for certain.

The church watched and waited and became increasingly worried about their association with the pop star and his behaviour.

Thriller had been the biggest challenge so far, when Michael had released the incredible video to the title track of his album.

He had been ordered in 1984 to explain himself, as church leaders feared the lavish production appeared to be promoting Satanism and the occult.

Their reaction troubled Michael to the point where he originally ordered the video be scrapped. Only last minute intervention from his management team and the suggestion that he issue a disclaimer saved the project from disaster.

Jackson told the faith's *Awake!* magazine on May 22, 1984 he would never make such a mistake again, claiming: "I would never do it again! I just intended to do a good, fun short film, not to purposely bring to the screen something to scare people or to do anything bad.

"I want to do what's right. I would never do anything like that again. A lot of people were offended by it.

"That makes me feel bad. I don't want them to feel that way. I realize now that it wasn't a good idea. I'll never do a video like that again!

"In fact, I have blocked further distribution of the film over which I have control, including its release in some other countries. There's all kinds of promotional stuff being proposed on *Thriller*. But I tell them, 'No, no, no. I don't want to do anything on *Thriller*. No more *Thriller*."

Despite the quick thinking of the Jackson management concern continued amongst the Jehovah's Witness community about his general behaviour.

Now as "Wacko Jacko" took hold, the elders saw the need to step in once again.

In the spring of 1987, Michael was summoned to a meeting by the elders of the church in Woodland Hills, California and told in no uncertain terms that the publicity that surrounded him was not befitting of a Jehovah's Witness.

As their most famous follower, the elders were greatly concerned about the long-term damage he might potentially bring to the religion. They also believed he was setting a terrible example.

Michael agreed to renounce the faith and a letter was set to key leaders of *Watchtower* instructing them to remain silent on the issue. They would not be drawn in by the media.

Michael's sister La Toya Jackson wrote about their faith in her autobiography, *LA TOYA – Growing Up in the Jackson Family*, which was published in 1991.

She said: "After Mother became a Jehovah's Witness, we no longer celebrated Christmas at home. So my grandparents, feeling sorry for us, took us to Christmas parties and gave us gifts and money. Although this went against my mother's religious beliefs, she permitted it, seeing how happy it made us.

"While my older brothers were dating, the opposite sex was the last thing on my mind. For one thing, Michael and I were very active in the Jehovah's Witness faith. By this time most of our siblings had basically given it up.

"Five days a week the two of us and Mother studied the Bible at home and attended the Kingdom Hall.... Every morning Michael and I witnessed, knocking on doors around Los Angeles, spreading the word of Jehovah.

"As my brother's fame grew, he had to don disguises, like a rubber fat suit he bought years later, around the time of *Thriller*. Michael's incognito easily fooled adults, but it was a rare child who didn't see through his costume.

"As an entertainer and idol of millions, Michael was always being reproached for such things as the length of his hair and for wearing widely flared bell-bottoms. My brother loves vivid colors, particularly red, causing one elder to criticize, 'The colors you wear are too bright, and you're attracting attention to yourself. You must stick with brown and black.' Some Witnesses refused to associate with us at all.

"Whatever long-standing reservations these Witnesses held about Michael being a pop idol crystallised the night he won those record-breaking eight honors at the 1984 Grammy Awards. The very next morning one elder issued him an ultimatum that my brother must choose between music and the religion. 'What you're doing is wrong,' the man declared.

"Truth be told, many Jehovah's Witnesses used to congregate outside the Kingdom Hall hoping to catch a glimpse of Michael Jackson, knowing full well this kind of adulation was forbidden."

She also revealed in her book how he had been told never to talk to his sister because she hadn't been coming to church.

She told how Michael said: "'La Toya, I ...' The words came out in a torrent. 'I can't talk to you ever again...' The elders had a big meeting, and they told me never to speak to you because you haven't been coming to the Kingdom Hall.

"Michael then excused himself, drove over to his friend Marlon Brando's house, asking his advice. Marlon advised him, `For heaven's sake, Michael, that's your sister. If that's the way they're going to do things, you don't need to be part of that. You can always get another religion, but you can never get another sister.'

"Michael decided to disobey the elders' edict and after that never attended any more meetings. To this day we've never discussed exactly what happened, but I know he subsequently severed his ties to the organisation through a formal letter."

Michael's renunciation of his faith that summer was a terrible blow for Katherine Jackson.

Officially it meant she was now forbidden to discuss spiritual matters with her son, and some followers even felt that former members are totally disowned by their friends and families.

Katherine would never disown Michael of course. She was a mother first and foremost, and whatever her son was becoming she still loved him absolutely.

CHAPTER 19

Neverland

As his life became a media freak show it was sometimes hard to remember Michael Jackson was still one of the world's greatest living musicians.

The success of *Thriller* remains unmatched and will probably now never be rivalled in terms of sales and success, given the changing entertainment market and the rise of digital downloads.

But in the summer of 1987 there was one man who believed he could smash *Thriller* into the ground. That man was Michael Jackson.

For his new album, *Bad*, anything less than the astonishing 38.5 million copies of *Thriller* sold would be a failure. He wanted 100 million sales. He insisted it could be done and ordered those around him to show positivity.

Settling down in the studio with Quincy Jones, he explained he intended to create a masterpiece, an even better album with even more incredible videos. He and Jones carefully considered 62 songs written by Michael.

J. Randy Taraborrelli also describes in his biography *Music and the Madness* how the pair discussed a duet for the track 'I Just Can't Stop Loving You' but Barbara Streisand felt she was too old and Diana Ross was angry with Michael after a tiff over a restaurant date with Elizabeth Taylor.

There was also a failed collaboration attempt with Prince for the title track of the album, which would include a bizarre Michael Jackson PR campaign with stories being planted over the pair's non-existent feud to fuel a frenzy ahead of the song's release.

Even before the album was recorded, the pressure was getting to Michael. He was desperate to succeed and frightened to fail. *Bad* had to be perfect.

The album was released in July 1987 with 'I Just Can't Stop Loving You' released as single in the same month. Critical acclaim did not reach the heights of *Thriller* or *Off The Wall*, but the single went straight to No. 1 in America and the UK, and the album did the same. The follow-up single, 'Bad', also went to No. 1.

An 18-month world tour kicked off in Japan achieving huge success, grossing $21 million. But wherever Michael went a media more interested in his "Wacko Jacko" creation than his music dogged him.

As the stories surrounding him grew more and more outlandish, Michael decided to put an end to them, trying to put the genie back into the bottle.

He wrote a letter to *People* magazine in America. It was handwritten on hotel stationary, poorly spelt and largely unintelligible

"Like the old Indian proverb says do not judge a man until you've walked 2 moons in his moccasins. Most people don't know me, that is why they write such things in which most is not true.

"I cry very very often because it hurts and I worry about the children all my children all over the world, I live for them.

"If a man could say nothing against a character but what he can prove, history could not be written.

"Animals strike, not from malice, but because they want to live, it is the same with those who criticize, they desire our blood, not our pain.

"But still I must achieve I must seek truth in all things. I must endure for the power I was sent forth, for the world for the children.

But have mercy, for I've been bleeding a long time now."

The letter did not have the affect Michael hoped for. Instead of winning the world's sympathy, he was widely ridiculed. His manager Frank Dileo was by now a worried man. For the first time he was beginning to believe his famous client was falling apart.

Meanwhile, the third single from the *Bad* album 'The Way You Make Me Feel' had also gone to No. 1. Michael's touring continued, the stage shows become bigger, better and more elaborate, yet it was clear Michael was personally losing public support.

People were buying his records but Michael Jackson needed much more than that. He wanted to be adored.

Michael had been spent his entire life being reminded by his father, Joseph, that the Jackson boys had to be winners in life. His father no doubt loved him and was proud of him despite his barbaric acts of violence, but he had never told Michael – leaving him to find the missing love and approval amongst his fans.

Even in the hours after Michael's death in June 2009 Joseph would show little in the way of kindness to his son during an interview he gave to America satellite channel CNN. The exchange left his fans staggered.

CNN: "Joe, I know the past few days have been tough.

Joe: "Ug? Tough. Yeah, tough. Remember, we just lost the biggest superstar in the world."

He also used the interview to promote his new record label Ranch Records and even mentioned that Michael only recently came to visit him on his wedding anniversary to Katherine. In death, as in life, Joseph's relationship with his famous son was all about his own selfishness.

Jackson's 'Bad' tour continued to be a huge success in America and Japan though ticket sales in Europe and Australia were affected by the constant tide of tacky headlines and bizarre stories that persisted about his personal life.

Even so, the third single from the album 'The Way You Make Me Feel' went straight to the top of the charts in America, as did the fourth, 'Man In The Mirror'; 'Dirty Diana' made it to No. 5, which is still a remarkable achievement.

Yet Michael remained frustrated. Anyone else would have been delighted. Another smash hit album with four singles topping the American charts, it was incredible success by the yardstick of any other recording artist.

But Michael wasn't any other recording artist. He was only interested in perfection. In his eyes, not only had *Bad* failed to reach the dizzy heights of *Thriller* it had also failed to be recognized by the industry. That hurt Michael to his core, where his childhood lack of self-esteem meant he was easily damaged.

"If Elvis is supposed to be the King, what about me?" he asked.

Don King's words of six years ago rang in his head: "You're the biggest star ever, but the white man will never let you be bigger than Elvis. Never. So you can forget that."

Despite – or perhaps because – of this, Michael's performance at the Grammys on March 2 in 1988 saw a sensational return to form. It reminded people that Michael Jackson was an amazing entertainer. His set was breathtaking and he literally stole the show.

But the experience then turned bitterly sour for Michael. The *Bad* album and all its singles had all gone straight to the top of the charts, but the Grammy judges ignored them. Michael Jackson didn't win a single award.

"Wacko Jacko", the Chimp loving, oxygen chamber sleeping, bone collector was eclipsing Michael Jackson the musician.

Far from seeing this moment as a wake up call and the moment to reconnect with reality, Michael's response was to retreat even further into fantasy.

He had recently found himself a remote ranch where could escape the increasingly relentless pressure – a space in which he could be the child his childhood never allowed, free from his family, safe in his own fantasy world.

Michael named his ranch Neverland after the place where nobody ever grows up. He had been obsessed with the story of Peter Pan since he had been a small child. Neverland Valley – its full name – would become the place where he could live as a child surrounded by childish things.

Jackson paid $17 million for the 2,700-acre estate in Santa Ynez Valley in March 1998 while he was touring with Bad. He had stayed there with Paul McCartney when they filmed the video for their record 'Say, Say, Say' years earlier, when the sprawling estate was known as Sycamore Ranch.

Now, Michael wanted his lawyer John Branca and accountant Marshall Gelfand to sign for the house. He believed if his name wasn't on the deeds then it would be impossible for the media to track him down and provide him with a place to hide.

He changed his mind less than a month later after being persuaded it was madness not to be the legal owner his own house.

Michael's biggest hero was Walt Disney and the Disneyland theme park he had created was one of his favourite places to visit in the world. Even if he did have to wear a disguise, it only made him more like his favourite characters, Mickey and Minnie Mouse.

Michael had developed the blueprint for Neverland while still living with his family in California.

He had lived at 4641 Hayvenhurst Avenue since May 1971 when his father had paid $250,000 for the six-bedroomed, five-bathroom house and the two-acre estate.

When Joseph had struggled financially in 1981 Michael had bought a share in the property and eventually the whole house. As he steadily took control over the family living space, he added more and more fantastical elements to the architecture as he began to live out his private fantasy world.

First of all, he knocked the original house down and rebuilt it in the style of a Tudor palace, drawing inspiration from properties he had seen in England and other cities in Europe.

The property included a white "wedding cake" style fountain on a brick-laid drive in front of a house bedecked with stain-leaded light windows.

Black and white swans swam in the garden ponds while llamas, peacocks, a giraffe and a ram also grazed on the grounds. There was even a snake called Muscles.

A model version of Michael's favourite place, Disneyland's main street was created next to the garage – and there was his own private amusement park complete with puppet figures that Michael treated as friends.

A huge swimming pool and outdoor hot tubs were to be expected but the house also boasted a 32-seater theatre, complete with a full library of Fred Astaire films and his bedroom suite featured five female mannequins – all from different ethnic groups and there were pictures of Peter Pan on all the walls.

The garden was crammed with exotic flowers, a waterfall and colourful ceramic tiles.

In the centre of the garage stood a giant clock with Roman numerals.

Now, away from his family and with a whole new space in which to indulge his fantasies, Michael Jackson set about transforming Neverland Valley into his own private wonderland.

Part funfair, part theme park, by the time he had finished it had merry go rounds, dodgem cars and miniature castles, an electric train, a ferris wheel, vintage video games, fire trucks, an ornate marble fountain and statues of playful children.

There was also a Red Indian village with canvas teepees and a model horse, a cinema, and his private menagerie had been extended to create an exotic private zoo.

Neverland Valley was also home to a treasure chest of fantasy memorabilia: a larger than life statue of Spiderman, the prop hands that Johnny Depp wore in the film *Edward Scissor Hands*; the car from *Driving Miss Daisy*, a model replica of the Disneyland castle.

The soft verdant countryside and four-acre man-made lake in sapphire blue made it look more like England than California.

There were life size mannequins of old ladies and children having tea; there was a horse-drawn carriage and a bicycle with a fridge on the front for ice cream.

In his private rooms, Michael's bed was covered with a £50,000 sequinned duvet. A print of the *Last Supper*, in which the singer sat in the place of Jesus, with Abraham Lincoln and Elvis by his side as apostles, hung on the wall above.

The theme park also paid homage to Hollywood and the days of the silver screen – ball gowns from actress from another age, oil paintings of Elizabeth Taylor. Several first editions, including one of JM Barrie's *Peter Pan*.

The Neverland library was crammed with 10,000 literary classics, including books on philosophy, history, psychology and sociology.

His lawyer Bon Sanger said he was privately extremely well read and the books were covered with notes.

"He was very intellectual but didn't flaunt it," said Sangar.

Michael was also an obsessive collector. If he fell in love with something, he bought it. And, of course, Neverland was also packed with stacks of Michael Jackson memorabilia.

From the fedora he wore in the video for 'Billie Jean' to the glittering red jacket he sported on the *Thriller* video, this also was Michael's own museum to himself.

The private zoo held a positive menagerie of strange and wonderful animals.

There was a 12 ft albino python, a tiny 34 inch stallion called Cricket, an elephant called Gypsy, a miniature sheep, pot bellied pigs, giraffes, elephants and crocodiles – and, of course Bubbles, the chimpanzee

At night endless strings of thousands and thousands of twinkling lights transformed the ranch into a fairytale place lit up like the night sky.

But with Michael now practically a recluse, Neverland differed in one large respect from Disneyland. It was empty. There was only Michael, his advisors and his animals. To complete the fantasy, there should be children playing on the rides, the sound of laughter and bustle. Michael increasingly sought only the company of children, and now he wanted them to come to Neverland and share his sacred fantasy space.

Michael began to invite children from all over the world to come to his estate. They arrived at the ranch railway station to the sound of Disney music blasting out from more than a 100 hidden speakers.

Michael himself used a fleet of child-sized diesel-powered cars and a Pope mobile-style electric buggy to get around the lush green acres.

It was where he took his friends for tree climbing water fights and, crucially, "sleepovers".

It was where Elizabeth Taylor married her seventh husband Larry Fortensky under a gazebo in a million dollar ceremony in 1991. And it was where he entertained child stars like Macaulay Culkin.

Culkin had become Hollywood's richest young actor at the age of nine after starring in the first *Home Alone* movie. He and Michael were both child stars who had worked their whole childhoods and had been suddenly catapulted to fame at a young age. By the time he was 12 Culkin was one of Michael's closest friends and even helped him design his Peter Pan palace.

By the mid-1990s Michael was spending in the region of $150,000 a year just on toys to supply Neverland and its visitors.

"It's like stepping into Oz," he once said. "Once you come in the gates, the outside world does not exist."

There was a private butler and a designated chef to see to every need, but for Michael and his mother – a frequent visitor to Neverland – one of the happiest rituals was a simple breakfast together on the flower-scented patio.

Child visitors would tuck into their meals in the large kitchen – or picnic on the extensive lawns.

Safety and security were paramount and CCTV cameras were carefully concealed in scores of pretty birdhouses scattered around the ranch.

In its heyday 54 full-time paid staff manned the estate with a payroll bill of £32,000 a month. Medical insurance alone ran to £74,000. Monthly vets bills often topped £41,000 with more than £1500 spent on elephant bedding and £5,000 in hay for horses and camels. The annual upkeep was estimated to be a staggering £2 million.

Money didn't matter to Michael. Now, safe inside his walled Neverland he was finally safe from his family, advisors, hangers on and the ever-intrusive media. In Neverland the outside world did not exist and for Michael the maintaining of his private fantasy was priceless.

CHAPTER 20

Moonies

Michael had left Hayvenhurst, but still his family's troubles intruded on his Neverland idyll.

Joseph Jackson had been a poor father, a terrible husband and, if possible, an even worse businessman – squandering millions on a series of poor investments.

Joseph had invested in oil and even launched his own brand of fizzy cola drink, 'JoCola', but appeared to rely heavily on his famous son's name to land any kind of business deal.

The Berwin Entertainment Centre Complex debacle was another in a string of bad deals.

Joseph had agreed to buy the Hollywood complex, which included a recording studio, nightclub and leisure facilities, with entrepreneur Gary Berwin. They would pay $7.1 million, with Joseph owning 85 per cent and Berwin the remaining 15 per cent.

Joseph opted to pay cash, handing Berwin a cheque for $7.1 million but with strict instructions not to cash it for a few days. He needed to move funds.

When he asked for a longer delay, then another, it became quickly apparent to Berwin this money would never arrive.

Joseph had expected to raise the money from Michael, but in fact his son had told him he wasn't interested in getting involved and advised his father that he too should walk away. He was not prepared to lend any money and the matter was closed.

Joseph Jackson was issued with a writ and warned to either pay the full amount or damages if he could not complete the deal. A court eventually ordered him to pay Berwin $3 million.

Berwin told Michael Jackson's biographer J. Randy Taraborrelli: "I couldn't imagine Michael Jackson, who earns all these millions, could not give his father the money. I couldn't believe that he would let his father go down like that.

"This building would have put Joseph on his feet once and for all and independently of the family. He would never had had to deal with the kids any more, professionally.

"I tried to appeal not only to Michael but also to the other kids, all of whom are isolated by hard-nosed lawyers. Not one of them cared about Joseph's security. As much as I grew to dislike Joseph, I also felt sorry for him. "Joseph indicated that money was not a problem. I had no reason to doubt him.

"Michael had just brought the Beatles' catalogue for $47 million, so I believed that the family had access to money. In fact Joseph laughed when I bought up the question of finances."

In fact, Michael's brothers and sisters' personal lives were in chaos. Hazel and Jermaine had divorced – only for Jermaine to move into his parents' home with his new girlfriend and their new baby. Tito and Dee Dee's marriage was also in trouble.

La Toya's attempts to break into the world of music were not going well. The harsh truth was she was not as musically gifted as the others.

Janet, however, did appear to have a gift. She was seen as having real potential but after her first two albums struggled she decided to seek a new direction.

She axed Joseph and teamed up with new manager John McClain, who in turn introduced her to Jimmy Jam and Terry Lewis and got to work on her image. With their help she sharpened up her clothes, lost weight and employed new songwriters. The result was a sharp and sassy album, *Control*, that became one of the best sellers of 1986.

Her single 'What Have You Done For Me Lately' was a massive hit. The song was supposedly about a neglectful boyfriend, but with Janet earning her first co-writing credits, friends believed it was actually a veiled attack on the rest of the Jacksons.

Control was a concept album all about Janet's new-found independence, and escaping the clutches of her famous family. It also marked the end of Janet's marriage to James DeBarge.

Hit singles including 'Nasty, Control', 'When I Think of You' and 'Let's Wait a While' followed.

Today, *Control* is regarded as one of the most influential R&B albums of all time, pioneering a mixture of rap, R&B, and swing that help in the rise of a new musical genre known as "new jack swing".

Ironically, while Michael was obviously pleased for his sister it did feel curious to have another groundbreaking superstar in the family.

But at least Janet was one of the few family members who didn't rely on Michael. All too often when things went wrong he was the first one they called. When money was tight they would call Michael. When they needed to give their particular business venture a boost they would use Michael's name or beg him to put in an appearance.

And the requests were getting more and more bizarre.

Around this time, the Jackson family – with the sole exception of Janet – attempted to do a deal with the Moonies, the Korean Unification Church widely seen as a cult.

The saga revolved around the Moonies' leader, Reverend Sun Myung Moon's attempts to have his church recognized as a respectable organisation. As part of his new PR offensive, the Reverend wanted to stage a special concert in Korea featuring Michael Jackson.

Reverend Moon approached the Jackson family through a Korean businessman called Kenneth Choi. He met Joseph and Katherine Jackson through their adviser Jerome Howard and explained that a $15 million payout was on offer for a concert in Korea.

He claimed the funds would come from a shipping company and Korean newspaper *the Segye Times*. In fact the Unification Church and therefore the Moonies owned the newspaper.

Michael Jackson and his brothers would play four two-hour concerts. Michael would have to open with the Korean national anthem and perform three numbers in Korean.

The Jacksons knew Michael would never agree to singing in Korean but given the money on offer they agreed to try and convince him to play the concerts.

If they succeeded they would be paid $7.5 million for the concerts. They would receive 100 per cent of ticket sales and they could keep all monies made from broadcasting the concert outside of Korea.

It was one hell of a deal. All they needed was for their famous brother to agree.

After the debacle of the 'Victory' tour, the family knew their chances of persuading their brother were slim, but one by one they tried to convince Michael. Finally, the family used their secret weapon – Katherine, the only one Michael couldn't say no to. But this time the strategy failed. The stark answer came back: "No".

The Koreans then began a new strategy, lavishing gifts upon the Jackson family, friends, associates, anyone who could potentially persuade Michael to take part.

They gave away cars and cash, bodyguards, pretty much anything anyone wanted. The pressure was beginning to build on the Jacksons. The Moonies needed Michael Jackson in Korea, and the Reverend Moon wasn't someone people said no to. They didn't care what it took.

Michael was sent expensive artwork, a white Rolls-Royce and the promise of an additional $8 million personal payment on top of the $7.5 million already offered.

The Moonies eventually offered to pay $1 million to the person – whoever it was – who could get this deal done.

Katherine asked Michael one last time, Michael relented. In the end his family needed him, and the simple fact was that the Moonies were never going to give up. He decided the best way to get his peace of mind back was to take a deep breath, do the concerts and get out.

Incredibly, given the lengths they went to secure Michael's involvement, and with the deal now done Reverend Moon attempted to change the terms. He announced that with fortunes they had already spent on bribing the family they couldn't now pay Michael the addition $8 million and offered $2.5 million instead.

In the farce that followed, the deal collapsed. Michael received a writ. Joseph, Katherine, Jerome Howard, Jermaine and Bill Bray were also named and ordered to return all the monies and gifts they had received.

Michael counter sued for $8 million and insisted that nothing given would be returned. For him, the whole affair left a bitter taste. The realisation that family members were happy to accept bribes to bring him alongside hurt him deeply.

He was also unhappy with his manager Frank Dileo and he decided it was time for a fresh approach to his business dealings.

Their relationship, once one of the best in showbusiness, had been showing signs of strain. Michael had been unhappy at Frank's media profile, which was growing because Michael refused to give interviews. Newspapers and television now interviewed Frank instead, and Michael felt his newfound television career was starting to affect his judgment.

He was also unhappy with Dileo's management of his *Moonwalker* video project. Including live footage, music, videos and a feature film starring himself and the actor Joe Pesci, the 90-minute production had cost a staggering $27 million to make. It was successfully released in Japan, but there had been distribution issues in the US that had caused other territories to back away from the project.

Even so, Michael remained King of Video – the film went straight to the top of *Billboard* music video cassette chart and stayed there for 22 weeks. It was only knocked off its No. 1 slot by 'Michael Jackson: The Legend Continues'.

The accompanying book, Michael's autobiography *Moonwalk*, shot to the top of the best seller lists selling 200,000 copies.

In 1989, Michael's annual earnings from album sales, endorsements and concerts alone were estimated at $125m

In fact, Michael barely had time to concentrate on his business affairs because his family was once more in the spotlight.

His sister La Toya was now threatening to expose the Jackson family's secrets with a book that would tell the truth about the siblings' childhood, warts and all. She had already been paid $300,000 as an advance from Putnam, the publishing house, and had promised there would be fireworks.

The most explosive allegation of La Toya's book was that his father Joseph had sexually molested Michael Jackson, and that La Toya had also suffered sexual abuse as a child. Even though the allegations were withdrawn from her autobiography La Toya did make the allegations during a tour to promote her book, causing great distress to her family.

It was a sensational – and unfounded – claim that was never pursued and was immediately and categorically denied both by Joseph and Michael. Her unsubstantiated claims were immediately rejected by her family. She later withdrew her claims.

Michael's lawyer John Branca warned Jack Gordon, La Toya's manager and partner, that Michael would sue her and the publishers if such a ludicrous claim were made.

It wasn't the first time La Toya had rebelled against the family. Only a few months earlier she had stripped naked for *Playboy* magazine.

Frustrated by sales of her albums, she blamed her manager and father, Joseph. She wanted to be as big as Michael but simply did not have his vision, commitment or raw talent.

Her parents had hired Jack Gordon to handle her affairs, but the couple were soon dating.

Gordon had a criminal conviction, having spent time in prison for attempting to bribe the Nevada State Gaming Commission. Joseph even claims Gordon threatened him after he questioned expenses on his daughter's account.

Jack Gordon took La Toya straight to Hugh Heffner, owner of *Playboy* magazine. She agreed to pose naked with a boa constrictor.

Joseph and Katherine were too ashamed to leave Hayvenhurst for a whole month. La Toya claimed publically that at least Michael approved of the photoshoot. Hearing her claim, Michael was furious and said he hated the pictures.

Now, La Toya's revenge was to expose her family to further horror.

And when she heard of their united dismay she made it clear the only way she would stop would be if they paid her.

Jack Gordon put a deal together that would cost Katherine and Joseph Jackson $5 million to stop the book. It was an astonishingly callous way to treat her family, however they might have behaved.

In the end, there was no pay-off from the family. Despite rumours Michael had tried to buy the publishing firm to stop the book, he was adamant he would not get involved.

La Toya was now told in no uncertain terms that her family – from whom she had been estranged since marrying Gordon in September 1989 – would sue her without a second thought if she continued with her claims.

La Toya – Growing Up In The Jackson Family, was published in September 1991. It was deeply critical of the family, with the exception of Michael. There were no allegations published, despite her threats, that he had been molested as a child and its view of him was largely positive. La Toya in effect withdrew her claim that her father Joseph had molested her as a child.

Michael, as ever, turned to work, persuaded by his team that it was time to release a greatest hits album called *Decade* to celebrate a brilliant ten years of unparalleled pop success.

John Branca negotiated an incredible deal with Sony Corporation who by now owned CBS Records, and the album was scheduled for Christmas release.

Jackson would receive an $18 million advance – $15 million that would be recouped from sales and $3 million that he would keep. It was the biggest deal in music history.

The deal would also see Sony establish and fund a customized Jackson Records label. Profits would be split equally and he would own half the stock. The label would be worth around $50 million.

Michael was also given a $5 million advance from Warner-Tamerlane Publishing Corporation, or Warner Bros for a publishing deal but, in truth, his heart was not in a greatest hits record. His relentless creative urge meant he really wanted to get on with creating new material, and felt a Greatest Hits album would disappoint his fans.

Michael was also interested in making and starring in a film; Prince had released *Purple Rain* and received great praise. He wanted to do the same and began working on a deal with producer David Geffen.

Geffen was a friend and trusted advisor to Jackson. He had made millions from running a record label and had a string of films including *Risky Business* and *Beetlejuice* as well as Broadway hits to his name. He was listed by *Forbes* magazine as being the richest man in Hollywood at that time, worth more than $100 million.

Geffen was to have a growing influence in the decisions taken by Michael Jackson.

CHAPTER 21

Surgery

In June 1990, Michael Jackson lay in the emergency room of St John's Hospital in Santa Monica, California – the place where on the weekend of his death 19 years later Farrah Fawcett would quietly slip away. Hearing of the news that he had been admitted suffering "chest discomfort" fans began flocking to the hospital, and President George H.W. Bush was immediately in touch.

Hordes of photographs and reporters rushed to the scene. Friends, family and some of the biggest names in show business sent flowers and cards. The rumour mill was working overtime. Was the King of Pop having a heart attack?

Michael had been complaining of chest pains and feeling dizzy in the days leading up to his admission on June 3, 1990.

He was weak, pale and apparently in a lot of pain. Medics ran a series of tests including one for HIV, which was negative.

Press interest grew; worried fans maintained an all-night vigil. Was Michael Jackson dying?

In fact, Michael Jackson had suffered a panic attack at most. And there are those who believe the entire event was staged to allow him to get out of various commitments – and for the pure attention.

Of course Michael was no stranger to hospitals and medical procedures. His obsession with his body, his face and his ready access to the money to pay for any operation he wanted had left him addicted to surgery.

By now he had made more than ten changes to his nose which now included a prosthetic nose-tip, which he hid with make-up.

Years of surgery had seen his nose collapse as a result of the trauma. It was the reason he was often seen wearing a surgical mask in public.

He was also diagnosed as suffering with the skin disease vitiligo in the 1980s. His dermatologist Dr Arnold Klein diagnosed him as having discoid lupus, an auto-immune disease that causes darkening or lightening of the skin on his scalp.

For years he had applied Porcelana in a bid to lighten the colour of his skin but now he was told he needed to avoid sunlight, hence he was by now often seen carrying an umbrella in sunshine.

He had suffered panic attacks when he was a child but they had got fewer and fewer as he grew older and learned to cope better with the huge pressures placed on his shoulders.

Now whether it was a panic attack or play acting, the situation had certainly been provoked by an awkward and stressful situation he found himself in with friends.

Michael had been negotiating a deal with Disney Studios over a project for their theme parks when David Geffen asked him to appear at the Universal Theme Park in Florida.

Steven Spielberg was also pressuring Michael to go to Florida but the bosses at Disney were not happy and told him to choose one or the other.

As the pressure mounted, Michael was admitted to hospital. He was eventually diagnosed as having Costochondritis – an inflammation of the cartilage connecting his upper ribs to his breastbone, and a common cause of chest pain. Doctors noted he was also suffering with over exertion and stress.

Apart from the family pressures and concerns over a new album Michael had lost his grandmother Martha Bridges that summer and he had to cope with the death of 18-year-old Ryan White.

Ryan had AIDS and had fought a long legal battle for the right to attend a normal school despite being HIV Positive. Michael was supportive of his fight for justice.

Michael was also growing increasingly paranoid. He had started secretly tape recording conversations, he scrambled telephone calls, and he was convinced staff members were not to be trusted. In fact, the only person he knew he could trust was his mother Katherine.

On June 23 1992, *Daily Mirror* photographer Ken Lennox took a shot of Michael in close-up at a press conference where he was announcing the formation of a charity and to a launch a worldwide tour for his *Dangerous* album. The offending picture revealed him as "a scarred phantom" said the *Mirror* "with a hole in his nose, one cheek higher than the other and an oddly sagging chin".

It ran it across a whole page under the headline "This is the real Michael Jackson".

Michael Jackson sued. At the High Court in London, *Mirror* Group Newspapers and the paper's former editor Richard Stott acknowledged that Michael Jackson was neither hideously disfigured nor scarred.

Jackson's solicitor, Marcus Barclay, told Mr Justice Popplewell the case had been settled "amicably" on confidential terms.

He told the court: "Representatives of *The Mirror* have since met directly with the plaintiff and have seen with their own eyes that the photographs which were published, albeit in good faith, do not accurately represent the plaintiff's appearance.

"The defendants regret the injury which has been done to the plaintiff's reputation and have agreed they will not repeat these allegations."

At around the same time Michael also became frightened of the idea that he might die.

Along with the spoon-bending psychic Uri Geller, one of his eccentric friends, he went to a conference on human cloning.

His then chauffeur Al Bowman remembers how excited the singer was as he "bounced out ...like a small child".

"I heard him and Uri talking in the back of the limo. He was talking about the prospect of being cloned. He grabbed Uri by both arms and told him: "I really want to do it Uri. I don' care how much it costs.'

There were rumours he contacted a bizarre religious sect called the Raelians to pursue the dream. The sect has a scientific arm called Clonaid, which believes cloning is the key to eternal life. There was no telling what Michael Jackson would do next.

Now, in a move that stunned the music world, he decided to split with John Branca, the lawyer who had single-handedly master minded his career – turning him from an emerging act worth around a million dollars in 1980, to a worldwide superstar worth more than $300 million.

Michael had already dismissed Frank Dileo and accountant Marshall Gelfand and he had become convinced that Branca was not devoting enough time to him.

Branca was paid by Michael on a monthly retainer. He had a host of other clients including the Rolling Stones and, unlike Frank Dileo, who had been told he was only allowed to work with Michael, he had been allowed to continue his work with other people.

Terence Trent D'Arby joined his client-list and that worried Michael. He believed the singer was a potential rival and ordered Branca to drop him. The order was refused.

Branca also felt he was deserving of more money from Michael. After all it was his brilliant negotiating skills that had made the singer all of his money. He asked for a share of the publishing company.

In the middle of all of this Michael was being told about a possible way out of his current deal with Sony. Under Californian law no contract can run for more than seven years. He had signed for the label in 1983 so he could effectively leave.

Branca told Michael it was a bad idea. He still owed them four albums under the terms of the agreed contract and Sony would almost certainly sue for damages. They would base their claim on the success of *Off The Wall*, *Thriller* and *Bad* and that could mean a claim for millions.

Geffen told Michael to ignore the threat of legal action and leave, possibly because he wanted him to sign to his record label.

In concert at Wembley,
15th July, 1988

The Jacksons' home in Gary Indiana

The Jacksons perform on stage at Roosevelt High School, behind the Jackson family bungalow in Gary, Indiana. From left to right: Reynaud Jones on lead guitar, Milford Hite on drums, Marlon Jackson on tambourine, Tito Jackson on rhythm guitar, Jackie Jackson singing, Jermaine Jackson singing, and at end of line Michael Jackson playing a set of borrowed bongo drums

The Jackson Six –
Pictured left to right
are: Jackie, Tito,
Marlon, Michael,
Jermaine and little
Randy jumping in
November 1972

ABOVE: At home
at 641 Hayvenhurst
Avenue, Los Angeles.
February 1973

RIGHT: Arriving at
Heathrow Airport in
February 1979

ABOVE: Signing his autograph at his home in April 1984

RIGHT: In concert at the Don Valley Stadium in Sheffield in 1988

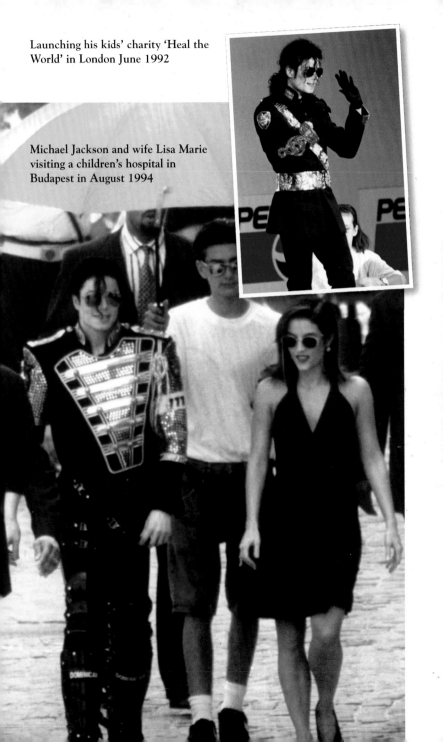

Launching his kids' charity 'Heal the World' in London June 1992

Michael Jackson and wife Lisa Marie visiting a children's hospital in Budapest in August 1994

The Michael Jackson statue on the Thames for the launch of the *HIStory* album June 1995

Leaving Santa Maria Courthouse March 2005: left with his mother Katherine Jackson and right wearing his pyjamas after arriving in court an hour late

At the O2 arena in London, where he unveiled plans for his comeback gigs – vowing they will be his last, March 2009

DAILY Mirror

Wednesday July 8, 2009

REAL NEWS.. REAL ENTERTAINMENT **45p**

SPECIAL EDITIO
FAREWEL
TO JACK

KING OF POPS

CENTRE STAGE Red roses adorn Michael Jackson's gold coffin last night

By RYAN PARRY in Los Angeles

MICHAEL Jackson's heartbroken children say farewell to their dad last night after taking to the stage at his extraordinary memorial.

Prince Michael, 12, Paris, 11, and seven-year-old Prince Michael II, who was clutching a Jacko doll, joined showbiz stars to sing their father's hit We Are The World.

But it was tearful Paris who captured the hearts of millions watching worldwide with a moving personal tribute.

She said: "I just want to say, ever since I was born daddy has been best father you could ever imagine. I just want to say I love him so much." Earlier Jacko's golden coffin had been transported to the LA memorial in an 18-car motorcade.

FULL STORY: INSIDE

'He was the best father you could ever imagin

— PARIS JACKSON AT LAST NIGHT'S MEMORIAL SERVICE

CENTRE STAGE Red roses adorn Michael Jackson's gold coffin last night

Incredibly, given the success Michael had experienced with Branca, he sided with Geffen. His newly appointed accountant Richard Sherman then informed his loyal lawyer that his work with Michael Jackson was over.

Michael now appointed a team of three lawyers, Bertram Fields, Alan Grubman and Lee Phillips, who were all associates of Geffen.

They put a new package together and re-signed with Sony; the contract was based on a framework that had been built by Branca.

Michael Jackson would potentially earn hundreds of millions from this new deal. Should sales reach the dizzy heights of *Thriller*, he would be paid $120 million per album thanks to a 25 per cent royalty rate.

In a deal worth around $50 million, he would also have his own label, 'National Records'.

CHAPTER 22

Jordie Chandler

Michael Jackson met Jordie Chandler by pure chance one spring day in 1992 when the car he was driving broke down on a Californian boulevard. The most famous man in pop cut a curious figure in black turban and white gym shoes, a veil across his face, kicking the car wheel in frustration.

Driving past just at that moment was the wife of a car rental worker, who called her husband, Mel Green, to tell him she'd seen Michael Jackson stuck on Wilshire Boulevard. Mel raced to the scene, calling his boss Dave Scwartz to say he was bringing Michael Jackson to the parking lot.

Dave, in turn, called his wife June, telling her to being should bring their young daughter and her son Jordie, from a previous marriage, in to Rent-a Wreck for a big surprise.

Jordie was a handsome brown-haired, dark-eyed boy with a massive creative talent. He was only 12 yet that same year he had had the idea for a spoof version of the hit film *Robin Hood: Prince of Thieves*.

His father Evan, June's ex husband, wrote the script for *Robin Hood: Men in Tights* and it was eventually made into a major movie.

Jordie was also a massive Michael Jackson fan. The first time he had seen his hero he was just five years old and out for a meal in a restaurant with his parents. He simply admired Michael from afar.

Then, after the star was badly burned in the Pepsi commercial, Jordie sent a letter and a photo of himself to the hospital where he was being treated. Michael later called him to say thank you.

Now, the prospect of him meeting Michael in person was too great an opportunity to miss.

June quickly brought Jordie down to see his hero and, with her encouragement, the pair swapped phone numbers. To June there appeared to be nothing wrong with a 33-year-old man befriending a schoolboy of 12.

Michael was known to be interested in children, saying he found them creative. Since the world viewed him as mysteriously asexual there was natural curiosity but no real condemnation.

Nearly a decade earlier at the age of 25 he had struck up a friendship with 12-year-old, tall, child actor Emmanuel Lewis.

Emmanuel was regularly entertained at the Encino estate and the two playmates would tell each other fairy stories and wrestle together on the floor until eventually the boy's parents had intervened.

Now, just a week after first meeting Jordie, Michael called him up on the phone to chat about video games and the arcade Michael had at his secret "hide-out" – an apartment in Century City, California.

It was the first of many telephone conversations.

In June of that year Michael set off on his 'Dangerous' tour, a grueling nine-month round of 39 concerts, for which he had sold the rights for a record $20 million.

Other children joined him on the tour at various points. Australian Brett Barnes, aged 11, visited him, as did nine-year-old Prince Albert von Thurn, the wealthy son of Gloria von Thurn und Taxis of Bavaria.

But he still found time to keep in touch with his newfound friend Jordie.

In long late-night conversations they would chatter on about all kinds of different subjects – but often about his favourite place in the world, Neverland.

"He would be calling me from various places throughout the world," Jordie later recalled. "On occasion these telephone conversations lasted as long as three hours.

"After I met Michael Jackson at Rent-a-Wreck he began calling me on the telephone. From about May of 1992 until about February 1993 I received many telephone calls from him. For at least part of this time Michael Jackson was on tour.

"Michael Jackson and I talked about video games, the Neverland Ranch, water fights, and famous people that he knew."

In February 1993, a few weeks after the tour ended, Michael appeared on the Oprah Winfrey TV show in a ratings-winning interview, which included a nighttime trip around his playground ranch.

The following day he rang and invited June Chandler, Jordie and Jordie's half-sister Lily for the weekend.

They played games, took jet skis out on the four acre sapphire blue lake, swam in the massive swimming pool, drove around in Michael's golf cart – and then went shopping to Toys R Us.

With the shop closed to the public Jordie and Lily piled three trolleys high with more than 10,000 pounds worth of toys and games.

"In about February 1993, my mother, Lily, my half-sister, and I went to Neverland at the invitation of Michael Jackson," Jordie said.

"The three of us stayed together in the guest area. I did not spend the nights with Michael Jackson. This was a weekend trip.

"I spent the entire weekend with Michael Jackson. We went on jet skis in a small lake he had, saw the animals that he kept at Neverland, played video games and went on golf cart rides.

"One evening he took Lily and me to Toys 'R Us and we were allowed to get anything we wanted. Although the store was closed, it was opened just for our visit."

A week later a limousine pulled up at June's house for a repeat visit but this time Brett Barnes was sitting on Michael knee. When the bags were unloaded at Neverland, Brett's were taken to Michael's room.

In late March the family were invited to see Michael again. This time they flew by private plane to his luxurious $3000-a-night suite at the Mirage hotel in Las Vegas.

June and Lily went to bed early in the room they shared while Michael and Jordie sat up to watch the horror movie *The Exorcist*.

"When the movie was on I was scared," Jordie would explain later. "Michael suggested I spend the night with him, which I did."

He later insisted that there had been no physical contact between the two that night.

Nevertheless when June saw Jordie's empty bed the next morning and realized what had happened she seemed angry, upset and concerned.

She made Jordie promise he would never do anything like that again.

But Jordie, by then 13, was upset and confided in Michael who tackled June head on. What was wrong with it, he wanted to know.

June shot back that it was completely inappropriate. But Michael considered Jordie his "soul mate". He described their relationship as totally innocent. He blamed adults with dirty minds. All children were innocent until "conditioned" by the adult world, he explained.

When he started to cry, June was left comforting him.

She agreed to trust him with her son – and the next day Michael rewarded her for that trust, with a $12,000 ruby and diamond bracelet from the jewellers Cartier.

In early April the family returned again to Neverland and this time there was no discussion. June and Lily stayed in the guest quarters while Jordie bunked up with Michael in his room.

According to Jordie's uncle Ray many more weekend "sleepovers" followed, by which time Michael and Jordie were regularly sharing a bed.

June remained worried about her son's friendship with Michael and when the star began calling again, she listened in on a conversation.

When it became obvious the two were talking in some sort of code she challenged Michael again and he invited her to discuss it in person at Neverland.

Michael, sitting in his pyjamas, told her he was lonely and asked to go back with her to her home. To show that she trusted him, he said, she should let him share Jordie's bed.

Meanwhile, Jordie's dentist father Evan was growing increasingly concerned about Jordie and Michael's friendship. Initially, he was simply unhappy that another man had influence in Jordie's life, but when he found out they were sharing a bed he was horrified and he and June argued.

But he had no real control over his son's movements.

He was upset that Jordie seemed colder towards him but when he could see how well June, Jordie and Lily appeared to get on with Michael Jackson he began to question whether he was right to be worried after all.

In May 1993 Michael took June, Jordie and Lily to the glamorous city-state of Monaco, for the World Music Awards.

The group was booked into the $2000-a-night Winston Churchill Suite at the prestigious Hotel de Paris. An American tabloid ran a picture story, calling them "Michael's new adopted family".

The following month, Evan, his five-year-old son Nikki (from another marriage) in tow, paid his ex-wife and his son a surprise visit and was amazed to find Jordie's bedroom packed to the rafters with toys, CDs and videos – and Michael himself lurking in the background.

When the star began to play happily with Nikki, Evan relaxed. He allowed Michael to buy Nikki toys and accepted a Cartier watch from the singer but he still had nagging doubts.

In the end, he confronted Michael about the relationship. What was it? He demanded to know. Michael neatly avoided the question, replying that it was "cosmic".

As Evan watched the two of them together over the next few days and weeks he began to think there was something to worry about after all.

By July he was concerned enough to apply to change the custody arrangements for Jordie, forbidding him from going near Michael and pushing for the boy to get psychiatric help to expose how much influence the star now had over his son's life and mind.

He also hired his lawyer friend Barry Rothman to investigate.

When Evan called a meeting with Dave Schwartz to discuss the matter Dave secretly taped the conversation.

"Jackson is an evil guy," said Evan....

"If I go through with this, I win big time. There's no way I lose. I will get everything I want and they will be destroyed forever... Michael's career will be over.

"It will be a massacre if I don't get what I want. It's going to be bigger than all of us put together."

Initially Michael laughed off the threats – but even so his own attorney Bert Fields interrogated Jordie about the relationship until he was clear in his own mind that nothing untoward had gone on.

As the legal wrangle began to unfold, June did not know what to think.

She was aghast when her lawyer told her he had met with police who described Jackson as fitting the classic profile of a paedophile.

When Evan drew up papers banning her from taking Jordie out of Los Angeles County she did not challenge them.

Michael felt betrayed and refused to speak to June on the phone. He handed the matter over to Fields and private investigator Anthony Pellicano to deal with, claiming that Evan was just jealous of his friendship with his son.

But on August 2 the matter took a dramatic turn. At his dental surgery, Evan gave Jordie the drug sodium amytal to take out a tooth that was bothering his son. In his woozy state the boy suddenly began to talk about sexual encounters between himself and Michael.

Stunned, Evan asked Jordie directly if Jackson had ever touched his penis. His son replied yes.

Two days later, witnessed by Pellicano, Evan Chandler and Michael Jackson had a showdown. Wide-eyed and anxious, Jordie tagged along.

Evan produced a psychiatrist's letter and read from it.

"The minor is in danger whether the relationship continues or ends," it said. The impact that would be caused to other family members of the minor should also be considered.

"These circumstances create the possibility that there exists negligence towards the child, even as far as prostitution."

He openly accused Michael of "fucking" his son. Jordie could not meet Michael's eye.

Pellicano countered with an utter denial. It was an insult and a lie, he said.

Evan told Jackson he would see him in court and with Jordie taking a last ever look at his hero, father and son left the room, and Michael burst into tears.

The following day there was a meeting between Evan, his lawyer Barry Rothman and Pellicano where the Jordie camp laid their case on the line. The demand? A cool $20 million.

Jordie was to get $5m in yearly installments for four years. Some would go to child abuse charities and Evan would retire and devote himself to his son.

If Michael refused his career would be over, said Evan. He would bring a case for sexual assault and push for the singer to be jailed.

Michael, through Pellicano, made a series of much lower counter offers, including a million dollar film deal giving Evan and Jordie more than $1m to write three movie scripts with the guarantee that a major studio would look at any others after that.

Meanwhile Jordie's mother, June, baffled by the negotiations, petitioned the court to have Jordie returned to her.

Evan played for time and arranged another session for Jordie with Dr Mathis Abrams, the psychiatrist who had provided the letter for the recent showdown.

The case he had originally outlined had not been hypothetical, he told Dr Abrams. There had been a case of sexual abuse and it involved his son Jordie and Michael Jackson.

Jordie opened up describing a catalogue of sexual contacts with Jackson including oral sex and masturbation.

A caseworker from Los Angeles Children Services and a police officer were called in and Jordie gave a detailed description of Michael's genitalia.

While Jordie remained with his father, Jackson set off alone to Bangkok, on the next leg of his 'Dangerous' tour.

On August 21, 1993, the day after his flight left for the Far East, detectives raided both Neverland and Jackson's Los Angeles "hideaway".

They found little. Michael's staff had spent the previous hours stripping the properties of anything incriminating or otherwise. But they did seize diaries, videotapes, photographs and address books and it wasn't long before the story hit world headlines.

Pellicano went public with the child molestation allegations to protest Michael's innocence and paint him as the victim of an extortion attempt.

He also arranged for two of Michael's young friends, Brett Barnes and Wade Robson, to appear on TV to say they had slept with Michael, often with no sexual overtones.

Michael, they said, was simply a highly sensitive and affectionate man with a soft spot for kids. It was, they said, "like sleeping with your mother".

He was someone they could eat fast food with, chat with, and sit around with watching TV. Both boys said that sharing a bed with the singer was just like a "slumber party" and that nothing untoward had happened.

"I was on one side of the bed and he was on the other," said Brett. "It was a big bed."

But the statements backfired badly. Many viewers were immediately uncomfortable with the idea that a man in his thirties was in bed with children at all.

In Bangkok the fall-out was having a shattering effect on Michael, while back home in Los Angeles his shocked relatives were hastily arranging a Jackson family press conference.

Michael was the victim of a cruel attempt to take advantage of his fame and success, they declared. He had their "unfailing" support.

He also had support from another unexpected quarter – the woman he had recently begun dating.

Lisa Marie Presley, the daughter of the Elvis, the King of Rock 'n' Roll, was now coming to the aid of the King of Pop.

CHAPTER 23

Evidence

Like Michael, Lisa Marie had had a difficult childhood. The only child of Elvis and actress Priscilla Presley, she was indulged by her famous father who showered her with jewels, provided her with her own golf cart to ride around the estate, and once flew her to Colorado aboard his private jet named "Lisa Marie" so she could play in the snow.

But in 1977, at just nine years old, Lisa Marie had watched her daddy die in front of her on the bathroom floor.

She may have been ten years younger than Michael but by the time the two met she was already married to musician Danny Keogh and the couple had two children, Danielle and Benjamin. After the upbringing she had had surrounded by her father's addictions, it was perhaps no surprise that Lisa Marie was a wild child, who had started using drugs herself at 14.

Michael and Lisa Marie met at a dinner at the home of artist friend Brett Livingston-Stone in February 1993. Michael listened to tapes of her singing and assured her he was impressed. She had real talent, he said and he would see what he could do to help.

They were the words Lisa Marie longed to hear and the couple struck up a telephone relationship – chatting on the phone almost daily.

Lisa proved supportive as the child molestation accusations grew. She believed the extortion story and Michael welcomed the emotional crutch.

His personal life was in absolute turmoil.

That year he gave a heartrending interview to Oprah Winfrey and spoke about his abusive father for the first time.

"There were times when he'd come to see me, I'd get sick. I'd start to regurgitate.

"He's never heard me say this," then looking at the camera, "I'm sorry. Please don't be mad at me…"

He added: "But I do love him."

As well as Lisa Marie, Michael leaned on several friends, most notably Hollywood star Elizabeth Taylor.

He had first met Taylor after sending her VIP tickets for one of his shows at Dodger's Stadium. She complained they were too far away from the stage and stormed out. He rang to apologize, weeping, and it marked the start of another long telephone-based friendship for Michael.

When they finally met for tea at Taylor's house, with Michael bringing along Bubbles the chimp, it was the start of a firm friendship.

The pair spent long hours together and in 1991 Taylor married her seventh husband Larry Fortensky in a star-studded ceremony at Neverland.

Now, Taylor was adamant that Michael was innocent of any abuse and in the midst of all the Chandler turmoil she and Larry flew over to Singapore in an attempt to boost their traumatized friend's morale.

She later held meetings at her house to work on his defence, though it was more of an exercise to keep Michael appraised of what was going on than a legal instrument.

When Michael moved on to Taiwan with his tour, his parents and some of his brothers jetted in to the tiny island country to show their faith in him.

The stress was having an effect on Katherine's blood pressure and she was desperate to comfort her son. But at first Michael refused point blank to see any of his family. He had no time for his father and could not face his brothers, or even Katherine.

He finally gave in and hosted a lunch for them all. He also agreed to take part in a Jackson family television programme, something he had previously refused to do. With his family so supportive, he no doubt felt he had to repay them in some way.

All the while, Michael was battling a secret addiction to prescription drugs.

He had recently had an operation on the head burn he had suffered during the Pepsi advert, his teeth were hurting after dental work and he was anxious and unable to sleep.

Now, he found the tranquillizers and painkillers didn't just deaden the physical pain but they also allowed him to escape the harsh reality of what was going on in his personal life.

And that reality was about to get even worse.

By October 1993 Los Angeles police had seized Michael's medical records and were threatening to conduct a strip-search of his body – to verify Jordie Chandler's description of his genitalia.

Amongst Michael's legal team there was in-fighting and backbiting. Michael added a new attorney to the team, the well-respected Johnnie Cochran.

Cochran's job was to settle the matter and to settle it without Michael having to go through the trauma of a trial. His family and his legal team knew he just wasn't in good enough physical or mental shape to survive.

In November 1993, Michael abandoned what was left of the 'Dangerous' tour and took off from Mexico bound for London. On arrival, he half walked and was half carried straight into rehab through the back door of the Charter Nightingale Clinic.

His medicines were confiscated and he was settled in on the entire fourth floor of the hospital, at a cost of $50,000 a week.

In a statement released the following day he revealed he had scrapped the remaining concerts and that he had become addicted to the medicines he had used for burns suffered during the making of the Pepsi ad.

"As I left on this tour I had been the target of an extortion attempt and shortly thereafter was accused of horrifying and outrageous conduct," his statement said.

"I was humiliated, embarrassed, hurt and suffering great pain in my heart.

"The pressure resulting from these false allegations coupled with the incredible energy necessary for me to perform caused me so much distress that it left me physically and emotionally exhausted.

"I became dependent on the painkillers to get through the days of the tour."

Michael started therapy sessions but within a few days had apparently been given permission to move out of hospital and continue his rehabilitation at the home of Elton John's manager John Reid.

There were business affairs for him to deal with – including signing off one multi-million-dollar deal with EMI to administer his ATV music catalogue that included Lennon and McCartney's songs.

Michael's friends feared his troubles lay too deep to be solved in a part-time "quick fix" treatment schedule. Yet by early December he had been officially discharged from hospital and was back in Los Angeles.

The fact that he arrived back in the US in the company of two young boys – Frank and Eddie Cascio – seemed a curious action given the furore still surrounding him, but Michael insisted he would not give up his friendship with children just because of sordid rumour. At least with the Cascio brothers, dad Dominic was always on hand as a chaperone.

His family was still standing by him. All except La Toya who called a press conference in the Israeli capital, Tel Aviv, where she was on tour, saying she believed the accusations against her brother were true.

"Michael is my brother and I love him very much," she told reporters.

"But I cannot and will not be a silent collaborator in his crimes against young children.

"If I remain silent then that means I feel the guilt and humiliation that these children are feeling and I think that is very wrong.

"Forget about the superstar, forget about the icon. If he was any other 35-year old-man who sleeping with little boys, you wouldn't like this guy."

Back in Los Angeles Michael's family, devastated at the apparent betrayal, called a press conference of their own to rubbish her claims.

For now La Toya stuck to her guns. As the La Toya music tour travelled the globe, so too did the media circus as she was widely interviewed about her views on her brother. One Spanish TV channel reportedly made plans to connect her to a lie-detector and then question her about why she thought Michael was a paedophile, but it was called off at the last minute.

If Michael was upset by the behaviour of his older sister, his worst nightmare was just around the corner.

The long-threatened strip search happened in late December 1993. Jordie had described Michael's genitalia in detail. He was circumcised, he said, he had short pubic hair, his testicles were marked pink and brown and there were brown patches on his left buttock.

The police now needed to know if the description was accurate.

A team of lawyers, doctors, police, a bodyguard and two photographers – one from each camp – waited in silence at Neverland as a tearful Michael finally emerged in his bathrobe and mounted a platform in the centre of the room.

When he was eventually persuaded to take off the robe, he was wearing swimming trunks underneath. He reluctantly removed those, only to reveal a pair of boxer shorts. How had his life come to that moment?

Those there tell how he pleaded with them: "Please don't make me do this".

But Michael's representatives were clear that the alternative could be far worse. He was not yet under arrest, and it was unthinkable that he be taken away in handcuffs as the world's press looked on.

As Michael slipped off the boxer shorts all eyes turned to his penis, but it wasn't immediately clear if he were circumcised or not.

He certainly had short pubic hair and patches on his backside. His testicles were marked pink and brown as the testimony stated, but it appeared he was not circumcised.

The District Attorney's photographer Gary Spiegel took several pictures before Michael called a halt and stormed off, only to be dragged back and re-photographed, then videotaped.

When one physician got out a ruler and made as if to start measuring, Michael's own doctor stepped in.

"That's it," he said.

Two days later Michael appeared live on CNN from Neverland to give an emotional four-minute speech. Wearing a red shirt and heavily made up, he looked directly into the camera and spoke.

"I ask all of you to wait and hear the truth before you condemn me," he said. "Don't treat me like a criminal because I am innocent."

He accused the media of "dissecting and manipulating" the allegations for their own ends.

He added: "I have been forced to submit to a dehumanizing and humiliating experience by the Santa Barbara County Sheriff's Department and the Los Angeles Police Department earlier this week.

"They served a warrant on me which allowed them to view and photograph my body, including my penis, my buttocks, my lower torso, thighs and any other area they wanted.

"They were supposedly looking for any discolouration, spotting, blotches or other evidence of a skin colour disorder called vitiligo which I have previously spoken about.

"It was the most humiliating ordeal of my life, one that no person should ever have to suffer. And even after experiencing the indignity of this search, the parties involved were still not satisfied and wanted to take even more pictures.

"It was a nightmare, a horrifying nightmare. But if this is what I have to endure to prove my innocence – my complete innocence – then so be it."

By 1994 a mountain of paperwork had been gathered in the Jackson – Chandler case, a complex mixture of evidence and hearsay in statements from hundreds of employees, former employees and boys Michael had known and befriended.

When attorney Larry Feldman also started pushing for access to Michael's financial records, it was apparently the last straw.

In January 1994 he paid over $22m to Jordie Chandler, Evan Chandler, June Chandler Schwartz and Larry Feldman.

With no one now willing to testify against the singer, no charges were brought against Michael Jackson for child abuse.

He himself tried to dismiss the pay-off. It didn't suggest guilt in any way, he said. He had done nothing wrong. He just wanted to get on with his life.

Elizabeth Taylor for one was delighted.

"Michael's love of children is one of the purest things I have ever seen," she proclaimed. "I always knew this would be thrown out of court and I am so grateful."

David Gest, the concert promoter who would later marry Liza Minelli also leapt to his childhood friend's defence.

"When the first allegations against Michael were made, we had a six-hour phone conversation. I told him to fight it.

"I believed he should prove his innocence. But defending yourself can cost a fortune. You could spend everything you have just to say: 'I told you I was telling the truth.' So I understand why he settled.

"I never doubted him. We spoke every day and Michael kept saying: 'I would never do this. You know me. I haven't done anything wrong.'

"I know he would never, ever harm a child. I always believed him and I hope I helped him stay strong."

Michael Jackson would later tell the *Daily Mirror*'s then editor Piers Morgan that only evil people could imagine he had abused children.

"I'd slit my wrists rather than hurt a child," he said. "I could never do that.

"No-one will ever know how much these wicked rumours have hurt me. If it wasn't for the children...I'd throw in the towel and I'd kill myself.

"I wouldn't care to live without children and without the inspiration they give me. They inspire me in all I do, every song I write, every dance I perform. People try and use that against me and it's just so unfair.

"I get very upset by it, it breaks my heart."

CHAPTER 24

Lisa Marie

A month later Michael and Lisa Marie Presley flew up to Las Vegas in Michael's private plane to see a Temptations' concert and spent the night together.

A fortnight after that she accompanied him to the TV show Jermaine had been working hard to put together for months, *The Jackson Family Honours Special*, a tribute to Elizabeth Taylor and Berry Gordy.

At the last moment, Michael refused to perform at the event and ended up being dragged into a messy lawsuit between the producers and the Jackson family.

Later that same month Michael took Lisa Marie to Neverland where he attended to her every whim. The two shared a candle-lit dinner on the terrace, they talked, they laughed, and they kissed – and may have made love.

By now and with the absence of his great friend Jordie, Michael was desperate for a new love in his life – he also badly wanted children.

A marriage would also help dampen the child abuse rumours that continued to follow him.

Being by now an experienced master of Public Relations, he may also have noted that to do it in secret, keeping the media guessing for weeks in a "did they, didn't they" controversy would create enormous interest and move headlines away from his past.

According to Taraborrelli, Michael gave Lisa her engagement ring in the living room at Neverland as they sipped wine and watched the Bette Davis classic, *All About Eve*.

"I walked over to her, reached in my pocket and pulled out this huge diamond ring," Michael told him.

"'So what do you think?' I asked her. 'You wanna?' She screamed out: 'Yes, yes yes' ."

Other reports suggest he proposed to Lisa Marie over the phone four months after they met.

"If I asked you to marry me?" he had apparently said, "Would you do it?"

Either way Lisa Marie said yes and on May 26, 1994, after a hasty divorce had gone through, the wedding ceremony went ahead in top secret at the elegant Case de Camp resort at La Romana in the Dominican Republic. Observers joked that it was Neverland meets Graceland, and that their wedding list was from Toys R Us.

Jackson had wanted to marry aboard an aircraft while flying high above the Caribbean island, but the country's laws forbade that, so instead the wedding went ahead on land.

It was a private affair conducted by Judge Hugo Francisco Alvarez and witnessed by Lisa Marie's friends Eva Darling and Thomas Keogh.

Family and friends including even Michael's close confidante Elizabeth Taylor were all kept in the dark. Even the bride's own mother Priscilla was not informed until after the service.

The ceremony itself took place in the Judge's house where Jackson was dressed all in black with a flamenco hat of the same colour and a cowboy belt with tacks.

According to some press reports at the time Lisa–Marie wore a short beige dress and carried matching flowers. Other sources say she wore black.

After the couple's wedding Judge Alvarez would later reveal some of the details of the cloak and dagger operation to the press.

He told how at the end of 1993 he was contacted by an unnamed friend in Miami and put in touch with Jackson's lawyers who proposed he officiate at the wedding of the singer and Lisa Marie.

He later met up with the legal team in Los Angeles where he signed a "statement of discretion" pledging not to reveal any details about the event.

But rumours of the match circulated widely.

It later emerged it was Michael himself who had let the secret slip. He told his mother Katherine, who told her daughter La Toya and it was La Toya who revealed the information to the world's press.

Eventually, two months after their marriage, Lisa Marie put out a statement confirming the reports.

"I am very much in love with Michael," it said. "I dedicate my life to being his wife."

There were those who suggested the marriage was a sham, and that the couple were not sexually involved. Certainly the timing, in 1993, appeared convenient in the wake of the child abuse allegations.

For her part, Lisa Marie fervently denied any claims the romance was fake.

"I'm not going to marry someone for any other reason than the fact that I fall in love with him. Period." she said.

During the two years they were married Michael and Lisa Marie appeared on TV together twice – in September 1994 and June 1995.

Their first showing as husband and wife was in front of 250 million viewers at the MTV Awards in New York.

As they walked onto the stage to uproarious applause Michael spoke.

"Just think, nobody thought this would last," he said, then her took her in his arms and kissed her full on the lips.

Nine months later they were interviewed on the US programme *Dateline* by reporter Diane Sawyer.

During the interview Michael refused to give specific details of the Jordie Chandler settlement, but he said: "I could never harm a child or anyone. It's not in my heart. It's not who I am and it's not what I'm even interested in."

Asked what he thought should happen to "someone who does that", he replied: "To someone who does that? What do I think should be done? Gee, I think they need help in some kind of way, you know."

He added: "I talked to my lawyers and I said, 'Can you guarantee me that justice will prevail?' And they said, 'Michael we cannot guarantee you what a judge or jury will do'.

"With that I was like catatonic. I was outraged, totally outraged. So I said, 'I have got to do something to get out of this nightmare, all these lies and all these people coming forward to get paid and these tabloid shows, just lies, lies, lies."

"So we got together and my advisers advised me. It was hands down, a unanimous decision to resolve the case."

Sawyer pressed on: what was a 36-year-old man doing sleeping with 12-year-old boys, she asked.

Lisa Marie, seeing her new husband stumble over the answer, leapt in.

"Let me just say that I've seen these children. They don't let him go to the bathroom without running in there with him.

"They won't let him out of their sight. So when he jumps in the bed, I'm even out (of the bed) you know?

"They jump in the bed with him."

But when Sawyer asked if sleepovers with children were now over at Neverland, Michael said no.

"No, because it's all moral and it's all pure," he said. "I don't even think that way... It's not what's in my heart."

"It's on the level of purity and love and just innocence, complete innocence. If you're talking about sex then that's a nut. It's not me.

"Go to the guy down the street 'cause it's not Michael Jackson. It's not what I'm interested in."

The interview then turned to the subject of their surprise marriage and whether it was a sham.

"You know it's crap," said Lisa Marie. "I'm sorry it's the most ridiculous thing I've ever heard."

Years later in a piece with *Rolling Stone* magazine she revealed how she was always telling Jackson: "People wouldn't think I was so crazy if they saw who the hell you really are, that you sit around and you drink and you curse and you're fucking funny, and you have a bad mouth and you don't have that high voice all the time."

In 2003, she told *Newsweek* Magazine: "He is not stupid. He's very charming when he wants to be and when you go into his world you step into this whole other realm."

And in a candid interview on American TV after they broke up, Lisa Marie was adamant she loved Michael – and was also sexually attracted to him.

Most people "just didn't know" him, she said.

"He was very quick the first time I met him to sit me down and say, look I'm not gay – I know you think this, I know you think that...."

"I was pulled in," she said. "I realized then he was so misunderstood. I fell in love with him," she said. "I did."

She insisted too that she was sexually attracted to Jackson and that they did have sex – "for a while".

After Jackson's death Lisa Marie reiterated her claims, insisting again the marriage was no sham.

It was, she said, "a situation where two unusual people who did not live or know a 'normal life' found a connection."

She went on: "I believe he loved me as much as he could love anyone. I loved him very much."

After Michael Jackson's death, Lisa Marie Presley wrote on her blog: "It was an unusual relationship, yes, where two unusual people who did not live or know a 'normal life' found a connection, perhaps with some suspect timing on his part.

"Nonetheless, I do believe he loved me as much as he could love anyone and I loved him very much."

Presley called Jackson "an incredibly dynamic force and power that was not to be underestimated."

She added: "When he used it for something good, it was the best and when he used it for something bad, It was really, REALLY bad."

For the two years they were married Michael, Lisa Marie and her two children divided their time between Neverland and Lisa's estate in Hidden Hills, California.

She never actually moved her family in to the Peter Pan palace – perhaps she already knew the marriage had a limited life, or perhaps she didn't want her own children to become part of the goings on at Neverland. Perhaps, she too enjoyed Neverland as a place where she could live out her own childhood – a time cut so unhappily short – and wanted to be childlike there herself.

As a committed scientologist Lisa Marie believed you were responsible for yourself, for the mistakes you made and for fixing those mistakes.

Michael was still very much blaming everyone else for the things that went wrong in his life. For the couple this difference in outlook became a constant source of friction.

Lisa Marie accused Michael of being selfish and whatever she might say loyally on television, friends say she was unhappy that he continued with his friendship with young boys.

They argued about the Cascio kids and the fact he insisted on spending time with them even after his relationship with Jordie Chandler had caused him so much damage.

When he took Eddie and Frank on holiday with him to Paris in July 1995 – and didn't take Lisa – it spoke volumes.

Two months later, that September, there were rumours in the press that their marriage was over.

Walking away from Michael, Lisa Marie has said, was one of the hardest decisions she ever had to make. Yet walk away, she did.

After 20 months, with the marriage turning increasingly "ugly" in her words, she ended it over the phone and filed for divorce citing irreconcilable differences.

She was considered as a witness at his child abuse trial but never took the stand. Later Lisa Marie released a statement saying she never saw her husband engage in "improper behaviour with children."

The divorce petition prompted an immediate revival in other Jackson stories – especially the Jordie Chandler scandal – and Santa Barbara District Attorney Thomas Sneddon was quoted as saying the criminal investigation into Michael Jackson was suspended, but not over.

There were reports of a videotape of Michael with a boy – though Michael always denied it and one was never revealed to the world. When writer Victor Gutierrez referred to it in Hard Copy (Paramount television), Michael sued and won.

It was not a good time for Michael. His marriage was crumbling and he spoke of horrible days and sleepless nights. His career had taken a dive and record sales had dipped dramatically since the height of his success in the 1980s.

Then, in 1995 he got a welcome musical boost. A double album *HIStory – Past Present and Future Book 1* was issued – a combination of 15 of his top hits and 15 new songs, including one of his most successful, 'You Are Not Alone', which shot to the top of *Billboard* chart.

The record went on to sell over 15 million copies worldwide – a major success.

The promotion for the album showed extraordinary hubris. This was a kind of arrogance not seen before in pop, with vast statues of Michael being unveiled in several European cities. Michael had not come back humbler from the child abuse allegations, he seemed to have simply retreated further into his fantasy world where he was a giant amongst men, out of the reach of all those who might do him harm.

On June 15 1995, in London, an enormous sculpture of Michael moulded to look like the statue of Liberty was towed down the Thames forcing the historic Tower Bridge to open to allow him to float by like a gigantic ocean liner.

The ten-metre-high sculpture made of steel and fibreglass and weighing two tonnes was towed by a barge to promote Michael's new album *HIStory*.

The River Thames incident prompted questions about Michael's apparently supersized ego, and when during a subsequent live performance he seemed to be comparing himself with Jesus, many thought he had gone too far.

At the 1996 Brit awards, Jackson was crowned Artist Of A Generation and introduced by Bob Geldof with the words: "When his feet move, you can see God dancing".

As Michael sang his hit 'Earth Song', surrounded by pictures of African children flashing up on giant screens, it was too much for Pulp frontman Jarvis Cocker. The normally mild-mannered Yorkshireman got up on stage and ran around, showing his trousered bottom to the audience and wiggling.

He later defended his actions saying he objected to Jackson's apparent belief that he was some sort of "Jesus like figure" with the power of healing. "It got my goat," he said.

Around the same time in the USA, a magazine was claiming Elvis had had a nose job – the source was supposedly Michael who said Lisa Marie had told him the secret.

She was livid.

When Michael collapsed in rehearsals for a 'One Night Only' concert at New York's Beacon Theatre and was rushed to hospital with suspected arrhythmia – an irregular heart beat – Lisa Marie at first refused to fly from Los Angeles to his bedside.

She cared little for him at that moment and when she did finally relent it was not a happy meeting. According to witnesses she stormed into the hospital in her black pea coat and dark sunglasses and the blazing row that then emanated from Michael's hospital room could be heard down the corridor.

In January 1996 the couple's divorce was announced on CNN.

She would later tell *Newsweek*: "I could tell you all about the craziness – all these things that were odd, different, evil or not cool – but it still took me two and a half years to get my head out of it."

Michael was once more on his own.

CHAPTER 25

Debbie Rowe

If Jackson was shattered by the departure of wife No. 1, Lisa Marie, it didn't take him long to find a second. He was convinced by now that he wanted children and being Michael was not prepared to wait. With one potential mother out of the door, he needed to find a new wife as quickly as possible.

Wife No. 2 was an entirely different proposition from the glamorous starlet Lisa Marie.

Deborah Jeanne Rowe was a blonde, fresh-faced, girl-next-door type – a nurse who had been treating Michael for his vitiligo long before their friendship developed into anything more.

She grew up in Malibu and joined Michael's entourage when she found work with his dermatologist Dr Arnold Klein.

In 1982 she had married Richard Edelman , a teacher from her former school Hollywood High and bought a small place in Van Nuys, California. Edelman subsequently set up a computer business that went bust with massive debts.

Her friends paint Debbie as an unusual figure. A leather-clad biker with a mouth like a trucker, she was a fan of beer and Tequila and stood out as one of the boys. She was a long way from the Princess type Michael usually preferred.

Michael first met Debbie in the early 1980s when he went to see if Klein could help with his vitiligo and was referred to her for treatment and advice.

He rang her regularly and sent her autographed CDs as gifts. They became friends. Debbie covered her apartment and office with pictures and CD covers of his.

Observers put it down to a "romantic crush", but Debbie refused to commit herself on how she felt about Michael. If she had any dreams of something more long term she was not letting on.

They remained friendly throughout the Jordie Chandler years and throughout his marriage to Lisa Marie.

Yet when that relationship started collapsing he challenged his wife: if Lisa Marie did not want to make a baby with him, he knew someone who would.

The divorce with Lisa was finalized in August 1996, and it seems that when Michael spoke of how he longed for children, Debbie offered to provide the means.

Straight after his divorce, Michael embarked on his 'HIStory' tour – 82 concerts in 35 countries in five continents over five months.

That same year, he also faced a new challenge to his name. The Anti-Defamation League issued a press release charging him with anti-semitism in the lyrics of the song "They don't care about Us," which included the line: "Jew me, sue me, everybody do me."

He changed the words.

Almost a decade later he faced more claims of anti-semitism when an answerphone message he left was made public.

The singer, referring to Jewish people, said: "They suck... they're like leeches... It's a conspiracy. The Jews do it on purpose."

Abraham H Foxman of the Anti-Defamation League said the comments were "hateful" and Jackson had an "anti-semitic streak".

"It seems every time he has a problem in his life he blames it on Jews," he said. "It is sad that Jackson is infected with classically stereotypical ideas of Jews as all-powerful, money-grubbing and manipulative."

Michael was only a few weeks into his tour when the story of Debbie and Michael's baby broke, appearing in British Sunday tabloid The News of The World on November 3 1996 under the banner headline "I'm Having Jacko's Baby".

Debbie would later claim that she was tricked into revealing the story through a friend who was secretly taping it.

In brief, the story said that the two had had sex but resorted to artificial insemination after she did not immediately fall pregnant.

Their first attempt at the Los Angeles Fertility Institute had ended in miscarriage but the second had resulted in a successful pregnancy.

Once the baby arrived, it said, Debbie would get a payment of $500,000 from Michael.

The world media went into meltdown, hunting down every possible angle on such a bizarre news event.

Debbie's father Gordon Rowe spoke out – revealing his daughter had told him the astonishing news by telephone.

"I only speak to her once in a while," confessed Gordon. "She said straight off: 'I'm going to have Michael's child.'

"After I recovered from the shock, Debbie said, 'Come on it's not so bad. We had the child by artificial insemination'.

"I said, 'Debbie, why artificial insemination? Isn't he capable of fathering a child like anyone else?' She laughed and said, 'Michael doesn't do anything like anyone else.'

"I said to her: 'Isn't this the same man who was charged with child abuse?' She said, 'He wasn't charged with anything, not at all'.

"Then she told me, 'Dad you have no idea who the real Michael Jackson is.

He is the most compassionate person I have ever met in my life. If you could only spend one day with him, you would love him like I do'."

Gordon, who had been divorced from Debbie's mother Barbara for 20 years and saw little of Debbie, later retracted every word of what he had said.

Michael then put out his own statement.

"The reports speculating that Ms Rowe was artificially inseminated and that there is any economic relationship are completely false and irresponsible," he said.

Debbie has always refused to discuss the matter. "Michael knows the truth," she has said. "He has to come clean."

Later there would be claims that not only was Michael not the children's father but Debbie was not the mother – simply a surrogate conceived through IVF using egg and sperm donors.

Whatever the complexities, nine months after the agreement was made, and under pressure from Michael's mother, he and Debbie were wed.

With her Jehovah's Witness faith informing her traditional morality, Katherine had been appalled at the prospect that her son was apparently fathering a child with a woman to whom he was not married.

There was already Michael's half-sister Joh'Vonnie in the family after Joseph's philandering, and she was horrified at the idea of history repeating itself.

So, in November 1996, in the middle of the 'HIStory' tour, Michael and Debbie both wearing black, tied the knot at the Sheraton hotel in Sydney Australia.

Held in a suite filled with orchids, roses and lilies, the ceremony was a simple affair, though with 15 of the couple's friends present it was somewhat bigger than Michael's wedding to Lisa Marie.

The bride, by then six months pregnant with their first child, was 37. The best man, a friend of the groom, was an eight-year-old boy.

The story ran that the youngster, whose name was Anthony, had recently lost one of his parents and needed "cheering up".

That night, like the previous one, Debbie slept on her own in her bedroom at the Sheraton while Michael stayed in another room with an "assistant".

Later the *Daily Mirror* published a photograph of Debbie on the hotel balcony, her head in her hands.

The headline ran: "Oh God. I've Just Married Michael Jackson". A week later Debbie flew back to Los Angeles alone.

The day before Valentine's Day in 1997, Michael Joseph Jackson Jnr – also known as Prince Michael I – was born at Cedars-Sinai Medical Centre in Los Angeles.

He spent a few hours in the special care delivery suite before being whisked home to Neverland where a team of nannies, nurses and bodyguards were ready and waiting.

In a statement, Prince Michael's ecstatic new father said: "I have been blessed beyond comprehension and I will work tirelessly at being the best father I can be.

"I appreciate that my fans are elated but I hope that everyone respects the privacy that Debbie and I want and need for our son.

"I grew up in a fishbowl and I will not allow that to happen to my child. Please give my son his privacy."

Six weeks later the proud parents posed for pictures with their baby son.

One nanny who helped care for the little boy in those early days told how staff rarely saw Debbie but lavished every possible care and attention on Prince Michael.

In Taraborrelli's book she revealed how the team did day-to-day exercise drills with the baby and even had to measure the air quality in his room.

Utensils were boiled and only ever used once before being thrown away. Toys were also discarded quickly for sanitary reasons.

Jackson was so delighted with his young son that a few months later Debbie became pregnant again while in the French capital.

She had arranged to join Jackson on the French, Austrian and German legs of his 'HIStory' tour and while she was in Paris she was apparently artificially inseminated again.

Meanwhile, Michael was still seeing his ex-wife Lisa Marie. She had struck up a friendship with his sister Janet and was curious about the new woman in his life.

Were she ever allowed in the bedroom, his new wife would have seen that Michael still kept Lisa Marie's photo on his bedside cabinet.

Lisa Marie arranged to fly out for the London and South Africa legs of the tour and the two strolled affectionately arm in arm together, water-skied and ate out together.

In February 1998, Michael took her out to the Ivy in Los Angeles for her 30th birthday. After a romantic dinner they walked through Beverley Hills and kissed through his silk mask – a picture captured by Paparazzi and plastered over the tabloids a few days later.

Their marriage might be over but their relationship was still close, even peculiarly intimate despite the facemask. It's possible that Lisa felt more comfortable with Jackson now he was married to someone else – however unusual that marriage might be.

It was perhaps the closest Jackson ever got to a normal kind of adult love.

In November 1997 Debbie announced she was pregnant with her second child – a girl. In April 1998 Paris Katherine Michael Jackson arrived.

This time Jackson just wrapped the baby in a blanket and fled.

As he explained in bizarre detail later: "I was so anxious to get her home after cutting the cord – I hate to say this – I snatched her and just went home with all the placenta and everything all over her. I just got her in a towel and ran."

It may well have been the final straw for Debbie, who was left exhausted in the delivery room without her newborn baby to hold. In any case, she had suffered a catalogue of pregnancy problems with Paris and could not bear him any more children.

"After Paris I couldn't have any more children," she said. " Michael was upset. He couldn't understand it. He wanted more babies."

"I always had this tug in the back of my head, the things I wanted to do," Michael said. "To raise, children, have children. I'm enjoying it very much."

On April 13, 1999, Michael Jackson gave his first newspaper interview in 20 years to Piers Morgan, then editor of the *Daily Mirror*. He spoke lovingly of his children Prince Michael and Paris, then two and one years old.

"I love my children so much," he said. "They have changed me and my outlook on life. I just wish people would leave me alone to get on with my life….

"To see my kids leaping round the room going mad to my sister Janet's music is just fantastic. It fills my heart with so much joy. As soon as Janet's songs with a good beat like 'The Knowledge' or 'Rhythm Nation' come on they both go crazy. You'd think a machine is moving them around.

"I start singing and there's screaming all over the house. I start dancing and Prince is all in the way trying to dance with me."

Michael went on to explain that he doesn't play his own music for his children, "I'm saving that for a surprise when they are a bit older," he smiled.

Michael also said he would love his children to go into the entertainment industry but was also aware of the consequences.

"It's going to be hard for them," he said. "When Lisa Marie wants to sing, people always compare her to her father, which is so tough. Of course, I'd love them to do something in the arts so I could teach them to sing and dance. But they'd have to want to do that without pressure from me."

Michael said the children were staying with a long-time friend at that moment.

"They are staying with a friend of mine who I went to school with. We go back a long way. My children are with hers having fun which is great. I call them all the time and we have great conversations. Hearing them say 'Dad! Dad!' is such a thrill."

Asked about his relationship with Debbie, Michael added: "I love my wife, and we have a happy marriage. Debbie is a nurse who loves her work, who loves taking care of people.

"Every day she wants to get up and look after others, to help them and make them better. That's why I love her, and that's what gives her bliss in life, God bless her."

In reality, Debbie Rowe had by now served her purpose as a vessel to carry and bear Michael's children, and was effectively sidelined. Six months after Paris' birth, she filed for divorce.

Some sources claim she was given a $10m settlement. Reports elsewhere said the payment was a clear pay-off – £4.2m over nine years for Debbie to give up any rights as a mother.

There was an initial agreement that she could see the youngsters once every 45 days but Debbie herself later applied to courts to end her parental rights completely.

Five years later, she spoke about her decision on GMTV, praising Jackson as an excellent father.

"He's a really wonderful caring man..." she told viewers. "There could be no other person that could be a better father and I resent anyone making allegations that he is not a parent and that he is not a proper parent.

"No-one has ever read more about parenting, no one has ever practised the art of parenting and parenting is an art. You earn the title 'parent'.

"Because you give birth, because you impregnate someone that does not automatically give you that title of mother or father. You earn the title. My kids don't call me mum because I don't want them to."

She continued: "They're Michael's children. It's not that they are not my children but I had them because I wanted him to be a father.

"I believe there are people who should be parents and he's one of them. And he is such a fabulous man and such a good friend and he's always been there for me. Always, from the day I met him.

"I could do something for him and this is what I wanted to do... People don't understand that – they think that something has to be traditional."

She said people had a false notion of what life was like in the 1950s. It wasn't then and wasn't now, she said.

"We have a non-traditional family and if it makes people uncomfortable it's a shame that they are not more open.

"We are a family unit. Michael and I will always be connected with the kids. I will always be there for him. I will always be there for the children.

"People make remarks: 'I can't believe she left her children.' Left them? I left my children? I did not leave my children.

"My children are with their father where they are supposed to be. I didn't do it to be a mother."

After the divorce from Debbie Michael decided to continue his drive to be a father – but this time without the added complication of a wife.

The surrogacy was carried out with a mystery woman who has never been identified – possibly with Jackson's own sperm. Prince Michael II, also known as Blanket, was born in 2002 and certainly bears an uncanny resemblance to his father.

Hidden by swathes of clothes every time they left the house, it would be February 2008 before the Jackson children were photographed "unveiled", offering a rare glimpse of their faces

Michael hoped to have even more children and pledged to call all the boys Prince Michael, each with a different number next to their names.

Now that Michael is no longer alive, whether Debbie continues to have a role in the life of their children is questionable.

She has sometimes claimed that she saw Michael regularly, that it was an "occasional friendship". But when she appeared in court to give evidence in 2003 she admitted she had not seen her ex-husband or their children for several years.

In 2006 she went back to court to win back her right to be a parent, complaining that Jackson had stopped paying her. He said she had breached a confidentiality agreement but the couple reached a settlement in secret.

Life for Michael meanwhile carried on in the same chaotic way – careering from one extreme to the other. Over the next five years he continued to live in the full glare of publicity and he continued to make music as well as the headlines.

His 1997 album *Blood on The Dance Floor – History in the Mix* was a big hit in the UK but did less well in the US and only sold 4 million worldwide. Meanwhile, his 2001 release *Invincible* sold 8 million copies, but was ultimately a commercial flop.

But Michael Jackson had always been a great stage performer and his 1997 'HIStory' tour was a phenomenal success; in 2001 he was reportedly offered $10 million to play two nights in Vegas. In the same year he starred in a short film *Ghosts*, a long form music video, in which he played a maestro with supernatural powers being hounded out of town by the mayor. The soundtrack to the video came from *Blood on the Dance Floor: HIStory in the Mix*.

During a speech he gave to Oxford University in 2001, promoting his "Heal the Kids" charity, he spoke movingly about his own early experiences as a father.

"What if they grow older and resent me and how my choices impacted their youth?" he asked his audience. "Why weren't we given a normal childhood like all the other kids, they might ask.

"And at that moment I pray that my children will give me the benefit of the doubt. That they will say to themselves: "Our daddy did the best he could, given the unique circumstances he faced.

"I hope they will always focus on the positive things, on the sacrifices I willingly made for them, and not criticize the things they had to give up, or the errors I've made and will certainly continue to make in raising them.

"We all have been someone's child and we know that despite the very best of plans and efforts, mistakes will always occur. That's just being human."

Elsewhere there were more suggestions of a new, more mature Michael, someone who had at least begun to grown up now he was a father.

"Wacko Jacko"? Where'd that come from?" he said in another interview. "I have a heart and I have feelings. I feel that when you do that to me, it's not nice. Don't do it. I'm not a wacko."

Yet only 12 months later, Michael was caught up in one of his most damaging controversies, dangling his baby son dangerously over a balcony.

When Blanket was just nine months old Michael caused public outrage when he was photographed carelessly holding his little son as if he were a toy five floors above the ground, his face covered with a white scarf.

Michael was due to attend the Bambi entertainment award ceremony, and about 200 fans had gathered at the entrance to the Adlon hotel, near the Brandenburg Gate, as Jackson's motorcade arrived in November 2002.

The reclusive performer had to fight his way through the crowd of fans to get into the hotel, in a scrum that injured one person.

Later, they watched in horror as he dangled the baby out of the window of his room on the third floor, holding it with one arm under its shoulders.

Many feared he would drop the infant, although after he brought the child back inside safely they cheered for him to appear again.

This time Jackson came out onto the balcony covering his face and threw a towel down to the crowd below.

The 2002 stunt was condemned by the NSPCC, and variously branded dangerous and stupid. Michael was dismayed, both by his own actions and the embarrassment it caused him, his family and his friends. He was also already facing another court battle – this time with music promoter Marcel Avram over missed New Year gigs back in 1999. What if the German Police decided to press charges?

Fortunately, the local police ruled that the balcony incident was not a crime and decided not to launch a criminal investigation.

By 2003, on a visit to London a package of drugs allegedly arrived for Michael from the US. As a result a private trip to London Zoo had to be cancelled.

The singer was so out of it, it was nearly impossible to rouse him. Even when

Uri Geller screamed at his friend to "Wake up!" Michael was too dazed to go out.

"I was so worried about him," Uri would say later.

"I told him, shouting and screaming, that he would die if things continued as they were."

"The trouble is nobody said no to Michael and that was a problem."

Michael's former British minder Matt Fiddes, claimed things were so bad at one point that he and Jermaine planned to kidnap him and wean him off the drugs he was addicted to.

"One minute it was like the world was his oyster but the next he'd be so down you thought he wanted to kill himself," Fiddes said. "His circle of doctors constantly had him under sedation."

Speaking after Michael's death, he told the *People* newspaper: "Michael had become dependent on his inner circle of medics and didn't want to know anyone else including his own family.

"We got together in the city centre hotel and Jermaine cried. 'They've brainwashed my brother. We've got to get him away'. He was devastated by what was going on.

"Basically it was a kidnap plot and the last throw of the dice as we saw it."

According to Fiddes, he and Jermaine flew together to the States, but Michael refused pointblank to even speak to them and the plan collapsed.

It was in a haze of prescription drugs that Michael now seized upon a new strategy to rebuild his tarnished reputation. He agreed to a TV documentary with the British journalist Martin Bashir – the man who had so famously interviewed Princess Diana in November 1995.

It was to trigger the greatest scandal of his life.

CHAPTER 26

Martin Bashir

Around 15 million UK viewers watched the screening of the documentary *Living with Michael Jackson* in February 2003. With unprecedented access to the star, it was the first time the viewing public had ever been given such an insight into Michael's bizarre and troubled world.

When the programme crossed the Atlantic, the number doubled. It was a major coup for Bashir who had been trying to persuade the reclusive Michael to do the interview for several years.

In the end, his success came from using Uri-Geller, the self-proclaimed psychic most famous for bending spoons, and a close friend of Michael, as a go-between.

There are conflicting reports over when the psychic and the singer first met, some suggesting the late '80s', while Geller himself told a newspaper he met Jackson three and a half years ago through Harrods department store owner Mohamed al-Fayed.

Michael had been best man at Geller's ceremony to renew his wedding vows in 2001.

Now Geller told him: "Michael, maybe it's time to open up to the world."

A meeting was arranged and Bashir managed to convince the singer he should do the show.

In a series of interviews over eight months, Bashir was offered unique and extraordinary access to Michael's personal life. A reclusive, private man opened up about his love life, his changing appearance, Neverland and his children, coming across as tortured, eccentric – and vaguely ridiculous.

There were some sympathetic moments, like the one where he spoke of the "bad, really bad" beatings he got from his father Joseph; or the times he longed to play in the ball park with his friend but had to record in the studio opposite instead, watching forlornly from a window.

It wasn't the whole truth. Bizarrely, Michael denied ever having had any plastic surgery on his face – insisting he only had an operation on his nose to help him breathe properly.

"I'm telling you the honest truth," he tells Bashir. "I don't do anything to my face." It appeared as if he believed his own untruths.

Michael was also filmed bouncing baby Blanket on his knee, talking about how much he loved him. He told Bashir he was really Peter Pan – "in my heart".

He was filmed climbing the so-called "Magic Tree" where he wrote many of his best songs, and spending thousands of dollars on gaudy baroque furniture and ornaments.

Michael repeatedly opened his heart, emphasizing his absolute love for children: "I'll say it a million times. I'm not afraid to say it," he said. "If there were no children on this earth, if somebody announced that all kids are dead I would jump off the balcony immediately. I'm done. I'm done."

Then, crucially, in a piece of footage that would go on to wreck the rest of his life, he also told a stunned Bashir how he invited disadvantaged children to his Neverland ranch and let them stay in his bed.

In the film, he held hands with a 12-year-old boy called Gavin Arvizo, who had survived cancer, and freely admitted sharing a room with him.

"I was, like Michael you can sleep in the bed," says Gavin. "And he was like, 'No, no you sleep in the bed,' and I was like, 'No, no, no, you sleep in the bed,' and then he said, 'Look if you love me then you'll sleep in the bed.' I was like 'Oh man!' So I finally slept in the bed."

As the cameras rolled, Michael told Bashir in an echo of the press statement he had put out in the wake of the Jordie Chandler affair: "I have slept in a bed with many children. Why can't you share your bed? The most loving thing to do is share your bed with someone.

When you say 'bed' you're thinking sexual. They make that sexual. It's not sexual. We're going to sleep.

"I tuck them in and I put a little music on and when it's story time I read a book. We go to sleep with the fireplace on.

"I give them hot milk you know, we have cookies. It's very charming, it's very sweet. It's what the whole world should do."

He admitted many children had been invited to his room, including the famous Culkin family, who he had called up after the success of the first *Home Alone* film.

Child actors Macaulay and Kieran Culkin and their other brothers and sisters had all slept in the same bed as him, he said. But he denied having had sexual contact with any of them.

"I think we understand each other in a way that most people can't understand either of us," Macaulay would later say.

Bashir also asked Michael about the 1993 Jordie Chandler allegations. But he refused to talk about them in any detail citing a "confidentiality agreement".

He had paid out the money to the Chandler family because he wanted to get on with his life, he said. He didn't want to go through a "long, drawn-out affair, like O.J. (Simpson)".

But that, in the end, was to be his fate.

When the programme went out in America, Michael was horrified, issuing a statement in which he said he felt betrayed and devastated at such a "gross distortion of the truth". His parents Katherine and Joseph arrived at Neverland to support their son.

Bashir strongly defended the programme, insisting the filming had not been "traumatic" for Jackson. He also said he had not set out to "ensnare" Jackson but that he had been honestly troubled by the relationship between the singer and the boy.

"If concerns are expressed about the way he behaves with children and it makes him careful in the future then that's a good thing," he added.

But Michael complained about the way it had been edited. It was a twisted reconstruction of innuendo and scandal, he claimed.

Michael now released his own video footage of Bashir's interviews which he had recorded himself showing Bashir describing him as a "spectacular" father.

Michael then decided to put out a two-hour documentary about his life, roping in friends and family to defend him on film.

As part of it he employed a videographer Christian Robinson to tape an interview with Gavin's family, showing hospital footage of Gavin, still hairless from chemotherapy and being pushed around in a wheelchair.

Narrator Maury Povich explained how the Arvizo family had been forced into hiding after the Bashir programme and Gavin's mother Janet Ventura-Arvizo declared: "I'm appalled at the way my son has been exploited by Martin Bashir.

"The relationship that Michael has with my children is a beautiful, loving, father-sons-and daughter one. To my children and me, Michael is a part of my family."

The Michael Jackson Interview: The Footage You were Never Meant to See was sold around the world. Even Debbie Rowe emerged from the shadows to talk about how excellent a father Michael was in a remarkable interview with GMTV in London.

Meanwhile, Michael tried to get on with everyday, if not ordinary life. He walked and played with his family at Neverland, he took his children shopping wearing masks supposedly designed to foil potential kidnappers.

But still the fall-out from Granada TV's Bashir documentary rumbled on.

Child welfare experts and teachers spoke out with concerns about possible inappropriate behaviour.

In the UK, the Children's charity Barnado's said that if anyone in the UK had revealed similar circumstances then an investigation would be launched by the authorities.

Principal policy officer Pam Hibbert said: "At Barnardo's we feel it is totally inappropriate for an adult man to share a bed or bedroom with a child that is not his own."

A spokesman for the NSPCC said: "His behaviour could be used as justification by people who want to harm or sexually abuse children as an excuse for their own behaviour". Across the Atlantic, Local District Attorney Thomas Sneddon said initially that under Californian law merely sleeping without "affirmative offensive conduct" was not a criminal offence.

The Department of Child and Family Services in Los Angeles however, began an investigation and it was decided experts would now formally interview the Arvizo family.

Michael's camp sent along an investigator and a friend to be with them. When the investigator was asked to leave, Michael and Gavin's mother Janet arranged to secretly tape record the proceedings.

The details from those recorded tapes were later published in J. Randy Taraborrelli's biography.

According to the tapes, the Arvizo family attributes much of Gavin's remarkable recovery to Michael.

Janet Arvizo meanwhile describes Michael as "like a father to my children". She adds: "He loves them and I trust my children with him."

She says she was completely aware of everything that went on at Neverland and Michael was never alone with the children. They might have sat on the bed together watching TV and snacking "but for the allegations they share a bed, it is no".

He was "a blessing" to them and had never been anything other, she said.

Gavin insisted: "Michael is like a father figure to me. He's never done anything to me sexually." His older sister Daveline, sobbed: "He is so kind and loving".

The DCFS closed their case. No action taken. The LAPD and the Santa Barbara Sheriff's Department followed suit.

But at some stage over the next few weeks the Arvizo family had a change of heart.

Janet Arvizo now brought in Larry Feldman, the same lawyer who had represented Jordie Chandler – and he organized for Gavin to see clinical and forensic psychologist Stan Ketz.

Over a number of sessions with Dr Ketz, Gavin apparently started remembering all sorts of events that he had hitherto forgotten or been too frightened to mention. The family claimed it was only with Dr Ketz that he had felt safe enough to reveal the full story.

According to records of the interviews Gavin said he drank alcohol every night – strong spirits like whiskey, vodka and rum. He was shown pictures of naked women on the computer and he once saw Michael naked. There was even a brief mention of masturbation and how Michael would go crazy if he didn't do it.

Gavin's brother Star went further. He said he and Gavin often slept in Michael's room with his brother in the bed, and they talked a lot about sex.

Daveline had seen Michael "rubbing" her brother and hugging him,

The children remembered drinking "Jesus Juice" from in-flight soda cans.

Dr Katz felt the stories were credible. He immediately reported the remembered sexual abuse to the police.

Within a matter of months there was another police raid on Neverland. This time it was much more high profile.

Early one November morning, while Michael was away in Las Vegas filming a video, up to 70 officials in a convoy of a dozen cars descended on the 2,700-acre ranch backed by armed police. They went through the property with a fine-toothed comb, discovering several locked safes, filing cupboards and a maze of secret rooms and cupboards from which the seized a litany of computer files, personal diaries and documents.

The singer later described the raid as his "darkest day". Film-maker Larry Nimmer, who was part of Michael's defence team told the *Daily Mirror* after his former employer's death in 2009: "Jackson was in Las Vegas on the morning of the raid but he felt his private sanctuary had been violated."

The following day a warrant was issued for the arrest of Michael Jackson. Michael arranged with police to fly home and a day later handed himself in to their custody. He was handcuffed, photographed and had his fingerprints taken by officers before being freed on $3 million bail.

Fans around the world held a candlelit vigil that night but were powerless to stop the wheels of justice turning.

After the arrest Michael claimed he had been "manhandled" and showed a photograph he said was taken after he left the police station, with apparent swelling above his wrists.

He told American TV show 60 *Minutes*, "(I was) manhandled very roughly. My shoulder is dislocated, literally. It's hurting me very badly. I'm in pain all the time. They did it to try to belittle me, to try to take away my pride.

"They put me in a certain position, knowing it's going to hurt and affect my back. Now I can't move – it keeps me from sleeping at night."

Michael also recalled: "Then one time, I asked to use the restroom. And they said, 'Sure, it's right around the corner there.' Once I went in the restroom, they locked me in there for like 45 minutes. There was doodoo – faeces – thrown all over the walls, the floor, the ceiling. And it stunk so bad.

"Then one of the policemen came by the window. And he made a sarcastic remark. He said, 'Smell — does it smell good enough for you in there? How do you like the smell? Is it good?' And I just simply said, 'It's alright. It's okay.' So, I just sat there, and waited."

When he finally called home to Neverland, he was told his private world had been devastated, Michael claimed.

"My room is a complete wreck. My workers told me. They said, 'Michael, don't go in your room'. They were crying on the phone, my employees. They said, 'If you saw your room, you would cry'. I have stairs that go up to my bed. And they said, 'You can't even get up the stairs. The room is totally trashed.'

"And they had 80 policemen in this room, 80 policemen in one bedroom. That's really overdoing it. They took knives, and cut open my mattresses with knives. C — just cut everything open."

Santa Barbara Sheriff's Department insisted Jackson was treated with courtesy and respect throughout the booking process.

A month later, in December 2003, Jackson was formally charged with seven counts of child molestation and two counts of administering intoxicating liquor to a minor with the intent of committing a crime.

The crimes were alleged to have taken place between 7 February and 10 March 2003 – curiously, during the days after the Bashir documentary was broadcast.

Jackson remained on bail and his lawyer said he was "unequivocally and absolutely innocent" and would fight the charges "with every fibre of his soul".

He told America's 60 Minutes in an interview that he would "slit his wrist" before hurting a child.

But after that programme went out to 27 million viewers he allegedly collapsed following a Morphine overdose. The late-night drama, kept secret until after his death was revealed by an unnamed medic who claims Michael's brother Randy called him in the early hours of December 29, 2003.

The doctor told the Daily Mail he was wakened by a call from Randy at 1.51am and asked to attend someone who was sick, since they couldn't call 911 for security reasons.

He found Michael dressed in his pyjama bottoms, propped up in bed but unconscious, he said. He checked his breathing and blood pressure, and then helped Randy take his brother to the bathroom.

"Randy said Michael had been under severe stress because of the television programme which had aired that night," the unnamed doctor said.

"I recall him saying that an earlier TV documentary had caused all manner of problems and that Michael had worked himself up into a frenzy of anxiety over this one."

Michael recovered with none of his fans knowing about his collapse and returned to business as usual. Once the authorities had returned his passport he even managed to fulfil commitments in the UK over Christmas and New Year.

On January 16, 2004, Michael Jackson appeared in court in Santa Maria, California, to officially deny charges of child abuse.

Katherine and Joseph, his sister Janet and brothers Jermaine, Tito and Randy were all there to give him support.

Michael hung around with fans outside, smiling and shaking hands, only to be firmly reprimanded for being 21 minutes late.

On that occasion, the Judge told him: "You have started out on the wrong foot here. I want to advise you that I will not put up with that. It's an insult to the court."

Later Michael emerged only to amaze fans by dancing on the roof of his car.

It was the start of the fully-fledged circus that would surround him when the case finally went to trial more than a year later.

CHAPTER 27

On Trial

On April 21, 2004 Michael Jackson was indicted by a Grand Jury and ordered to stand trial. If convicted he faced up to 20 years in jail.

The same evening, a special episode of *South Park*, the acerbic cartoon series was broadcast on US television featuring an eccentric family called the Jeffersons clearly based on Michael Jackson.

To date it is the only episode to feature 'Kenny' speaking audible lines, as he is disguised as 'Blanket' and not wearing his trademark parka.

Nine days later, on April 30, Michael appeared in court and pleaded not guilty to ten child molestation charges including a fresh charge of conspiracy to abduct a child.

The new conspiracy count included 28 allegations of "overt acts" including false imprisonment and extortion.

This time Michael took a new approach to appearing in court. He arrived early wearing a crisp suit, and his only display of bravado was to briefly flash a two-fingered victory sign to his screaming fans before leaving the courthouse.

Even so, almost half Santa Maria's 110 strong police force were needed on crowd control duty that day and they were backed up by as many as 50 sheriff's deputies. Hundreds of Michael's fans were determined to show their support daily.

The judge said the $3 million bail order would remain in place and adjourned the hearing until May 28. Further delays followed as the lawyers prepared their cases and a date was finally set for January 31, 2005.

But the death of defence lawyer Thomas Mesereau's sister delayed the start and when on February 15, Michael was rushed to hospital apparently suffering from flu, the trial was put back for another week while he was treated.

Finally, on February 22, the jury was selected and sworn in and the People v Jackson got underway.

Outside the Santa Barbara courthouse, it was a melee of press, TV reporters, photographers, paparazzi, and music fans.

The Judge, Rodney Melville, conscious that the case could descend into a media circus, had refused to let the hearings be televised so while TV reconstructions abounded (with lookalike Ed Moss in the starring role) there was not quite the soap-opera style hype that had surrounded cases like the OJ Simpson murder trial.

Nonetheless Jacko fans worldwide followed the proceedings with a mixture of concern and growing fascination.

Gavin Arvizo had been born into a poor family, one of three children, living in downtown Los Angeles.

He had one thing in common with Michael Jackson – a childhood tainted by violent abuse. His father David, a lorry driver, was a violent man who beat the children's mother, Janet, and them with disturbing regularity.

Janet and David split in an acrimonious divorce and in 2004 she remarried, to US Army Major Jay Jackson.

Gavin might never have met his idol, Michael Jackson. But at the age of ten he was struck down with an aggressive form of cancer.

Surgeons removed a massive 16 lb tumour from his stomach, his spleen and a kidney and while he was recovering in hospital a comedy club owner asked him what would really make him happy.

Gavin wanted to meet famous people – and Michael Jackson was on the list.

Michael got to hear about the brave little boy who was a huge fan – and rang him. Gavin couldn't believe it was his idol on the other end of the telephone.

The pair became friends and Michael invited the family to Neverland. Before long he had brought the Arvizos inside his fantasy world in a way that had loud echoes of Jordie Chandler.

He was soon paying for Gavin's medication, taxis to chemotherapy visits and splashing out on endless gifts and toys. But the relationship foundered and after a handful of visits contact ceased, leaving the boy devastated.

Then in 2002, Jackson rang Gavin again.

"You want to be an actor, right?" he said to the boy. "I'm going to put you in movies."

"The movies" turned out to be Bashir's documentary.

CHAPTER 28

People vs Jackson

Even if the cameras weren't allowed in, the People vs Jackson trial was compulsive viewing for the US public. It was perverted music megastar against defenceless sick child, or a tacky attempt at extortion against the most maligned and misjudged man in showbusiness, depending on the viewer.

Prosecutors casually unpicked Jacko's innocent "Peter Pan" world at Neverland – steadily exposing it as a booze-soaked paedophile's palace where victims were groomed for abuse.

The defence countered, painting Gavin as a wild teenager with behavioural problems, a disruptive who stole alcohol and watched pornography.

On Day One, the jury was told how Michael abused Gavin, then 13, plying him with alcohol and exposing him to "strange sexual behaviour" during visits to his Neverland ranch.

Thomas Sneddon, prosecuting, said: "The private world of Michael Jackson reveals that, instead of cookies and milk, you can substitute wine, bourbon and vodka."

Thomas Mesereau, defending, claimed Michael had been the victim of an extortion attempt by Gavin's mother Janet, who used her sick son to prey on celebrities for money.

On Day Two, TV journalist Martin Bashir took the witness stand and the jury watched the two-hour *Living with Michael* programme.

Mr Mesereau told them there was no DNA evidence of the alleged abuses.

On Day Three, a former Jackson employee told the court how the star's team was "extremely agitated" after the broadcast of Bashir's documentary highlighted his friendships with children.

Public relations executive Ann Gabriel said the show, in which Jackson admitted sharing his bedroom with children, had become an "absolute disaster" for the singer.

Asked by the prosecution, how she would rate its negative impact on a scale of one to ten, she replied: "A 25."

The following day Gavin Arvizo's sister told how her brother asked if he could sleep in the singer's bedroom during one of his first visits to Neverland and the family agreed.

She also revealed how at the time of the alleged abuse, Michael repeatedly took the boy into a private room during a trip to Miami. Her brother, she said, would "act jumpy" afterwards.

On day five, the jury was shown video footage of Gavin and his mother praising Michael and insisting there was nothing untoward about his relationship with the boy.

But three days later Gavin's younger brother Star gave evidence, describing how Michael lay on a bed masturbating himself and his brother.

Star told the jury he had twice seen Michael sexually molesting his brother. He also said that, on one occasion at Neverland, Michael had entered a bedroom, where the boys were sitting on the bed, naked and in a state of arousal.

On March 9, Michael's accuser, by then 15, faced the singer across the courtroom in an emotionally charged atmosphere – the centrepiece of the show trial.

According to some observers Gavin seemed singularly unimpressed by the man in the dock. Others report that he could not look Michael in the eye.

Gavin described how on his first visit to Neverland, Michael had suggested he and his younger brother sleep in the entertainer's bedroom. "He told us to ask our parents ... at dinner. My parents said yeah."

Gavin also agreed with previous testimony from his brother that the singer and an assistant showed them pornographic internet sites on that first night at the ranch.

The prosecution argued that Michael administered alcohol to the boys to help commit a crime.

But the defence pointed to discrepancies in Star Arvizo's story. They held that the two boys were "running wild" through the main house, breaking into the wine cellar and drinking alcohol of their own volition.

Day Nine saw farcical scenes after Michael failed to arrive at court in time and headed instead to hospital, complaining of a bad back.

The Judge, furious at his no-show, threatened to arrest him and take away his bail unless he was there within 60 minutes.

Just over an hour later Michael appeared, dishevelled, dressed in his pyjamas and slippers, a suit jacket thrown over the top. The bizarre photographs of him were flashed around the world.

As the trial continued Gavin told the court how the singer masturbated him to ejaculation.

"He asked me if I masturbated and when I said I didn't he said he would do it for me."

The two, who had been drinking alcohol, then got under the covers of Michael's bed, the boy said. "That's when he put his hands in my pants and started rubbing me."

The second time Jackson fondled him, said Gavin, the singer had tried to get him to do the same to him. "He grabbed my hand to get me to do it but I didn't want to."

Under cross-examination the boy defended his claim that Michael had not helped him through his cancer. He had dumped him half way through, he said.

As Thomas Mesereau detailed the gifts and hospitality the singer had offered, Gavin replied that to him, then an 11-year-old boy, "it felt like my heart broke" when Michael stopped calling.

On May 11, the former child actor Macauley Culkin took the stand and firmly rejected any suggestion Michael ever molested him.

The charges against the singer were, he declared, "absolutely ridiculous".

Culkin had his own struggles with celebrity, and was just nine when he met Michael. But he insisted any sleepovers he had at Neverland were entirely innocent and was amazed that he had not been approached earlier to defend his friend.

He told lead defence lawyer, Tom Mesereau, that he had only learned of the allegations by watching coverage of the trial on television.

"I just couldn't believe it," he said. "It was amazing to me that nobody even approached me and asked if these allegations were true."

The most specific accusation came from Frenchman Phillip LeMarque, Jackson's former chef, or self-styled "majordomo", or head of staff, who told the court he had seen the singer with his hand in Culkin's trousers during a night-time video-game session.

Mr LeMarque had been ordered to bring some food, but was so stunned by what he saw he "almost dropped the french fries".

The incident happened in 1991 about "three or four o'clock in the morning", said Mr Lemarque. He had been summoned from his bed to make some late-night chips for the singer.

He said he walked into the room and saw Jackson at a *Thriller* video game with Culkin.

"He [Jackson] was holding the kid because the kid could not reach the controls. His right hand was holding the kid and the left was down the pants."

But Culkin, who was by then in his twenties, painted a very different picture of their relationship. They had formed a friendship because they were both child stars who shared a unique bond forged by the difficulties early fame entailed, he said.

"We're a part of a unique group of people," he told the court. "He'd been through that before, so he understood what it was like to be put in that position I was in, to be thrust into it."

Asked whether he had witnessed anything untoward going on between Mr Jackson and other boys who frequently stayed at Neverland, he replied: "I've never seen him do anything improper with anyone."

It clearly did no harm to Michael's case. But his greatest ally – and the witness who probably did most to destroy the prosecution case – was his ex-wife and the mother of his two eldest children, Debbie Rowe.

The former nurse – who was at the time involved in a bitter custody battle with Jackson – had been expected to give evidence against him, admitting their marriage had been nothing but a ploy to improve his public image.

Instead she told the court he was easily manipulated and might well have been the victim of "opportunistic vultures".

The defence also pointed to a number of dents in Gavin's credibility as a witness.

All the Arvizo children had taken acting lessons in the run up to a 2001 lawsuit against American retailer J C Penney and there was a suggestion they been coached to back up a "far-fetched" story.

In August 1998 the family had been detained for shoplifting after walking out of a department store with armfuls of clothes.

The shoplifting charges were eventually dropped but Janet Arvizo counter-sued for $3m, claiming she and the boys were beaten up by three security officers during their arrest. She also said she had been sexually molested.

JC Penney settled at the last minute for $137,000 but the store's lawyer branded it simply a "scam to extract money".

The Jackson case was another "shakedown" he said. "Shakedown part 2."

After the jury retired to discuss the verdict, a stressed Michael spent a two-hour session in a blood circulation device at his Neverland ranch.

An interview with Michel's nutritionist Dick Gregory in the *Daily Telegraph* claimed the star lay on a bed while inflatable "spaceman" cuffs wrapped around his calves, thighs and buttocks pumped blood from his lower limbs to his heart.

After spending June 1 in court with the family, he travelled back to Neverland with them and gave Michael a massage on his lower back.

"I told him this was serious and he had to get to hospital because he needed IVs of electrolytes. His condition was so bad that he had four IVs that night."

The next day, Gregory went on a $1,500 shopping trip for vitamins and herbal remedies to prepare a "smoothie" Jackson could take each morning and evening.

He also told how Jackson used Enhanced External Counter-Pulsation (EECP), a little-known technique for boosting blood circulation.

"It's ideal for patients who are suffering from stress and fatigue," said Sara Soulati, the medical technician who conducted the two-hour EECP.

"Mr Jackson had the treatment for two hours and after we finished he jumped up smiling and gave me a big hug. He said he hadn't smiled for a long time and told me he would want me to come back after the whole trial thing had settled down."

In the end it took the Jackson jury a week and a half to decide that the Arvizo brothers' story just did not quite add up.

The world held its breath as the verdicts were announced just after 10pm on June 14, 2005.

In the hushed courtroom, the atmosphere was electric as the jurors – eight woman and four men – filed in one at a time in a deafening silence.

In a stern voice Judge Melville told the court he would stand for no reaction – be it delight or despair – and Michael sat quietly, contemplatively, staring ahead as the ten envelopes containing the ten verdicts were each opened, then read out by the court clerk

Ten times the words "Not Guilty" echoed around the chamber. At least one juror wept.

Jackson was cleared on all ten counts of abusing Gavin Arvizo, plying the boy with alcohol to molest him, and conspiring to abduct his family.

As the news went public, the crowds outside went wild. One woman fan released a white dove as each not guilty verdict was repeated on live TV broadcasts. Someone else released white balloons. Others scattered confetti.

But inside the building it was a different story. Jackson's biographer J. Randy Taraborrelli had one of the best seats in the house and watched his friend closely.

What hit him like a thunderbolt was the sudden realisation that Jackson was on so many different drugs he didn't even realize what was going on.

He vividly remembers the blank, flat, empty look in Jackson's eyes.

"I smiled at him," he recalled. "He smiled back. But his eyes were empty. It should have been the happiest day of his life but it was as if he wasn't even there to enjoy it. Michael Jackson was gone."

Moments later Michael left the courtroom slowly, under the protection of a black umbrella. He held his hand to his heart, blew kisses to the screaming mob, then stepped into his black SUV vehicle to be driven back to Neverland, with many of his supporters following him. They were ecstatic and they wanted a party.

In the UK, nearly 8 million people watched the BBC's main evening news that night for live coverage of the culmination of the four-month trial.

It was the largest audience since the last week of 2004, when BBC1's coverage of the tsunami disaster pulled in an average of 7.8 million viewers a night.

One man told how he "cried like a baby" when the verdicts were announced. "It was the most beautiful day of my life," he said.

Michael was said to be "at peace" after the verdicts were delivered. In reality he looked exhausted and emotionally drained. The experience had cost Michael dearly – and not only the £25,000 he had spent on tailored suits for his court appearances.

Gregory the nutritionist described the elaborate cocktail "smoothie" of vitamins and herbs he prepared for Jackson after he underwent a series of intravenous feeds of electrolytes in hospital because he was so badly dehydrated.

He had joined Michael's entourage on May 31, 2005 after flying out because he was so alarmed by what he had seen of Jackson on television.

"I could tell that he wasn't drinking nearly enough. He was in court all day so he couldn't take liquids on a regular basis. And stress leaves you even more dehydrated than normal and wipes out your appetite."

Now, he told the *Daily Telegraph*: "My greatest fear is that Michael will go into a slump now this is all over, even though he's been cleared.

"It's like an enormous hangover after a huge party. That would be very dangerous for a man in his physical condition. It could kill him.

"Three of the biggest killers in America are sleep deprivation, dehydration and lack of physical fitness. Michael is suffering from all of them."

Around the world, supporters expressed their relief and their faith in the US justice system and Debbie Rowe issued a statement: "I would never have married a paedophile." She added, somewhat unclearly: "And the system works."

Any euphoria Michael might have felt was short-lived, as the jury went public in post-trial media interviews describing how they had reached their decision

Some said they it was their belief that Jackson may, after all, have molested boys. Their verdict did not necessarily exonerate the singer, merely reflecting the fact that the evidence was too weak for a conviction.

Raymond Hultman, 62, said: "I feel that Michael Jackson probably has molested boys. I can't believe that this man could sleep in the same bedroom for 365 straight days and not do something more than just watch television and eat popcorn. That does not make sense to me.

"But that does not make him guilty of the charges that were presented in this case and that's where we had to make our decision."

Mr Hultman was one of three jurors who voted to acquit only after the other nine persuaded them of the reasonable doubt.

The jury foreman, Paul Rodriguez, said the jury had given credence to some past allegations against Jackson presented during the trial to demonstrate an alleged pattern of abuse. But the singer was not on trial for these.

"There are not too many grown men we know that would sleep with children but we had to base it on the evidence presented to us," said Mr Rodriguez . "There were a lot of things lacking."

And 79-year-old grandma Eleanor Cook confided: "We had our suspicions, but we couldn't judge on that because it wasn't what we were there to do."

The negative publicity was a severe blow to Jackson's hopes for public rehabilitation – and a come-back for his fading career. He had already started looking at doing a show in Las Vegas.

The singer's lawyer Tom Mesereau immediately hit back, insisting his client had vowed to change his life – and never to sleep in the same bed as young boys ever again.

Mesereau, pledged that his client would now make radical changes to his lifestyle.

"He's not going to do that any more," he said. "He's not going to make himself vulnerable to this any more. He's going to take it one day at a time. It's been a terrible, terrible process for him."

Later Jackson issued his first public statement. "Thank you to my family, friends and fans for all your love and support," he said on his website.

"I will never forget. I love you all. Michael."

CHAPTER 29

Aftermath

Back in the United States, as the small town of Santa Maria cleaned up in the days after the trial ended, its 80,000 plus citizens were still rubbing their hands. The whole Michael Jackson circus had brought in millions of dollars for the town. Hotels and inns were filled to capacity with lawyers, journalists and Jacko fans.

Ordinary citizens rented out prime locations in homes and gardens with one man charging TV crews £1,300 a day for a space on his flat roof opposite the court building.

Restaurants, cafes and bars had been packed to the gunnels. One internet cafe said its takings were up 1,000 per cent. With the summer season barely begun, they had already made a year's money.

Michael Jackson, on the other hand – despite his acquittal – found himself with little to celebrate. For the next two weeks he disappeared inside the sanctuary of Neverland and there was no glimpse of him. After living out his daily life for the cameras during the weeks of the trial, Michael had gone into hiding.

But he was not entirely alone. One woman had remained at the centre of the Jackson family life almost throughout.

On and off for 17 years, throughout the sex scandals and the marriages, there was one person Michael could always trust. Pretty matriarch Grace Rwaramba was the nanny who had cared for Michael and his children. Now, it seemed as if she might be something more.

Born in Rwanda, Grace arrived in America as a young woman and studied in Massachusetts before marrying an American man, Stacey Adair, in Las Vegas in 1995.

The couple appear to be separated, though not divorced and it is has been mooted the union was one of convenience.

Grace was 24 when she started working with Michael in 1991 dealing with insurance for his employees and is thought to have had a brief liaison with his brother Jermaine.

Then, in 1999, she became his first nanny and an integral part of the family. She had been with all three children from the day they were born, and as she cared for them so her relationship with Michael also grew.

Soon their romance was an open secret among staff and it was made very clear that it should not be revealed.

At that time, Grace had no interest in fame – in fact, she actively avoided it.

Insiders spoke of her and Michael as being "like a married couple", who would row over how the children were being brought up.

"Everything is done Grace's way," observed one member of staff.

When Grace took the children to meet Debbie at a hotel one day, Debbie was said to be stunned – and unhappy – to hear them call her "mom".

Now, in June 2006, it was announced that Jackson had begun a holiday in Bahrain to relax after the unimaginable stresses of his child abuse trial. He took Grace and the children with him.

Michael's brother Jermaine had ties with the country after he and the King's son, music-loving Sheikh Abdulla bin Hamad Al Khalifa, worked together on plans for a charity song.

Michael was described at the time as "a long time friend" of the royal family.

The singer, his children and his personal staff flew into the Gulf State on a private jet. "He is here in Bahrain on a friendly visit to relax and enjoy the hospitality," said a Bahrain official.

Over the next four months, apart from a couple of short trips to the UK, Michael settled more or less permanently into his new Middle Eastern tax-haven home – and into Bahrain's lavish lifestyle.

According to some reports, denied by his office, he paid out over 3 quarters of a million pounds for a paradise man-made island where he bought two villas, both with seaside views.

He was rumoured to have added a Bentley and a Rolls-Royce to his fleet of luxury cars as well as a Jeep for the kids. He was also said to be funding the construction of a mosque.

But the self-exiled King of Pop continued to keep an extremely low profile. So much so that in January 2006 bemused shoppers in the Bahrain capital Manama spotted him out with his children, disguised as a woman.

Leila al-Aradi, an assistant at Mothercare, told the *Independent* newspaper how she looked on in disbelief as the three Jackson children – led by a local woman invisible beneath an abaya, a traditional head-to-toe robe – dashed around the store for an hour trying out clothes and toys, until, arms full, they made for the checkout.

As they stood there, Ms al-Aradi noticed the woman in the abaya was wearing men's shoes. "I looked up at him and mouthed: 'Michael Jackson'," said Ms al-Aradi. "But he wagged his finger to caution me against saying his name aloud."

In a nearby showroom sales assistant Latif Muttath began serving what he took to be a rich local woman. Until, that is: "I looked at the person's shoes and found they were men's shoes. That's when I guessed it was Michael Jackson." he said.

Bahrain's citizens had mixed reactions to Michael Jackson's arrival in their country. Some clearly disliked Michael's eccentric, effeminate, American ways. But as long as he was a friend of the ruler's son there was little to be done about it.

Meanwhile, the relationship between Jackson and the Sheikh was beginning to show stresses and strains.

After his multi-million dollar trial, and the $20 million payout to Jordie Chandler, Michael's debts were beginning to rack up. But even as Michael was heading into financial dire straits he appeared in complete denial, still obsessed with spending money like water.

"It was the beginning of the walk down a tragic path", said his then publicist Michael Levine. Emotionally, spiritually, psychologically and legally, he said, and also financially.

During the Arvizo trial one accountant revealed Michael regularly spent $30 million a year more than he earned. He had been forced to sell half his stake in his ATV music catalogue for $195 million, dramatically weakening his hold over his prized possession.

Without another hit album, he used money from the deal to secure a loan. In 2001 he borrowed $200 million from Bank of America but allegedly sold that on to Fortress Investments – to whom he was paying a rumoured 20 per cent interest rate.

Even Neverland was being rented out in part, as he had to hire out some of the land for cattle grazing to scrape together money.

Yet at the same time in 2002 he spent £60,000 on a hotel bill during a brief stay in New York.

He clearly could not afford the life he was continuing to live. And meanwhile, he was becoming more and more isolated, not even seeing his dysfunctional family.

In October 2005, Michael visited London as the guest of the controversial Harrods owner Mohamed Al Fayed. He, Grace and the children all checked into a £2,500-a-night suite at the Dorchester hotel on Park Lane before taking in city sights including Madame Tussauds, the musical *Billy Elliot* and posing for photographs with Al Fayed at Harrods.

Granted a rare interview, the *Daily Mirror's* showbusiness editor Fiona Cummins recalled that Michael had a "surprisingly firm" handshake. Michael, who was wearing no makeup, unexpectedly hugged her.

"I love it here always," Michael told her. "I'm looking for a place to live. I've always liked the UK and I just love the fans here."

Instead, Michael returned to Bahrain.

Come Christmas 2005 and Michael invited a number of friends out to visit him out in the Persian Gulf, including the former *Oliver!* child star Mark Lester and his family.

Despite Michaels' financial problems, Lester returned with 22 crates of gifts from the star "everything from iPods, phones, cameras, computers, laptops and PlayStations to trampolines and water slides for our garden."

Lester had met Michael after receiving a telephone call from his manager asking if he could meet him in 1982 just before the *Thriller* album was released. He was at home in London with his sister and was stunned by the conversation.

"A few days later we went to see him at the Montcalm hotel in Park Lane," he remembered. "He came over, gave me a hug and said, 'Mark, it's so nice to meet you'.

"I was very nervous but we had tea and then ordered up burgers and chatted. We shared a common baseline. He was much more famous than me but we had both been child stars and we were the same age. He said that in the teeny mags in America it would be him on one page, me on another and David Cassidy on another. He always used to say we were like the positive and negative, the black and white."

However, when the Sheikh appeared to be left with the hefty bill for Michael's extravagant Christmas, the relationship between him and his long-term guest appeared to sour.

Soon, Michael was renting a £7,000-a-month ranch-style house in four acres in the more modest suburb of Sanad – not the choice of the super wealthy. It seemed the Sheikh had put his foot down over the limitless bills Michael was racking up.

In early 2006, 2 Seas, a record label based in Bahrain, announced it was to release Jackson's new album – his first since 2001.

The label, the statement said, was a joint enterprise between Jackson and the King of Bahrain's son. But in May 2006 Jackson left Bahrain and come September his US spokeswoman Raymone Bain said he was no longer linked with the label.

The Sheikh promptly sued his former friend for $7 million.

It would take another two years for the case to come to court and in the meantime Jackson became something of a nomad, beginning a period of restless travel. In June 2006, accompanied by his three children and usual entourage, he flew on a scheduled Aer Lingus flight in to Cork on the southern tip of Ireland.

Michael had always had an affinity for Ireland. He loved the rolling green countryside and was at one stage planning a leprechaun theme park to be twinned with his US Neverland ranch, though it never went ahead.

He flitted across the country staying either in sumptuous hotels or boarding with friends. Sometimes he lodged with his dancer friend Michael Flatley at his imposing castle home at Castlehyde in County Cork. Sometimes the family stayed with friends of Grace, the nanny and now suspected girlfriend.

Other times, Michael checked into the luxurious Coolatore House near Grouse Lodge recording studios in Westmeath, or the seven-bedroom Luggala Castle in Co Wicklow, a 1,500-acre estate complete with private chefs and butlers, all at a reported cost of over £25,000 a week.

While in Ireland he worked on various projects: recording an album, and trying to organize a concert in Rwanda to raise funds for African Aids victims.

He also made secret visits to a plastic surgeon. Dr Patrick Treacy has since refused to say what procedures he carried out but does admit that his appointments with Michael were well outside of normal working hours at Dublin's Ailesbury Clinic.

"We had to see him at the clinic at around 2 or 3 o'clock in the morning," Dr Treacy said, adding that was "the norm" for certain celebrities.

He painted a picture of a caring man who was deeply moved by the tale of two children Gavil and Millie Murray, then aged four and six, who were badly burned when their car was petrol bombed in Limerick.

"He wanted me to go in and see the children in Crumlin Hospital and give him an update," he said. "He had a genuine concern for children, not in a sexual way, but in a loving way."

He spent the November in a recording studio outside Dublin working with the Black Eyed Peas' Will.I.Am.

When he wasn't recording he told friends he was up early in the mornings making porridge for the kids, busy walking in the grounds, and horse-back riding.

There were rumours Michael was so happy in southern Ireland he was house hunting there. On the Emerald Isle, there was the expected curtain twitching but nothing like the full-on goldfish bowl existence he had learned to live with elsewhere.

Over the years, Michael had become used to disguising himself "because people act as if they personally know me".

"When I'm travelling people will sleep outside my hotel," he said. "I make sure they've blankets and food. I love connecting to my fans. I love them all."

Irish people seemed to stop short of actively bothering and targeting the star, preferring to just acknowledge him. But, however hard Michael tried to escape his former existence and move towards something resembling normal life, there were constant reminders of home.

Around that time Debbie went back to court trying to win back her right to be a parent. For the court papers, it didn't seem that she particularly wanted the children she had given birth to, it was just that an increasingly broke Michael had stopped paying her.

For his part, Michael claimed Rowe had breached a confidentiality agreement. In the end, the couple reached a settlement in secret.

In November 2006 Michael flew over to London for the World Music Awards for what would become his final public performance.

As usual he was the subject of intense media coverage, with press and television crews camped outside his hotel.

As he arrived on stage in his trademark black he was greeted with a standing ovation. Yet moments later he was being booed off after a shambolic performance that saw him warbling for just a few shaky seconds.

Devoted fans had queued for hours, expecting to hear him sing his hit single 'Thriller'. Instead he sang four lines from "We Are The World" – and they barely saw him. Even the most fervent fans felt bitterly cheated.

Later in the ceremony, Michael reappeared with a 50-strong choir of young people to sing two further choruses of the same song, but many fans were disappointed and he was forced to issue a statement saying the performance had been the result of a "misunderstanding" with organizers.

For what turned out to be his farewell performance, it was a chaotic affair, a final example of the almost constant misjudgements of his later life and a tragic testimony to the shell that remained of Michael's former genius.

In late December 2006 Michael flew to America, and between Christmas and New Year he gave a short speech at the funeral of one of his best-loved idols, James Brown, in Augusta Georgia.

By early 2007 he had moved again – this time to Las Vegas. He was now planning to stay in the US, said his spokeswoman Raymone Bain. She added that he was also planning a series of events in Japan for the coming March – his latest comeback strategy and an attempt to at least face up to his rapidly escalating debts.

As of March 31, 2007, Michael was said to be worth $236 million. But the reality was that less than $700,000 of his money was in cash.

In Tokyo guests paid $3,400 each in exchange for handshakes, hugs and a photograph at a VIP party. They got on average 45 seconds each.

In May there were reports Michael was being paid £5 million just to show his face at the 25th birthday party of HRH Prince Azim of Brunei in London.

By the end of the year he had come up with an even more lucrative strategy aimed at raising cash and also finally returning himself to his once firmly held status as a musical legend without parallel.

London's new state-of-the-art 02 arena – once the ill-fated Millennium

Dome in Greenwich – had already been the scene of a series of remarkable comebacks and reunions, including rock legends Led Zeppelin and Michael's own contemporary, Prince.

Now, Michael Jackson announced a full-scale return to the stage with a series of 50 concerts at London's O2 Arena.

The King of Pop was returning from self-imposed exile after years of rumours, court cases and interferences that had nothing to do with the music.

"I've been in the entertainment industry since I was six years old," he said. "As Charles Dickens says: 'It's been the best of times and the worst of times,' but I would not change my career.

"While some have made deliberate attempts to hurt me, I take it in my stride because I have a loving family, a strong faith and wonderful friends and fans who have, and continue to support me."

The truth was he was broke.

Neverland was rumoured to be on the market at a cut price $20 million.

Jackson's people denied the reports but the once glittering, opulent estate was falling into ghostly, dilapidated disrepair.

After his acquittal on child molestation charges in July 2005, Michael had decided he simply could not bear to return to his Peter Pan palace. It was no long the place of his dreams, but the stuff of nightmares. It was at the heart of every accusation made against him in court, and its place in his heart as an innocent, childish haven was now stained forever.

Michael's coat had been left hanging on a hook in the hall as if he were a dead man whose grieving staff could not bear to clear away his belongings. But in reality, he was still alive – he had just walked away.

For a while his loyal retainers had stayed on, carrying on the upkeep of the vast house and gardens. But they couldn't continue to work for nothing and when the pay cheques stopped coming they were forced to leave.

By March 2006, Michael was facing a bill of £180,000 in unpaid wages and some of his now unemployed staff faced the prospect of losing their homes.

According to one report, former Neverland chef Rudy Lozano was forced to take a new job running a fast-food stall. Others faced a similar decline in fortunes, having left what was almost a Royal household for menial jobs in gas stations and cafes.

The mammoth maintenance task was taken over by around half-a-dozen of Michael's friends and relatives. But it was simply too big a job.

The once green grass dried to a burned yellow, opulent buildings began to mould and decay, candy-striped canopies were ripped, and the glorious flower-clock that had welcomed new arrivals at the station was overgrown, the clock stopped, numbers missing. Electricity was only on in parts of the house. There was no one to play cowboys and Indians in the Red Indian village; the teepees were faded in the sun

Worse still, there was no longer enough food for the animals, water standing stagnant in their troughs after months of neglect. The exotic animals – once Michael's pride and joy – went to other homes. Michael's one-time companion and even confidante, Bubbles the chimp, was dispatched to a monkey sanctuary and the horses were sent to a children's riding school.

At this time, animal rights activists released shocking pictures apparently showing some creatures languishing in squalid and cramped conditions at the all but deserted estate.

The concerned activists produced photographs that appeared to show animals surrounded by their own faeces.

Other pictures included a giraffe apparently standing in a pool of its own blood while a crocodile swims in a pool little wider than itself. Elephants appeared to be walking among their own excrement, with no sign of keepers.

A spokesman for animal rights' group PETA – People for the Ethical Treatment of Animals – called on Jackson to close down the zoo immediately.

Lisa Wathne said: 'These photos make it clear that the animals are being held in what can only be described as cruel conditions. They are abysmal and little more than holding cells. My message to Michael Jackson would be to close this place down and relocate the animals to an accredited zoo or sanctuary."

PETA sent a letter to the U. S. Department of Agriculture urging it to launch an investigation into conditions.

Martin Dinnes, owner of Dinnes Memorial Veterinary Hospital, is claiming that the singer owes him £51, 800 in unpaid bills. Mr Dinnes's lawyer, Brenton Horner, said that his client had helped Jackson acquire the animals and continues to treat them regularly.

Jackson denied the cruelty claims and US officials insisted an inspection of Neverland had left them satisfied.

A spokesman said: "I'm unaware of any violations of the Animal Welfare Act."

Finally, when Michael failed to pay insurance costs and his debts on the property had risen to $25 million the authorities in Santa Barbara ordered that the building be completely closed down.

After years of financial difficulties, Michael was now facing bankruptcy.

At the same time the legal battle with Sheikh Abdulla bin Hamad Al Khalifa was also reaching a climax. According to the Sheikh, in 2005 he and Jackson had struck a deal whereby he would help revive the pop star's career with songs he had written himself in return for loans to help him get back on his feet

The loans provided would effectively be paid back by way of the music contract they had agreed.

According to Michael there was no valid agreement and the money the Sheikh gave to Michael and his family was "a gift".

The case was finally settled in November 2008 but not before much of it had unravelled in London's High Court in the presence of lawyers for both sides.

Sheikh Abdulla had begun to support Jackson financially in 2005 when it became apparent the singer was in serious financial difficulties.

In November 2008 Michael reportedly became a Muslim and changed his name to Mikeel. But the conversion was never fully confirmed and even when Michael died mystery still surrounded his true religion.

It's possible Michael simply allowed the idea to circulate while he was in Bahrain, but also possible that the conversion happened as reported in a ceremony at a friend's house in Los Angeles, with him sitting on the floor as an imam officiated.

The shahada ceremony is said to have taken place while Jackson was recording an album at the home of Steve Porcaro, a keyboard player who composed 'Human Nature' on the *Thriller* album.

Michael apparently warmed to the idea after friends David Wharnsby, a Canadian songwriter, and Phillip Bubal, a producer began talking to him about their belief.

Michael's brother, Jermaine, now known as Jermaine Friday, said Michael had taken interest in Islam since his own conversion in 1989.

"When I came back from Mecca I got him a lot of books and he asked me lots of things about my religion and I told him that it's peaceful and beautiful," he said.

"He read everything and he was proud of me that I found something that would give me inner strength and peace I think it is most probable that Michael will convert to Islam.

"He could do so much, just like I am trying to do. Michael and I and the word of God, we could do so much."

Sheikh Abdulla set Michael up with a recording studio at Neverland before sending him his compositions, and paid him $35,000 to cover bills at the ranch before advancing $1million at the request of one of his aides.

He then made numerous payments to Michael, including covering his $2.2 million legal bill after the 2005 child abuse trial

He also paid for a recording studio to be built in Bahrain for the two to make music together, while paying Michael's travel and living expenses in the country.

Incredibly he also spent £175,000 flying out a psychiatrist to help him sort his problems out.

In recompense, said his QC Bankum Thanki, the two men entered into a "combined rights" agreement under which Jackson would release songs through their jointly owned record label. An autobiography and a stage play were also planned.

The Sheikh's lawyers claimed that when Jackson went to a recording studio in London to record the track 'I Have This Dream' for victims of Hurricane Katrina, his vocals were not strong enough. When he had failed to turn up at a final recording session, the Sheikh had given up all hope that the record would be released.

Now his lawyers were claiming repayment of the advance, damages for breach of contract and interest. And Michael Jackson faced the appalling prospect of another day appearing in the dock.

At the High Court, Michael's lawyers insisted there was no valid agreement and the Sheikh's case was built on "mistake, misrepresentation and undue influence".

The singer admitted he signed a document which he understood gave him a substantial shareholding in the 2 Seas recording company. But he challenged the Sheikh's description of him as "an experienced businessman" and said he never read the terms of the document and was never advised to take independent legal advice.

He also claimed the Sheikh, exercised "undue influence" over him when he was emotionally exhausted after his highly-publicized criminal trial.

A deal was reached as Michael prepared to board a plane to Heathrow to give evidence.

But by May, Michael was being sued yet again – this time for £29 million by his former publicist and business manager Raymone Bain.

The trained lawyer, who worked for the singer for five years, claimed the singer failed to honour "financial obligations" outlined in a "contractual agreement" between the pair.

The lawsuit, filed at a court in Washington D.C, held that Jackson had agreed to give Bain 10 per cent of the profits from deals she orchestrated, but had failed to do so.

Bain said it was with "deep regret" that she had been forced to take action against someone she greatly "admired and respected".

As legal wrangles followed scandal and his finances continued to collapse, and even his beloved Neverland had become a ghostly tribute to his former glories, it is perhaps not surprising that Michael's always fragile health was rapidly deteriorating too.

The singer had become addicted to Morphine and Demerol while in the throes of his 2005 trial. Now it emerged he was suffering from a rare lung condition, Alpha 1 – which could kill him without an emergency transplant.

A book by writer Ian Halperin claimed the condition had become more acute and developed into emphysema, leaving him barely able to speak, never mind sing, dance or perform on stage.

Without his trademark mask his appearance was "distressing", Halperin claimed. The always slightly built Michael was now skeletal, his skin was badly pockmarked and his nails discoloured.

He used wigs to disguise his thinning grey hair and he was 95 per cent blind in one eye. Whether or not it was poetic licence, Halperin gave him six months to live.

Michael was also facing foreclosure on his once-beloved Neverland. At Christmas 2008, in the depths of personal despair or perhaps through a haze of prescription drugs, he announced he was to sell the ranch and auction off its contents.

By spring 2009, the entire treasure trove – even the wrought iron, gilt-edged gates – had been packaged up ready to for a four-day sale in Los Angeles. It was the first time ever Michael had sold off any personal effects, all that remained of a tarnished dream.

Before the Los Angeles sale, the Neverland auction lots went on show in Ireland – a two-week window in to the once weird and wonderful world of the King of Pop.

Several hundred of the 2000 or so lots were displayed at the Silverware Museum of Style Icons, a purpose-built showroom in Newbridge, Kildare – and the only European venue chosen for the privilege.

The theatrical show attracted in the region of 25,000 visitors.

As Michael Jackson's music played on a loop in the background, crowds walked the lots surveying the sad remnants of a pop empire.

There were gem encrusted jackets and Mickey Mouse diamond brooches. There was the famous white glove he wore for his world-stopping 'Billie Jean' performance, a collection of five crystal gloves seen in his short film, *Ghosts*, and the jacket he wore on the 'Dangerous' tour.

There were statues of imagined children who would never turn against Michael Jackson, barefoot and climbing trees, their heads thrown back in eternal laughter, unable to see what Neverland had become.

There was the rhinestone-covered equestrian hat Michael had worn during the 1981 'Triumph' tour with the Jackson Five, and a pair of rhinestone-embroidered acrylic tube socks worn on the same tour. A sketch of Elvis Presley – his late father-in-law and his idol – drawn by Michael's own hand. Even the star's MTV Moon Man award, was on view.

The Newbridge venue had been chosen by Martin Nolan, the co-owner of Julien's Auctions, the Los Angeles company conducting the sale.

He had been given the difficult job of emptying and cataloguing the contents of Neverland – a job that needed a team of 30 people and took almost 90 days.

The scale of the task overwhelmed Nolan when he first arrived at the run-down estate. In one case a crane had to be hired to dismantle some of the elaborate fairground rides. In another, it cost thousands of dollars to remove a marble fireplace, imported from an Italian castle.

The contents were stored in anonymous warehouses to cut the risk of theft. Together the haul was estimated to be worth around $25 million.

A marble chess set supported by gilt horses on marble pillars had a guide price of up to £2300. The Superman statue was on sale for £1,000. Models of Snow White and the Seven Dwarves were expected to attract bids of at least £700 – even the Magic Kingdom drinks cooler was expected to fetch £850.

There was a price tag of up to £21,000 on a self-playing piano. The carved marble fireplace was set to make over £10,000 and a golf cart featuring an image of Michael as Peter Pan was on for up to £4,200.

Bidders from around the world were expected to battle it out for the memorabilia; David Beckham, Brad Pitt and Angelina Jolie were rumoured to be among those interested in buying the ranch itself.

A couple of Jackson fans from Newcastle even tried to muscle in – hoping to buy it for £15 million and lease it back to their hero on the cheap.

Jackson viewed the sale as "cathartic", Nolan claimed at the time.

"He's closing a chapter in his life and moving on," he said.

The truth was that the sale heaped humiliation upon humiliation for a man reeling from the reality of his debts and tumbling fortunes.

Michael had already defaulted on payments on a £1.3 million second mortgage he had taken out on the Jackson family home at Hayvenhurst, throwing the security of Joseph and Katherine's home into jeopardy. To lose Neverland as well would have been a very bitter pill to swallow.

But in April 2009, just two months before he died, in a classic act of not following through on his declared intentions, Michael suddenly called off the auction of the house and its contents.

Initially he tried to claim that his effects had been effectively stolen by the auction house but auctioneer Darren Julien fought back saying it had cost him £1.4 million to promote the sale.

A US judge threw out Jackson's legal bid to scrap the auction, but he managed to strike a last-minute confidential financial rescue deal with the investment group Fortress and pulled the plug.

It seemed to do little to lift Michael's mood.

Not for the first time, he sacked Grace Rwaramba, the nanny – secretary-lifecoach-nurse who had been with him throughout everything.

Grace not only looked after the children but every aspect of Michael's well-being, fielding his calls, shaving him, trimming his nails, getting him to eat, even pumping his stomach clear of prescription drugs when she had to.

At one point there had been rumours the couple might marry. In fact, over the years Grace was routinely sacked and there were a catalogue of rows over the children.

When Grace, the last normalizing person left in Michael's life and his last remaining stabiliser, left for the last time, Michael's family and friends begged her to go back.

The housekeeper hadn't been paid and the children were being neglected, they told her.

"I was getting calls telling me Michael was in such a bad shape," she remembers. "He wasn't clean. He hadn't shaved. He wasn't eating well. I used to do all this for him and they were trying to get me to go back."

On the day Michael died, the 42-year-old was in London in talks with interviewer Daphne Barak – and about to reveal many of the hidden secrets of the Jackson clan.

CHAPTER 30

Appledore

A month before Michael Jackson's death, the sleepy village of Appledore in Devon installed a huge, 6ft bell on its sea wall, as part of an art installation.

Created by sculptor and musician Marcus Vergette, the bell's clapper is rung by the rise of the water at high tide. As the effect of global warming increases and sea levels rise, the bell will strike more frequently.

When the Jackson family announced its intention to move to Appledore a summer earlier in 2008, the portents were already ringing out for their more famous brother.

As Michael battled his growing money problems in the wake of the 2005 child abuse trial, his mother Katherine, then 78, brothers Tito, Jackie and Jermaine and sisters Janet and La Toya were considering starting a new life in a converted barn in rural England.

So too was Tito's girlfriend Claudia Lynx, Tito's sons and a whole assortment of other family members. The theory was that Michael would soon join them for a new life across the Atlantic.

The whole family was being followed by a fly-on-the-wall Channel 4 documentary crew for a programme called *The Jacksons are Coming*. The premise was that at 54 Tito had fallen in love with the seaside town and wanted to design and build his own glass-panelled home in Appledore.

For five weeks during that waterlogged summer, Tito rented a luxury home, enjoying conversations with the locals over cream teas as he hunted for a potential development site.

Some Appledore villagers were said to be upset at having their quaint town turned into a "celebrity playground" but others liked the incongruity of it all.

As life under the lens in Los Angeles wore thin and the family's financial problems continued, the Jacksons were already aware of Britain's potential as a new sanctuary – and a new market ripe for exploitation.

Britain had welcomed the family with open arms from their childhood, when the Jacksons sold out tour after tour in the UK.

In 2007, Jermaine Jackson had appeared in the C4 *Big Brother* house in the same year Jade Goody had insulted Bollywood icon Shilpa Shetty to enormous ratings. After he came second to Shetty, the resultant exposure sent the Jackson Five into the pop charts for the first time since 1988, with 'I Want You Back' charting at No. 58. His sister La Toya would become a housemate in the same show within a matter of months.

During the sleepy summer months, it was a godsend for the UK media, drawing headlines like 'Blame It On the Scrumpy'.

The Appledore project, filmed by Jane Preston for the production company Studio Lambert, had come at a good time for the cash-strapped Jacksons.

Tito had been reportedly performing with his blues band in tiny venues for as little as £250 a night. Now, *The Jacksons Are Coming* was rumoured to be earning him £50,000 plus a cut of the film sales.

The lure for the broadcaster was not Tito but that the other Jacksons would "drop in" along the way. Ageing mum Katherine, brothers Jackie and Jermaine and sisters Janet and La Toya were all keenly expected and duly came.

But it was Michael – always the financial lure for the rest of his family, always the ultimate prize – whose presence was dangled tantalizingly in front of broadcaster and viewers.

As ever, it appeared the Jackson family's attempts to exploit a financial opportunity had ended in them being exploited themselves. "I'm used to it," Tito told an interviewer afterwards. People try and use you because of the family name, and I just deal with it because I've been dealing with it all my life."

The film ended in a massive showdown, having become less of a celebrity vehicle and more a quirky, often sad, window into the Jacksons' dysfunctional world. Michael's ghost hung over the project, a disembodied voice at the end of the telephone who never set foot in Devon.

Now, the siblings planned a lucrative Jackson 5 comeback tour, but once again their brother was determined to go it alone. Not only did he refuse to join then, but also almost in the same breath he announced his own mammoth £50 million world tour. It was a hard moment for his family to take.

"My brothers and sisters have my full love and support," Michael said in November 2008. "But at this time I have no plans to record or tour with them.

"I am now in the studio developing new and exciting projects that I look forward to sharing with my fans in concert soon."

In truth, Michael had allowed his solo career to run parallel to the Jacksons for several years and, although the others may not have reached the phenomenal heights of his success, they all flourished to some degree in his shadow.

In return, the family usually showed up when they were most needed. At the height of his child molestation trial they famously turned up in a chauffer-driven double-decker bus dressed from top to toe in white in a bizarre show of solidarity.

While Michael's life had been lived out in the spotlight, a series of soaring highs and crashing lows, his brothers and sisters' lives had been more curious than astonishing, but with their own share of family heartbreak.

In 1991, Jermaine had released the single "Word to the Badd"; an attack on Michael after he felt his brother had forced a postponement of work on his album in favour of his own.

He later went on TV to criticize Michael for dangling baby Blanket from the hotel balcony in Berlin, and even at one point was alleged to have planned writing a book that would air his fears that his brother might, after all, be guilty of child abuse.

The proposal was allegedly put forward to publishers after Jackson's arrest on suspicion of child molestation in 2003 – but before his acquittal two years later.

In it, Jermaine was to make the claim: "I don't want to tell you my brother's innocent. I am not certain that he is. He has a thing for young children. Does he really know what he does with these kids?"

Jermaine had married Berry's daughter, Hazel Gordy, on December 15, 1973 in a lavish ceremony that drew comparisons to a royal wedding. But the fairytale marriage had not lasted.

An affair with Maragret Moldanado followed, and the couple were together eight years until Jermaine abruptly married Alejandra Genevieve Oaziaza, the mother of two of Randy Jackson's children.

Their relationship caused further rifts in the family and Jermaine and Alejandra divorced in 2008 after a complicated and bitter legal wrangle.

Jermaine had eight children in all, most of whose names began with the letter J – most notably Jermajesty, whose made-up-name almost seemed to rival Blanket for its utterly comic ring.

He released his first solo album in 1972 while continuing to perform with his brothers. A couple of hit singles followed including 'Tell Me I'm Not Dreaming' and the dance track, 'Dynamite', and he duetted with Whitney Houston and Pia Zadora.

He had 13 top ten singles with the Jackson Five and was inducted into the Rock and Roll Hall of Fame as a member of the band in 1997 – but his career never reached the dizzy heights of his baby brother's.

Jermaine converted to Islam in 1989 and was always one of the mildest-mannered and softly spoken members of the family.

He had a relatively low profile in the UK until his appearance on *Celebrity Big Brother* in 2007. He was caught up in the Shilpa Shetty race row after branding Jade Goody's mother Jackiey Budden "white trash".

By the time his brother died in 2009, Jermaine was in financial straits owing a small fortune to the taxman and sharing his time between his parent's home and his girlfriend's pad in Los Angeles.

La Toya Jackson was the sibling that most looked like Michael – and most sounded like him too when she spoke.

The fifth of the nine children she apparently also shared her little brother's penchant for plastic surgery – though they never admitted it – and it was a standing joke that you never saw them together.

Bookmakers William Hill even once offered 2,000-1 odds on the fact the siblings were really one and the same.

Michael and La Toya spent a great deal of their childhoods together – at first "evangelizing" door to door for the Jehovah's Witnesses and later living together in New York while he was filming *The Wiz*

La Toya later had success with her own album and notably provided the opening scream on her brothers' hit 'This Place hotel'. She also joined the Paris Moulin Rouge and had an acting role on the TV series *Counterstrike*.

But the younger of Michael's sisters was ostracized from the family in 1991 when she published a warts and all biography, *La Toya: Growing up in The Jackson Family*.

The book made scathing attacks on several members of the family and accused her father Joe of physical and verbal abuse.

Even more incredibly, La Toya claimed on the *Donahue Show* in America that her father had sexually molested her sister Janet. Janet was furious and described the claims to *Ebony* magazine as a "bunch of crap" and the claims were eventually retracted.

LaToya later claimed that she had been forced to make the allegations by her former husband and instead described her father as a "disciplinarian" rather than a bully.

La Toya also destroyed the Jackson's clean-cut image by posing naked for *Playboy*, described Michael's marriage to Lisa Marie Presley as a sham and said child sex allegations against Michael were probably true.

In 1996 she made headlines after being savagely beaten with a chair by her husband, Jack Gordon, her former manager. She finally divorced him in 1997 after brother Randy came to her rescue.

Her single 'I Don't Play That' in 2007 failed to chart on any *Billboard* listing, and she was voted 11th worst artist ever by one US magazine.

But in 2009, two years after her brother Jermaine's near success on *Celebrity Big Brother* she was paid £103,000 to take part in the show. The fourth celebrity to be evicted, she was also the first to be cheered by the normally baying crowd that gathers at the studio to greet evictees.

During the show, La Toya appeared to be trying to make amends, and certainly not to cause any more problems among her family.

She claimed her sister Janet hadn't missed an episode of *CBB*, and insisted her famous brothers were intending to reunite on stage.

When she described life in the Big Brother house as similar to growing up with the Jacksons, it seemed as if she were telling the truth.

But when she said that, far from her 1991 allegations, every day of her childhood was " fun, great, great fun," she seemed to be rewriting history.

But it seemed the Jackson trait of cashing in on every opportunity was still present. After the show, she allegedly tried to charge £55,000 for meets and greets with CBB fans.

Just before Michael's death, La Toya – who lives with her boyfriend in Beverley Hills – appeared in the controversial film *Bruno* – the gay fashion writer creation of British comic Sacha Baron Cohen. Her scene shows Cohen's alter ego joking about Michael as they both eat sushi off a naked Mexican immigrant.

On the night of Michael's death, Cohen cut the scene from the premiere – in an unexpected mark of respect. And there were mixed reports over whether it would be restored for the movie's worldwide release in July 2009.

Janet Jackson, on the other hand, always remained loyal to Michael.

At the height of the 2005 child molestation case she wore a T-shirt emblazoned with the words: "I'm a Pervert too" in solidarity.

Latterly she has tried to maintain a dignified silence about the strange eccentricities of her younger brother and in a recent round of interviews any questions about him were banned.

"I've finished talking about Michael," she said. "I've done it all my career."

Janet was the youngest of the Jackson clan and probably closest to Michael – both emotionally and professionally.

The second most successful female artist ever, she was a mere toddler when the Jackson Five were signing their lucrative record deals with Motown.

By the age of seven, however, she was appearing alongside them and at ten she was in the American sitcom *Good Times*.

She was just 16 when she made her first album in 1980 but it was her third, the Platinum-selling album *Control*, the tale of her battle to escape her family, which brought her global success and is still recognized today as a ground-breaking album.

It went to No. 1 on both the pop and R&B charts and six of the nine tracks were released as singles. In 1989 she released 'Rhythm Nation 1814' and the world tour that followed set her on the road to stardom.

The $32 million deal she signed with Virgin in the early 1990s was then the largest in history and the first record she made with them, 'Janet', was a huge success. So much so that she later renegotiated for a reported $80 million.

In 1995 Janet recorded the hit duet 'Scream' with Michael and the accompanying video – set inside a futuristic space pod – became the most expensive ever at a cost of more than $7 million.

Alongside her pop success there were also TV acting roles in shows and sitcoms like *Diff'rnt Strokes* and *Love Boat*. And in 2000 Janet was paid a reported $3 million to appear with Eddie Murphy in *The Nutty professor 11*.

Other albums followed including *The Velvet Rope* and in March 2004 she released *Damita Jo*, a reference to her two middle names.

But her sexually explicit lyrics did not always sit well with prudish middle America and her reputation was further tarnished during an incident at the half time show of that year's Super Bowl, when her top was "accidentally" torn open by Justin Timberlake – exposing her right breast to nearly 100 million viewers.

The resulting controversy was put down to a "wardrobe malfunction" but prompted CBS to cancel its invitation to Janet to perform at that year's Grammy Awards and the row rumbled on for years with the TV network eventually being fined £371,000 for apparently failing to protect the public from that fleeting glimpse of her nipple.

In the run up to Michael's death, Janet's career did suffer some setbacks. In 2008 she was forced to cancel several concerts in North America after being struck down with vertigo and her opening act rapper LL Cool J dropped out as a result of so-called scheduling conflicts. Meanwhile, a tour of Japan planned for 2009 was postponed because of the global financial crisis.

But at the time of Michael's death she was due to reprise her film role of Patricia in the movie *Why Did I Get Married Too* and at the last count was still worth an estimated $150 million.

Closest in age to Michael, Marlon Jackson, just a year older than his brother, was almost removed from the Jackson Five in the early days because his father felt he sang out of tune and missed dance turns. But once the group signed with Motown in 1969 he did sing – and sang co-lead on a number of hits before deciding to leave the group a year after his younger brother.

He was also considered by many to be the best dancer and was inducted into the Rock and Roll Hall of Fame with the rest of the Jackson Five.

He just 19 when he sprang a major surprise on the family while the brothers were performing in Las Vegas in August 1975 – secretly marrying 18-year-old Carol Parker.

He didn't break the news to his family until the following January – and it hit them like a bombshell.

Michael was particularly hurt by Marlon's decision. The pair were really close and yet he felt he had been excluded from what was supposed to be the greatest day of a man's life.

Marlon tried to explain his decision. He had seen the drama caused by his father when his other brothers had married and didn't want that for him or Carol. His other brothers were equally dismayed while Joseph was furious.

The couple had three children and unlike the rest of his brothers, Marlon managed to avoid divorce. While Marlon's own solo career failed to take off, he produced songs for all three of his sisters before embarking on a career outside showbusiness.

He bought a part-share in a cable network, The Black Family Channel, which aimed to open up family friendly TV to the black community and also set up his own Californian real estate company.

Often described as the least dysfunctional of the brothers, he left many open-mouthed when, just months before Michael's death news broke, that he was planning to invest in a "slavery theme park".

The controversial £2.4 billion plan was to build a luxury resort and slavery theme park in the historic port of Badagry, Nigeria – including a building to house Jackson 5 memorabilia.

Critics condemned him for exploiting a painful history.

Others simply wondered at his ability to find the money since there had been reports just months earlier, that he was broke at 51 and stacking shelves in a supermarket.

In the original line up of Jacksons, it had been Jackie, the eldest, who had been considered the most talented and debonair.

Along with Michael he was the lead singer of the group, and later as a solo artist he recorded a self-titled debut in 1973 and 'Be The One' in 1989.

Jackie, like Jermaine, enjoyed the attention of female fans at the start of his music career. But in 1974 he stunned the family by announcing his plans to marry Enid Spann, who at 26 was three years his senior.

They had two children – daughter Brandi and son Siggy, a rapper who performs under the name DealZ – before the couple finally divorced in 1987.

Jackie was unable to take part in the majority of the Jackson's 39 city 'Victory' tour in 1981 thanks to a knee injury but he did appear on the stage for the final show in Los Angeles.

In later years he has managed Siggy's rap career and started an internet clothing business .

These days, Randy Jackson, the former member of Jackson Five is sometimes confused with the more visible Randy Jackson the American Idol judge.

Randy – or "Little Randy" as he was nicknamed" – was the second youngest of the nine and while they were touring he was improving his piano playing back home.

At the age of 16 he wrote one of the group's most successful singles 'Shake Your Body (Down to the Ground)', and remains a consummate musician playing congas, drums, keyboards and guitar as well as singing.

Randy worked with Michael on the *Off The Wall* album and later formed his own band Randy and the Gypsys.

His career was interrupted briefly in 1979-80 when he was badly injured in a car crash, an accident that left him disabled for a time.

The story of what happened later featured in African American magazine *Jet* under the headline: "Randy Jackson Walks Again. Talks About His Future."

He has three grown up children from two different relationships. But in the spring of 2008 one newspaper report in *The New York Post* claimed he was struggling financially – and waiting in vain for a $1.7 million gift from Michael.

Meanwhile, it said, he was earning money doing odd jobs, including fixing cars at a Los Angeles garage.

Tito Jackson, the boy responsible for the family's first foray into music, has always stayed loyal to Michael.

Sometimes described as "the quiet" Jackson or the most serious, he has always been happy to fly the family flag. He was a huge supporter of his younger brother and featured on several TV programmes defending him against critics.

He hosted an acquittal party for Michael after the 2005 court case in which he was cleared and in January 2009 was guest of honour at the Michael Jackson tribute show *Thriller Live!*

Sadly, after Michael died, Tito said he regretted not having spoken to him for a while.

Tito was the first of the brothers to marry, wedding his childhood sweetheart Delores "Dee Dee" Martes when he was just 18. Their marriage lasted 16 years.

Six years after their divorce, Dee Dee was found drowned in a swimming pool. Her new partner Donald James Bohana was eventually convicted of second-degree murder over the death and sentenced to at least 15 years in prison.

Tito was the last of the Jacksons to go solo and reinvented himself as a blues musician, though his appearance on TV in Appledore is thought to have been his biggest earner for some time.

The only Jackson to really get away was Maureen "Rebbie" Jackson – the oldest of the siblings and often described as the "forgotten" Jackson.

Rebbie lives in Las Vegas with her businessman husband Nathaniel Brown. The couple married in 1968 and they have three children, all of whom are singers, and a grandson London Blue.

She later had some success on the R & B chart with Michael producing one of her greatest successes, 'Centipede'. She also sang on the film soundtrack to the film *Free Willy 2*.

"She sings great and she dances like a cat," Michael once said of her. "We're going to see some great stuff from her".

When Michael came out of exile in Bahrain and Ireland it was to Rebbie's city of Las Vegas that he headed.

CHAPTER 31

The Final Curtain

As plans for the 02 concerts finally got underway loyal fans camped outside the arena close by the Thames in London's Greenwich, ready to fight to get their hands on just one of the 750,000 coveted tickets. They sold out within hours.

Michael had often insisted he would not be moonwalking into his dotage. "I don't care about long tours – not the way James Brown or Jackie Wilson did," he said. "They just kept going, killing themselves."

Ironic then that during a press conference in the run up to the 02 tours, he declared: "The moonwalk is coming back. I've still got what it takes. I'll prove everyone wrong.

"This is it. I just went to say these will be my final shows… This will be it. When I say this is it, I mean this is it.

"I love you, I really do. You have to know that. I love you so much, really from the bottom of my heart.

"I'll be performing the songs my fans want to hear. This is the final curtain call and I'll see you in July."

In fact, while a frail and ill Michael must have been cheered by the continuing loyalty of the Jacko faithful he must have also been dreading the return to live performance.

He hadn't enjoyed a tour in years, hating the continuing performances he had been effectively forced into by his brothers, always preferring studio work – interested in ideas and one-off performances like his 'Billie Jean' moment, not the hard slog of long tours that reminded him of his father's early beatings.

Michael was so desperate to improve his fitness for the 50 concerts he hired *Incredible Hulk* star Lou Ferrigno. The actor and muscleman visited Michael's Bel Air mansion three times a week to put the singer through his paces.

The two became firm friends, playing pranks on each other and sharing stories about their difficult childhoods.

Michael even taught Ferrigno the secret of the Moonwalk. "I'm sworn to secrecy though," Ferrigno has said since. "I can't give the secrets away."

In February Michael had undergone a full five-hour medical and passed with flying colours. But he still wanted to be fitter.

"I would go to his house with an inflatable exercise ball and 3lb dumbbells," said Ferrigno. "He did not like the dumbbells. He said he didn't want big shoulders and big muscles like me.

"I laughed and said: 'Michael there's no way you will get big shoulders from 3lb dumb bells.'

"He ate only one meal a day, always in the evening " added Ferrigno. "He'd wake up and not have anything for the whole day and when he did eat it was always vegetarian."

"He wore whatever he put on first thing. So if he put pyjamas on he would wear them for the rest of the day. But it was always with a suit jacket, that was the Michael Jackson signature."

By spring, Michael had already delayed the opening four nights because he said he needed more time for dress rehearsals.

But rumours were now swirling around the delays. There were suggestions whatever preparations Michael was making with Ferrigno he was still a long way from being up to such an exhausting schedule – and that he was actually contracted to appear for only a matter of minutes each night.

A week before his death, the publicist for Jackson's brother Tito hinted at more serious medical problems, saying that Jackson's tour would probably be scrapped. "Michael is not mentally, physically or spiritually ready for these shows. There's something missing in his soul," he said.

His close friend Bryan Michael Stoller said Michael was so frail and exhausted towards the end he wanted to quit singing altogether.

"It was almost as if he'd lost his love for music," Stoller said. "I've never seen him looking so bad."

Then, four days before he died, Michael made a desperate call to a nurse demanding a powerful sedative – but refused to go to hospital.

On June 21 he begged 56-year-old Cherilyn Lee, a Californian nutritionist and registered nurse: "Please come, I need you now," he said. As members of his staff phoned, he complaining one side of his body was overheating and he had odd symptoms.

But Nurse Lee was in a hospital in Florida and unable to help.

"I was afraid. The symptoms were one side of his body felt cold, the other hot.

"That could have meant something going on with the cardiovascular system, but more the nervous system. He needed to go to hospital."

She also told Michael the medication he wanted, Dipriva, which experts say can cause heart attacks if overdosed, was unsafe.

"If you take this you might never wake up," she told him.

Yet the following day his friend and dermatologist, Arnold Klein claimed he was "dancing for the patients in my office".

On the morning before Michael died he performed a three-hour rehearsal – and AEG's chief executive Randy Phillips tells a completely different story.

"He was really excited, super-charged," Phillips said.

On Wednesday June 24, 2009 Phillips claims he was getting goose pimples as he watched Michael throwing himself into dance routines in rehearsals for the O2 shows.

"He was like a kid in the candy store," he said. "He was so up for it.

"I walked him to the car and he put his arm around me and, speaking softly like always, he said to me: 'Do you know what, we are here, we are going to make it. I love you for doing this and now I know I can do it.'

"He was riveting – dancing as well or better than the 20-year-old dancers we surrounded him with," he said. "He looked great.

"I thought this was going to be the greatest live show ever produced. I thought we were home free."

Meanwhile, photographer Kevin Mazur, who captured many of the final rehearsals on film, told the *Daily Mirror* he was blown away by Michael's energy.

"I was thrilled that the magical Michael Jackson was back," he said.

It was never to be. On June 25, 2009, 12-year-old Prince Michael watched in the bedroom of the family's $100,000-a-month rented mansion as his father started "fooling around". It took him a few moments to realize he was actually dying. The young boy was so shocked and traumatized he went into a sort of trance. "The horror of it all is that Prince thought his dad was just being his dad and clowning," said family biographer Stacy Brown. "But it was real, and he watched as they worked on him."

This account doesn't quite fit with what emerges later that the doctor, alone, found Michael unconscious in his bedroom.

At around 1.30pm, Los Angeles time on Thursday June 25, 2009, Michael Jackson was pronounced dead.

CHAPTER 32

Michael Jackson is Dead

"Michael Jackson Dies."

The singer had been dead just 18 minutes when the shock news flashed up on celebrity gossip site TMZ on Thursday June 25 2009.

The Hollywood-based website announced his suspected heart attack within an hour of the call to paramedics, at about 1.30pm local time – 9.30pm in London. It claimed the singer had gone into cardiac arrest, quoting a cardiologist at UCLA hospital as its source. There was absolute chaos as Michael had arrived at the hospital, the web report said. People were screaming, "You've got to save him! You've got to save him!"

TMZ reported his death at 2.44pm. Jackson had only been declared dead by a doctor at 2.26.

Traditional media were slower to respond, and the BBC and Sky News held fire, reporting only "unverified" claims as they desperately tried to get official confirmation of the death.

And while they waited, millions of fans clamoured for news, sending search engines like Google into an unprecedented spin, smothering the Iranian democracy crisis that had previously been flooding social sites like Twitter, into silence.

Among American users alone, 36 out of the top 100 search terms were linked to Jackson's death and his music. For the first 30 minutes Google thought it was under cyber attack.

At 2:51pm the LA Times weighed in with its death report. But it was another two hours – 4.25pm – before US news network CNN declared Michael Jackson was dead following a statement from the coroner's office.

News of Michael's death practically wiped out coverage of all other news stories for two days as the family battled to shield his children, from the flood of media reports about their father – his debts, his drug-use, his failing health.

As anticipation for the memorial built up, hundreds of Jackson fans camped outside the family's Encino home. As the scenes became more and more surreal, one Michael impersonator, Irishman Tommy O'Malley, performed a moonwalk in tribute.

Like many events in Michael Jackson's life, his last hours and moments remain shrouded in mystery.

Two men were certainly with Michael in the final chaotic moments before he died. One was cardiologist Dr Conrad Murray. The other, Michael's bodyguard, Alberto Alberez.

Dr Murray, who lives in a $1m home in La Vegas, is licensed to practice in California, Texas and Nevada. He had been treating Jackson for up to three years and moved into the singer's rented mansion in Los Angeles two weeks before he died after sending out a letter to his patients explaining he was leaving indefinitely.

He was reportedly put on the payroll by concert promoters AEG to support the O2 gigs and Jackson is said to have insisted personally that Dr Murray come to London.

He is the man who found Michael collapsed in his bedroom and began desperate CPR.

According to newspaper reports he retained a firm of lawyers after going "missing" for more than a day after Jackson's death – despite riding in the ambulance with him and speaking to family members at UCLA.

He also failed to sign Michael's death certificate. In the hours after the death, detectives impounded his car with its bags of medicines inside.

After finally tracing him on Saturday June 27, Dr Murray was interviewed for three hours in the presence of his attorney.

But Police said he simply provided useful information as a witness in the case. He was not a suspect.

In an interview with the LA Times Dr Murray's lawyer Edward Chernoff, said Jackson was already unconscious when the doctor entered his bedroom and that he "wasn't breathing."

He described it as "fortuitous" that the doctor went to see Michael on the second floor of his rented home in Holmby Hills, Los Angeles.

"There was no Demerol. No OxyContin," said Mr Chernoff, who was present when Los Angeles police interviewed Dr Murray for three hours.

"He checked for a pulse. There was a weak pulse in his femoral artery. He started administering CPR."

Murray had not "furnished or prescribed" Jackson with Demerol, said Chernoff.

Dr Murray was stunned by the 50 year-old's death, he said. "He was the one who suggested the autopsy to the family while they were still in the hospital. He didn't understand why Michael Jackson had died," he said.

Meanwhile, bodyguard Alberto, described as a stocky 15 stone 5ft 11 "gentle giant", was also quizzed by detectives after the event. It was he who had raced to find a phone – there wasn't one in the bedroom – to call 911.

The full panic-stricken call to emergency services was released to the media a few days later.

Operator: What is the nature of your emergency?

Caller: Yes sir, I need an ambulance as soon as possible, sir.

Operator: OK sir, what's your address?

Caller: Los Angeles, California 90077

Operator: Is it Carolwood?

Caller: Carolwood Drive, yes.

Operator: OK sir, what's the phone number you're calling from?

Caller: Sir, we have a gentleman here that needs help and he's not breathing. He's not breathing and we're trying to pump him, but he's not ...

Operator: OK, OK. How old is he?

Caller: He's 50 years old, sir.

Operator: 50? Ok. He's unconscious? He's not breathing?

Caller: Yes he's not breathing sir.

Operator: Ok and he's not conscious either.

Caller: No, he's not conscious sir.

Operator: Alright, is he on the floor, where's he at right now?

Caller: He's on the bed, sir, he's on the bed.

Operator: OK let's get him on the floor.

Caller: OK.

Operator: OK let's get him down to the floor. I'm going to help you with CPR right now. We're on our way there, we're on our way but I'm going to do as much as I can to help you over the phone. We're already on our way. Did anybody see him?

Caller: Yes we have a personal doctor here with him sir.

Operator: Oh you have a doctor there?

Caller: Yes but he's not responding to anything. He's not responding to CPR or anything.

Operator: Ok, well we're on our way there. If your guy's doing CPR as instructed by a doctor, he has a higher authority than me. Did anybody witness what happened?

Caller: No, just the doctor, sir, the doctor's been the only one here.

Operator: OK so the doctor's seen what happened?

Caller: (aside) Doctor, did you see what happened, sir? (To operator) If you can please ...

Operator: We're on our way, I've dispatched these questions on to our paramedics and they're on their way there sir.

Caller: Thank you sir. He's pumping his chest but he's not responding to anything sir, please.

Operator: Ok, we're on our way, we're less than a mile away. We'll be there shortly.

Caller: Thank you sir, thank you.

Operator: Ok sir, call us back if you need any help.

Caller: Yes sir

Speaking shortly afterwards at the UCLA Medical Centre, a clearly emotional Jermaine Jackson stepped slowly up to a lectern to make a sober announcement.

"My brother, the legendary King of Pop Michael Jackson, passed away on Thursday June 25 2009 at 2.26pm," he said. "It is believed that he suffered cardiac arrest in his home.

"His personal physician, who was with him at the time, attempted to resuscitate my brother as did the paramedics who transported him.

"Upon arriving at the hospital at 1.14pm a team of doctors including emergency physicians and cardiologists attempted to resuscitate him for over an hour.

"They were unsuccessful."

Michael's family had reached the hospital in time to witness the desperate battle to save his life.

His 53 year-old sister La Toya raced to the hospital sobbing hysterically after hearing how he had been stretchered in.

"Why?" she cried

Janet, who had just flown in from a film shoot, sat quietly in the corridor, tears streaming down her face.

Joseph, 79, arriving from Las Vegas, sat with his grief-stricken wife Katherine and they were joined by Rebbie, Jackie, Tito, Marlon and Randy.

Rebbie's singer son Austin, 23, and Hollywood star Elizabeth Taylor also rushed to the hospital along with Jermaine's manager and close friend Frank Dileo, who had once managed Michael too. Michael's nephew Austin was also badly hit. He wept uncontrollably as the man who had been his "mentor" slipped away.

According to those who were there the family walked into the operating room one by one to say a final goodbye to Michael, who looked "at total peace and in harmony".

Broken-hearted Katherine sat by her son's side for hours, clutching his hand and kissing it. She was the last to leave.

As Michael would no doubt have wished, the children Prince Michael, 12, Paris, 11, and seven-year-old Prince Michael II, remained at their rented Bel Air house as the drama at the hospital unfolded, oblivious to the pain that was to come, watching Disney movies as their father's life ebbed away.

But later they too went to see his body – and say farewell. Family friends reported that Paris screamed, "No, no," as she heard the news.

Later, she was said to have told *Oliver!* star and long-time friend of Michael Jackson, Mark Lester: "Mark, don't worry, Daddy has gone to live with the angels now."

When the family finally left the hospital they went back together to the family home at Encino, 20 minutes away, to comfort each other and discuss funeral arrangements.

Later, tears rolling down his cheeks, Jermaine spoke movingly about his brother's premature death, "I wanted to see Michael, I wanted to see my brother, and to see him there lifeless and breathless was very emotional for me," he said.

"But I held myself together because I know he's very much alive – his spirit is. That was just a shell, but I kissed him on his forehead and I hugged him. I felt really empty.

"I said, 'Michael, I'll never leave you. You'll never leave me'."

He said letting Michael's children say a proper goodbye was also "the best thing to do".

"At first I was against it, but what do you say if you don't show them?" Jermaine said.

"It's very tough. We have lost our brother, the world is mourning, we are mourning. It's unreal."

He added: "I've always felt I was his backbone, someone to be there for him. Things he couldn't say, I would say them for him.

"He went too soon. I don't know how people are going to take this, but I wish it was me."

He was a gift from "Allah", he said.

Joseph Jackson described Michael's death as: "one of the darkest moments of our lives".

He said: "Our beloved son, brother and father of three children has gone so unexpectedly, in such a tragic way and much too soon. It leaves us, his family speechless and devastated to a point where communication with the outside world seems almost impossible at times."

Joseph said his son seemed to be in robust health hours before he died as he chatted to fans at the gates of the house he was renting in Los Angeles.

"He was waving to everybody and telling them he loves them and all the fans at the gate.

"A few minutes after Michael was out there, he was dead. Michael was dead before he left the house. I'm suspecting foul play somewhere."

The Black Television Entertainment Awards went ahead in Los Angeles as planned – rearranged at the last minute to pay tribute to Michael.

Joseph, his face crumpled, sat quietly in the audience.

After the ceremony he voiced his fears again: "I have a lot of concerns. I don't like what happened."

Michael's sister Janet made a surprise appearance on stage to speak movingly about the very raw death of her beloved brother.

Her voice breaking, she said: "To you, Michael is an icon. To us, Michael is family and he will forever live in all of our hearts.

"On behalf of my family and myself, thank you for all your love, all of your support. We miss him so much. Thank you so much."

But as the Jacksons rallied together trying to cope with their anguish in the glare of the spotlight, there were also practicalities to deal with: the autopsy, decisions about the children – and the estate.

And outside their front door the rest of the world was going "Jacko" mad.

Outside, as it had for all of Michael's life, chaos and confusion reigned. There was information and misinformation. Fittingly, it was hard to determine where truth ended and fiction began.

Michael had been rehearsing for the 'This is It' tour at the Staples Center – the tour that would have brought him to London's O2 arena.

Footage and photographs were now released showing him apparently as fit and agile as he ever was, sporting a satin suit and skipping and whooping across the stage.

The first autopsy took three hours and confirmed Michael was using some prescription drugs but revealed no initial sign of foul play.

Toxicology and other tests were ordered, though as of writing, those results are not expected for up to six weeks.

Some reports suggested that Michael Jackson was allegedly being injected daily with the synthetic painkilling drug Demerol – a drug he nicknamed his "health tonic".

Other reports suggested that when police conducted two searches of Jackson's house they found the anaesthetic Propofol.

And there were claims that detectives wanted to question his dermatologist Arnold Klein about the drugs he prescribed – as well as his wider entourage of doctors, quacks, alternative therapists and other potential drug suppliers.

Any doctor or member of staff who supplied the singer with his cocktail of powerful painkillers, sedatives or anti-depressants could face prosecution.

Meanwhile in the UK, graphic details from the post-mortem then appeared in the *Sun* newspaper, which described them as "harrowing".

It claimed Michael was a virtual skeleton when he died, with his 5ft 10in frame reduced to 8 stone 10oz and nothing in his stomach except partially dissolved pills.

His hips, thighs and shoulders were riddled with needle marks, allegedly the legacy of injecting painkillers three times a day for years.

His body was marked with surgery scars from up to 13 cosmetic operations, said the paper. He was balding, his hair now just a "peach fuzz" covering his scalp.

He had bruises on his knees and cuts on his shins and his back, while the bridge of his nose had disappeared and its right side partly collapsed.

Michael had been left with three broken ribs as rescuers carried out frantic CPR – and there were four injection marks close to his heart, where attempts had been made to pump adrenaline directly into the organ to restart it.

But within hours the autopsy story was being roundly branded a fake across scores of websites.

The Los Angeles County coroner said: "The report that is being published did not come from this office. I don't know where that information came from or who that information came from. It is not accurate. Some of it is totally false."

Dr Tohme Tohme, spokesman to the King of Pop in his final months said he spoke to Michael on June 23, 2009. The singer kept fit, never ate red meat and didn't drink or take drugs, he said. He was in perfect health.

Godfather to Michael Jackson's three children, Mark Lester also said he refused to believe that painkilling drugs killed the singing superstar.

Michael had promised Mark he would dedicate his opening London show to Mark's daughter Harriet and invite her on stage. He claimed the singer was fit and healthy and looking forward to performing.

He told the *Mail on Sunday*: "Michael was absolutely sharp as a razor, really focused. It's the best I've known him in a long time.

"He said he couldn't wait to get back on stage and that his kids were going to see him perform – it was one of the main reasons for him doing the shows. That's why the whole thing is such a shock. '

"I've never seen him taking anything or any evidence that he was on something.

"I'm an acupuncturist. One time he got a bad spider bite that wasn't healing. I offered to treat it but he said, 'No, I hate needles, hate them.' That's why I find it so bizarre that he was supposed to be having these injections."

Lester said he had spoken to the singer just four days before he died and told of his excitement about his comeback tour.

He added: "We were on the phone for about an hour and all of the kids spoke to him. We were talking about the show. He said he'd been rehearsing and he'd just done a Pop Idol-type competition with the dancers.

"We wanted to sit at the front and he said we could have the whole front row. He was supposed to be coming over next week for rehearsals.

"People have said he was suffering from stage fright but I don't think Michael ever had stage fright. Performing was what charged him.

"He told Harriet he wanted her to come on stage with him when he sang his song 'Dirty Diana'. He was really fired up. I asked him what was in the show but he didn't want to tell us too much. He said, "I want it to be a surprise. You're going to be amazed by it."

"He was so excited. His children had never seen him perform and he wanted them to see Daddy at what Daddy did best."

Lester insisted any talk of Jackson committing suicide was nonsense.

He added: "There's no way he would have done that."

Within days of the death there were dozens of TV specials about Michael. His fans even got themselves into a frenzy over the apparent appearance of his "ghost" in a Live CNN programme, *Inside Neverland*, which featured an interview between interviewer Larry King and Michael's brother Jermaine.

A strange shadow resembling Michael's figure appeared on a wall in the singer's former home and walked across the corridor.

Private photographs and videos began to appear online – pictures and films that depicted Jackson as an ordinary family man. Michael at Neverland for Christmas 1998 or with his family at his Holmby Hills house in Westwood, California in late 2008.

Meanwhile, Michael's body had been released to the Jackson family, who had hired a private pathologist to carry out a second autopsy in response to unanswered questions about the star's death.

CHAPTER 33

Tributes

One by one they fell from the skies. Stars that lost their light the moment they learned of Michael Jackson's death.

It is often easy to forget that celebrities have their heroes too. Legends of stage and screen have idols just like the people who look up to them.

Michael Jackson was a King amongst Kings.

During his life and career he forged personal friendships with some of the most famous, most important people in the world, from Presidents to Princes, actors and actresses.

Those never met him felt just as close. They had his albums, were influenced by his music, his videos, his look.

His talent has inspired so many and his death affected the whole of the showbiz world.

His great friend, screen icon Elizabeth Taylor, was at first too devastated to even discuss his death. They had enjoyed a lifelong friendship.

Dame Elizabeth, said: "My heart... my mind... are broken. I loved Michael with all my soul and I can't imagine life without him. We had so much in common and we had such loving fun together.

"I was packing up my clothes to go to London for his opening when I heard the news. I still can't believe it. I don't want to believe it.

"My life feels so empty. I don't think anyone knew how much we loved each other. The purest most giving love I've known.

"Oh God! I'm going to miss him. I can't yet imagine life without him.

"But I guess with God's help, I'll learn. I keep looking at the photo he gave me which says, 'To my true love Elizabeth, I love you forever'. And, I will love him forever."

President of the United States Barak Obama had been to see Michael Jackson in concert and described him as a "spectacular performer" and "icon" and sent condolences to his grieving family.

And former South African president Nelson Mandela, for whom Jackson sang at his birthday concert in 1998, issued a message through his foundation.

He said: "The Nelson Mandela Foundation regrets the untimely passing of Michael Jackson. His loss will be felt by his fans worldwide."

Venezuelan president Hugo Chavez called Jacko's death "lamentable news" and former South Korean president Kim Dae-jung, who had met the singer, said: "We lost a hero of the world."

Former Philippine first lady Imelda Marcos cried at hearing the news. She had supported him throughout his child molestation charges and subsequent acquittal in 2005.

She said: "Michael enriched our lives, made us happy. The accusations, the persecution, caused him so much mental anguish.

"He was vindicated in court, but the battle took his life. There is probably a lesson here for all of us."

French First Lady Carla Bruni-Sarkozy said: "I don't think anyone can be indifferent to Michael Jackson, my husband included. I will enormously miss his voice, songs and presence in our world."

The news of Jackson's death flew around the world via Twitter and Facebook, news wires flashed and satellite television covered the event live.

Many of the star's showbiz pals in the UK were attending his close friend Elton John's White Tie and Tiara ball, including Justin Timberlake who was performing on stage, unaware of the drama that was unfolding.

When he was told, the 'Cry Me a River' star broke down in tears backstage. He has modelled his career, dance moves and singing style on Jackson.

The 28-year-old, said: "We have lost a genius and a true ambassador of not only pop music but of all music. He has been an inspiration to multiple generations."

Elton performed a special version of 'Candle In The Wind' in Michael's memory as his guests were left shocked and stunned by the news.

Britney Spears, 27, had been planning to watch Michael perform at one of his shows scheduled for the O2 Arena in London.

She said: "We were going to be on tour in Europe at the same time and I was going to fly in to see him. He's been an inspiration throughout my entire life."

Mariah Carey, 39, revealed her shock in a Twitter update along with a host of other stars including P Diddy who had earlier felt so rocked by the blow he telephoned a US talk show to reveal his "heart is hurting."

He added on Twitter: "Michael Jackson made me believe in magic. I will miss him."

Mariah, added: "I am heartbroken. Let us remember him for his unparalleled contribution to the world of music, and the joy he brought to his millions of devoted fans."

British pal Uri Geller, 62, said: "I want to wake up tomorrow and find out this was a horror film."

"I am so very sad and confused with every emotion possible. I am heartbroken for his children, who I know were everything to him, and for his family. This is such a massive loss on so many levels, words fail me"

British singer Lily Allen, 24, wrote on her Twitter site: " No f****** way!" when the news broke while Miley Cyrus, 16, and MC Hammer, 47 also left Twitter tributes.

American superstar actor and singer Jamie Foxx paid a special tribute to Michael at the American BET awards that were redesigned in the wake of his death.

He moonwalked onto the stage wearing a red jacket and white glove while a Jackson 5 medley was played for the crowd.

The organizers of the awards ceremony, held just hours after his death, changed their planned show in a bid to honour the singer. His family attended and his sister Janet Jackson spoke on behalf of the family.

Foxx and R&B star Ne-Yo Jackson sang 'I'll Be There' while photos of the star were showed to the crowd. Foxx said: "No need to be sad. We want to celebrate this black man. We gonna go through all of Michael Jackson."

Guests were invited to share their memories of Jackson and Sean "Diddy" Combs, or Puff Daddy added that Jackson had "knocked down barriers" for black artists like himself, adding: "Love you, Mike."

Beyone Knowles was best female R&B artist and said: "This is for you, Michael Jackson. I have to thank Michael for being my future and hero."

Ne-Yo, said: "He's the man who made it possible for me to be on the stage. I love you and I miss you."

Hip hop star Lil Wayne said: "We all know none of us in this room would be here if it wasn't for Michael Jackson."

Backstage, singer Ciara talked about speaking to Jackson on the phone but the pair never met. She was in tears as she added: "He meant so much to me."

Madonna paid a special tribute to Jackson at the O2 Arena in London where he was due to play his comeback tour with a look-a-like Michael.

A picture of a young Michael was raised on stage while Madonna performed 'Holiday' before the impersonator came on wearing a trademark sequined jacket, white T-shirt, white glove and white socks.

The music switched to 'Wanna Be Starting Something' as the look-a-like performed the trademark moonwalk.

Madonna, said: "Let's give it up for one of the greatest artists the world has ever known.

"I don't know what we could have done together. I could have carried his bags for him, maybe. I don't know what artist wasn't inspired by him.

"To work with him and become friends and hang out with him was exciting for me. I used to love picking his brains about music and stuff.

"I can't stop crying over the sad news. I have always admired Michael Jackson. The world has lost one of the greats but his music will live on forever.

My heart goes out to his three children and other members of his family. God bless."

Jackson was known for the Moonwalk dance but the original moonwalker, Apollo 11 astronaut Buzz Aldrin, sent his condolences via Twitter, adding: "Sad to hear of Michael Jackson. He was a talented performer."

Jarvis Cocker – who famously stormed the stage while Michael Jackson performed at the Brits – claimed Jackson's death was a 'tragedy' insisting his genius was that he "he invented the Moonwalk".

He said: "If there's a tragedy about the whole thing, I would say that if he had kept making records like he did in the mid 1980s up to now, that would have been great. But he didn't do that."

Director Steven Spielberg said: "Just as there will never be another Fred Astaire or Chuck Berry or Elvis Presley, there will never be anyone comparable to Michael Jackson. His talent, his wonderment and his mystery make him a legend."

Sir Paul McCartney said: "It's so sad and shocking. I feel privileged to have hung out and worked with Michael. He was a massively talented boy man with a gentle soul.

"Michael Jackson was my generation's most iconic cultural hero. Courageous, unique and incredibly talented. He'll be missed greatly".

Macca collaborated with Jackson on 'Say Say Say' and 'The Girl Is Mine' in the '80s. But they fell out when the American bought the publishing rights to Lennon and McCartney's songs.

Jackson's first wife Lisa Marie Presley said:" I am so very sad and confused with every emotion possible. I am heartbroken for his children who I know were everything to him and for his family."

Jacko's close friend Lisa Minnelli said:" I'm just devastated. Every Tuesday night we had dinner. I loved him, he was just sensational, a great, great friend and curious, curious man and a dear, dear friend."

Close friend, singer Diana Ross, said:" I can't stop crying, this is too sudden and shocking. I am unable to imagine this. My heart is hurting. I am in prayer for his kids and the family."

Italian legend Sofia Loren, a friend of the singer, said:" There will never be another Michael Jackson. The world has lost an icon."

Berry Gordy, the founder of Motown Records, where Jackson made his name as a child star, said: "Michael was and will remain one of the greatest entertainers that ever lived."

At one of his shows, Stevie Wonder altered the lyrics to his classic hit 'I Just Called to Say I Love You' in tribute to Michael.

California governor Arnold Schwarzenegger said:" Michael was a pop phenomenon who never stopped pushing the envelope of creativity. Though there were serious questions about his personal life, Michael was undoubtedly a great entertainer."

Former Guns N' Roses guitarist Slash played on Jackson's song 'Black Or White' added:" He was a talent from on high."

American Idol judge Paula Abdul said:" We have all lost a legend who has touched each of our lives through his music and showmanship over the past five decades."

Mariah Carey said:" I am heartbroken. I feel blessed to have performed with him several times and to call him my friend. No artist will ever take his place. His star will shine forever."

Cher added:" He was a great singer. He was a genius, like Ray Charles, like Stevie Wonder. They just have this gift."

Oscar-winning film director Martin Scorsese said:" When we worked together on *Bad*, I was in awe of his absolute mastery of movement and of music. It was like watching quicksilver in motion."

Celine Dion said:" I am overwhelmed by this tragedy. It's such a loss. It feels like when Kennedy died."

Bee Gee Robin Gibb said:" If even a small portion of the praise that is bestowed on Michael Jackson now in death was given to him last year, in life, he might well still be with us. One consolation is that he will triumph by his legacy."

Alice Cooper said:" He was the Fred Astaire of his time."

Harrods' owner Mohamed Al Fayed said:" The last I saw him I was really worried about him but he didn't listen to anybody. When I showed him around my store, he liked my statue. So now I'm going to have a Michael Jackson memorial here."

Dame Shirley Bassey said:" I have very fond memories of Michael, with one dinner in particular where he renamed me Lady Goldfinger. He was the King of Pop."

Peter Andre said: "Michael Jackson dying is absolutely devastating. I am totally shocked. MJ, you're the best."

Hollywood couple Ashton Kutcher and Demi Moore posted separate tributes on Twitter. Demi was "greatly saddened" while Ashton wrote: "RIP. Sending love and light to family and friend but especially his kids."

Kutcher's pal, musician John Mayer, who dated former *Friends* star Jennifer Aniston, posted: "Dazed in the studio. A major strand of our cultural DNA has left us. RIP MJ."

Quincy Jones, who produced Jacko's legendary album *Thriller*, said:" I am absolutely devastated at this tragic and unexpected news.

"He had it all – talent, grace, professionalism and dedication. I've lost my little brother today, and part of my soul has gone with him."

R Kelly, said: "I am truly saddened that my mentor, brother and friend will no longer be with us physically. At the same time I feel so blessed to have been touched by his music, his dance, his lyrics and his pure genius."

Singer Beyonce Knowles said:" Michael Jackson made a bigger impact on music than any other artist in the history of music. He will always be the king of pop."

Thousands of fans flocked to websites linked to the star around the world leaving flowers, praying and crying on each other's shoulders.

In London people headed to the Lyric theatre, where the *Thriller* musical is being staged. Producers said last night's show would go ahead as a tribute to the star.

And in Los Angeles hundreds of fans went to the UCLA Hospital while others paid their tributes at his Holmby Hills home and at his former Neverland Ranch – which could now be opened up to the public as early as next year.

On the Walk of Fame in Hollywood, mourners left tributes and lit candles but on the wrong star – that of US radio host Michael Jackson. Jacko's star was covered by a red carpet ahead of the *Bruno* film premiere.

CHAPTER 34

Legacy

After the accolades, the in-fighting soon began. It was now open season on Michael's millions, particularly since the most recent will, a five-page document, appeared to date back to July 2002 – and leave everything to a family trust.

Katherine was granted limited powers over the singer's estate soon after his death.

On the eve of the funeral the family made a court application to postpone naming lawyer John Branca and music executive John McClain as those who would shepherd Jackson's estate into a private trust.

But within days her lawyers were back in court trying to delay the appointment of the two men as temporary administrators of the estate.

In the 2002 will Branca and McClain were named as executors to oversee Jackson's estate. It was estimated at £310 million, but some reports said it was only $100 million more than he owed.

Katherine and those close to her wanted more time to see if a newer will might emerge. But lawyers for the two men argued they needed to be in control of Jackson's diverse financial interests and its liabilities – including refunds due on the series of London concerts that had been immediately cancelled, and several lawsuits.

One allegedly accused Katherine of "a race to the courthouse that is, frankly, improper". In the end, Katherine lost her case.

As Grace Rwaramba prepared to board a plane home from London to comfort Michael's orphaned children she claims she got a call from one of the Jackson family which shocked her to the core.

She told interviewer Daphne Barak: "The relative said, 'Grace, you remember Michael used to hide cash at the house? I'm here. Where can it be?'

"I told them to look in the garbage bags and under the carpets. But can you believe that? They just lost Michael a few hours ago and already one of them is calling me to know where the money is!

"They also told me the children were crying and asking about me. They can't believe their father died. Now the youngest has been saying, 'Why Daddy? God should have taken me not him'."

Michael's children were also at the centre of widespread speculation.

As they struggled to come to terms with their father's death, it was unclear what would happen to them.

For a long time Debbie Rowe had continued to live at the Beverley Hills mansion Jackson had bought her and even studied for degrees in criminal law and psychology but she hated the fame and notoriety and felt hounded by the Paparazzi. Eventually, in 2006, she had sold up – and moved away.

Today, fatter and 50, Rowe breeds horses on a ranch in rundown Palmdale, California. Her boyfriend is a policeman in the murder squad.

After Michael's death there were initial reports that Rowe would fight "tooth and nail" to win custody of her children from Jackson's 79-year-old mother Katherine.

It was also alleged that she would take out a restraining order if necessary to keep Joseph Jackson away from her children.

"They are my flesh and blood," she told a TV reporter. "I'm going after my children."

But within hours she was denying the claims – insisting she would be happy with more access than she had had in recent years.

Meanwhile, Michael's apparently secret love affair with Grace Rwaramba was finally exposed to the public glare. Matt Fiddes, Jackson's former British minder, revealed the singer had a secret long-term girlfriend.

"I'm not going to name who she is but I think the family were aware that there was someone special in his life who he loved and adored and had his ups and downs with."

Michael's personal photographer Ian Barkley, who travelled the world with him for three years, admitted it was Grace.

"Grace loved Michael and he loved her," Ian told the *Sunday Mirror*. "The kids called her Mom. For some time she's been present in his life.

"I imagine she's distraught right now."

Stephen Lachs, a retired judge who oversaw the custody arrangements, said that Debbie had not given up her parental rights. Unless there were strong reasons to the contrary she would be the "presumed parent and guardian" of Michael and Paris. All the indications were she wouldn't take it up.

Michael's 2002 will favoured his 79-year-old mother to care for all three children, and, for their part, the children were said to want to stay with their grandmother.

The will stated that in the event of Katherine being unable to look after them their guardian should be singer Diana Ross.

The family's lawyer Brian Oxman, however, predicted the children's young lives would be the subject of a lengthy legal battle with "all kinds of discussions" taking place about their future.

Jermaine came out in strong support of his mother's custody claim.

"She's up to it," he said. "She'll have someone with her to make sure she's doing the right things. I thought it was a great will, because the children are fine. My mother's the perfect person to be there for them."

On June 28 a Los Angeles Superior Court judge approved Katherine's appointment as temporary guardian pending a hearing the following week. In court documents she claimed the children had no relationship with their biological mother Debbie Rowe.

A guardianship hearing was set for July 13.

Away from the courtroom Michael's star, so tarnished in the later years of his life, was starting to rise again. As practically every radio station around the world played his music, records sales went through the roof. Within days, five of his albums were in the Top 10 and 13 singles had made the Top 40. His hits album, *The Essential*, rose 19 places to become the UK's No1 selling album.

For a few hours it was all about the music again and nothing else, as the world once more thrilled to the sounds of 'Beat It', 'Billie Jean' and 'Thriller', and fans wept to ballads like 'Ben' and 'I'll Be There'.

But all too quickly, the story began to move on.

There was talk of Michael's brothers putting together a tribute tour: The Jackson Four. And of resurrecting the bombshell documentary *Living With Michael Jackson* for a rerun on ITV – possibly without the footage of Gavin Arvizo.

It was suggested that previously unseen footage could now be added to the two-hour film to guarantee even bigger ratings.

An ITV source said: "It feels like now would be a good time to revisit the documentary in some form. The appetite for information on Jacko is bigger than ever.

"It may not have been all positive for Jacko, but it showed him at home and talking about his personal life in a way he had never done before, and now will never be able to do again. People can watch the footage and make up their own minds."

In fact many people around the world already had.

One US congressmen risked a major backlash by putting a two-minute rant on Youtube branding Michael a "pervert" and "a paedophile".

But Michael's fans either never believed the rumours or were not interested in raking over old, uncomfortable ground. They simply wanted somewhere to properly pay their respects to the now deceased King of Pop.

Standing beside Joe Jackson outside the house – by now the site of a makeshift memorial of flowers and balloons – civil rights leader Al Sharpton said the family was being "careful and deliberate on how they plan the celebration of his life."

Early proposals for the body to lie in state in a "fairytale glass coffin" at

Neverland were shelved after authorities rejected the plans.

Instead a private burial was arranged at the Forest Lawn Memorial Park in Glendale, Los Angeles County.

It was announced that on Tuesday July 7, at 10am local time, there would be a star-studded memorial to the singer, a musical extravaganza at the Staples Center – home of the Los Angeles Lakers Basketball team, and the place where Michael until only days earlier had been rehearsing for his 'This Is It!' tour.

Tickets were allocated by lottery and in the ensuing chaos, more than 1.6 million applied. There was outrage at first when the event was limited to those in the US but promoters AEG promptly opened it up worldwide. Fans were outraged when some memorial tickets found their way onto eBay.

A computer-generated programme selected the lucky 8,750, who received two tickets each. A total of 11,000 would be at the event itself, while 9,000 went to the Jackson family for relatives, friends and celebrity guests. A further 6,500 would watch from the Nokia Theatre opposite.

Flights to Los Angeles were packed with travellers, including hundreds of Britons, willing to pay up to £1,000 for an air ticket. Hotels across the city of angels were also full.

The memorial was broadcast live on multiple television networks.

More than one billion people switched on.

Even after Michael's funeral had been held, in Los Angeles, assistant chief coroner Ed Winter said investigators were holding Jackson's brain, or part of it, and that it would be returned to the family for interment after further tests.

The entertainer's death certificate did not give a cause of death. The document, which was filled out with information given by Michael's younger sister La Toya, listed Jackson's occupation as "singer", and his industry as "entertainment".

It stated he had been in the business for 45 years – and gave his race as "black".

The certificate stated that he was to be temporarily interred at the Forest Lawn cemetery where his family held a private memorial service.

Where Michael Jackson's body – or his ashes – would finally end up, is at the time of writing, still unknown.

CHAPTER 35

The Memorial

Draped with red roses, Michael Jackson's coffin was carried by his brothers into the hushed auditorium of the Staples Center, watched by one billion people in countries across the world.

The glittering, gold-trimmed casket was placed at the front of the stage covered in wreaths.

Outside, the Staples Center and at Michael's former homes in Encino and Gary Indiana, as well as in neighbourhoods like Harlem in New York, the pavement was deep in flowers, recalling for British audiences the death of Diana, Princess of Wales.

"The press were hard on her in the same way they were hard on me," Michael had once told the *Daily Mirror*, discussing phone calls shared by two people living in the permanent glare of the flashbulb. "She needed to talk to someone who knew exactly what she was going through.

"She felt hunted in the way I've felt hunted. Trapped, if you like."

The gold commemorative programme for the event featured a tall, healthier Michael from happier times, arms outstretched and his face split by a wide grin.

This was Michael Jackson's final performance, the reunion of which his brothers had dreamed for so many years.

In his memory his remaining brothers, Marlon, Jackie, Jermaine, Randy and Tito – still a Jackson Five – each wore a single white glove glittering with rhinestones.

While Michael had always worn right-hand gloves, his brothers varied the hands, suggesting they had only invested in three pairs of the gloves.

Messages came in from across the globe including from Nelson Mandela and Diana Ross.

"Michael was a giant and a legend in the music industry, and we mourn with millions of fans worldwide," a message from the South African former President, read out by Smokey Robinson, said. "My wife and I, our family and friends, send you our condolences during this time. Be strong."

There followed a dazzling array of musical legends, from Stevie Wonder to Berry Gordy, Lionel Richie to Mariah Carey, but it was Michael's own clear singing voice, his music and his performances up on the big screen that shone the brightest of all.

The other most memorable moment came from his 11-year-old daughter,

Paris-Michael Jackson, in a rare glimpse of a child often shrouded in scarves and facemasks since her birth.

"I just want to say ever since I was born, Daddy has been the best father you can ever imagine," Paris told the audience, thrust briefly into the limelight before disappearing into the waiting arms of her aunt Janet Jackson. "And I just wanted to say I love him so much."

Little Marlon, now a grown, even elderly man, also caused the audience to choke back tears, asking Michael to hug his lost twin brother, Brandon, who had died within 24 hours of his birth.

The public memorial for the King of Pop started a little after 10am, or 6pm for the 6-million-strong British audience. The event followed a private family funeral at Forest Hills Cemetery from which a motorcade of around 20 vehicles escorted the family and loved ones to the Staples Center.

Along the route the highways were filled with a ghostly silence as roads were closed to normal traffic and fans lined the streets to catch a glimpse of Jackson's hearse.

Had he been alive, the scenes Michael Jackson caused everywhere in life would have been frenetic, even frightening. But in death, this was a surprisingly controlled ending with none of the expected drama. There was no pandemonium, no uncontrolled fans, and no breakdown of public order. Just the quiet grief of thousands of Michael Jackson watchers meeting for the last time to honour their hero.

Across America, more than 16 TV networks carried the memorial live but many people preferred to leave their homes and became part of the national event, joining others in Harlem and Times Square in New York, and in the Jackson family birthplace in Gary, Indiana.

In London, many of the fans who had bought tickets to the 'This Is It!' concerts, gathered outside the O2 Arena in Greenwich.

In Los Angeles, the world media took up its positions: Britain's BBC2, France's TF1, Germany's RTL, Australia's Nine and NHK from Japan.

Screens were erected outside the O2 World Arena in Berlin, and on the Champs-Elysees in Paris. Across Sweden's larger cities, daylit squares held candlelit memorials.

At the ceremony, the Civil Rights leader Al Sharpton claimed that Michael Jackson was part of the trajectory that had led to America electing its first black president.

"Those young people grew up from being teenage, comfortable fans of Michael's to being 40 years old and being comfortable to vote for a person of colour to be president of the United States of America. Michael did that."

Before the service began, Barack Obama briefly interrupted a visit to Russia.

"I don't think there's any doubt he was one of the greatest entertainers of our generation, perhaps any generation," he told CNN. "I think, like Elvis, like Sinatra, like the Beatles, he became a core part of our culture.

"There are certain people in our popular culture that just capture people's imaginations. And, in death, they become even larger."

Meanwhile, former US President Bill Clinton paused during an aid mission to Haiti to remember Michael's performance at a 2002 fundraiser for the Democratic Party in New York.

"He basically helped save my party from terrible financial distress," Clinton remembered.

Inside the venue where Michael had made his final live public appearance only days earlier to promote the 'This Is It!' tour, Smokey Robinson began the memorial by reading statements from friends who could not attend the ceremony, including Diana Ross and Nelson Mandela.

After Robinson exited the stage, the arena lights dimmed as the packed arena gave Jackson a moment of silence.

Mariah Carey was the first performer to take to the stage; her tribute a rendition of the Jackson Five hit 'I'll Be There' with Trey Lorenz.

Then, the musician-turned-actress Queen Latifah took the podium to reminisce about the King of Pop, explaining why for young black Americans he had long ago reached iconic status.

"Michael was the biggest star on earth," she said. "He let me know that as an African-American, you could travel the world — there was a world outside of America, other people."

She also recited a new poem by Maya Angelou, black America's Poet Laureate, written about Jackson, titled 'We Had Him'.

"Sing our songs among the stars, and walk our dances across the face of the moon. In the instant we learned that Michael was gone, we know nothing... with the abrupt absence of our treasure, though we are many, each of us is achingly alone, piercingly alone.

"Only when we confess our confusion can we remember that he was a gift to us, and we did have him.

"In Birmingham, Alabama and Birmingham, England, we are missing Michael Jackson. But we do know that we had him."

Lionel Richie chose a religious track for his tribute performing 'Jesus Is Love,' a song he had once sung with the Commodores.

Motown founder Berry Gordy, co-writer of 'I'll Be There,' and Michael's surrogate father figure in the early years of his career, told of Michael's "special" qualities.

The "King of Pop" wasn't a title big enough for Jackson, Gordy said. Michael was the "greatest entertainer who ever lived."

He added: "From the first beat of Billie Jean, I was mesmerised. And when he did his iconic moonwalk, I was shocked. It was magic.

"Michael Jackson went into orbit, and never came down. Though it ended way too soon, Michael's life was beautiful. Sure, there were some sad, sad times, and maybe some questionable decisions on his part, but Michael Jackson accomplished everything he dreamed of."

Berry was one of the only people at the memorial who mentioned Michael's questionable decisions, with the characteristic honesty that Michael respected.

"This is a moment that I wish I didn't live to see come," Stevie Wonder told the crowd. He wove the words "Michael, why didn't you stay?" into the song 'Never Dreamed You'd Leave in Summer'.

After tributes from a heavily pregnant Jennifer Hudson and family friend the Rev. Al Sharpton, John Mayer led the band through a poignant rendition of the *Thriller* ballad 'Human Nature.'

Brooke Shields read a passage from Antoine de Saint-Exupéry's *The Little Prince* and told the crowd that Jackson's favorite song was Charlie Chaplin's 'Smile.'

"To the outside world, Michael was a genius with unchallenged ability," she said. "To the people who were lucky enough to know him personally he was caring and funny, honest, pure, non-jaded and he was a lover of life.

"He cared so deeply for his family and his friends and his fans. He was often referred to as the King. The Michael I knew reminded me more of the Little Prince.

"Michael's sensitivity was even more extraordinary than his talent. His true truth resided in his heart. Michael saw everything with his heart. To his family, his brothers and sisters, Katherine, Jo and to his children, Prince, Paris, Blanket, my prayers are with you.

"Michael's favourite song was not one of the countless masterpieces that he gave us but it was a song that Charlie Chaplin wrote for the movie *Modern Times*, it's called 'Smile' and there's a line in the song that says, "Smile, though your heart is aching".

"Today, although our hearts are aching, we need to look up where he is undoubtedly perched in a crescent moon and we need to smile."

It fell to Jermaine Jackson amongst all his family to take the microphone for the performance of 'Smile.' Somehow, Michael's favourite brother managed to maintain his composure, faltering only towards the end.

Martin Luther King III and Bernice King were followed by Texas Congresswomen Sheila Jackson-Lee, who held up a framed piece of paper – Resolution 600 – a motion she would be putting to the House of Representatives officially recognizing Jackson as a musical icon, legend and humanitarian.

RnB star Usher sang 'Gone Too Soon' from Michael's *Dangerous* album, breaking through the invisible barrier to actually touch the silver coffin of his idol.

After a video of the Jackson Five performing 'Who's Lovin' You,' Smokey Robinson, who originally wrote the song walked proudly to the podium.

"That's my little brother over there," Robinson said, indicating the coffin strewn with flowers. "But he's not really gone. He's going to live forever and ever and ever."

Among the stars at the memorial was an astonished 12-year-old Welsh schoolboy called Shaheen Jafargholi who shook off understandable nerves to sing 'Who's Lovin' You', a Welsh daffodil pinned to his lapel.

Shaheen, from Swansea, made the finals of Britain's Got Talent in 2009 and has since played Jackson in the stage show *Thriller Live*. Michael had apparently seen him perform on YouTube, and he said Michael had been a "huge inspiration".

The performances concluded with 'We Are The World' as had the rehearsals for the 'This Is It!' Concerts at the same venue.

The Jackson family then lifted Michael's casket, with a lone spotlight illuminating the space at the microphone stand he had filled only days earlier, as the Staples Center lights faded.

It was Michael Jackson himself who once said: "If you enter this world knowing you are loved and leave knowing the same.... then everything in between can be dealt with."

Whatever the tragedies and wrongdoings and sad misfortunes of Michael Jackson's life, there was no doubt that he died loved by millions.

POSTSCRIPT 1

Whatever Happened to Bubbles?

The story of Bubbles the Chimp is one of the most enduring in the Michael Jackson mythology. Surreal, insane and poignant by turns, it seems a fitting postscript to the life of a man whose life roller coastered between all three.

Michael Jackson revealed in a television documentary that at one time he planned a special party at Neverland for his best friend, Bubbles. As guests, he invited the most famous animals on the planet, including screen legends Cheetah the Tarzan monkey, and Lassie and Benji the dogs.

Michael rescued three-year-old Bubbles from a cancer research clinic in Texas in 1985. The singer's fascination with animals meant he already kept Llamas and other pets at the family home in California, and his collection was growing more exotic.

Bubbles and Jackson became almost inseparable. Perhaps it was the chimp's obvious dependency on Michael or the fact that chimp loved to play.

Whatever the reasons Michael went everywhere with him, even dressing him identically to himself. The unlikely pair shared hotel suites and even went to restaurants together.

Bubbles had a special crib in the corner of Jackson's bedroom and was claimed to have shared the singer's private bathroom.

Later, staff suggested Bubbles actually wore a nappy and had a tendency to foul on the floor and hurl faeces at the walls of their Neverland Ranch.

Music producer Quincy Jones, said: "The public perception of what Michael is as a human being has been highly exaggerated. Those articles are hard for me to relate to. For instance, Bubbles is more fun than a lot of people I know. I saw Bubbles at a wedding in a tux. He has great table manners."

Bubbles shared a bedroom suite with Jackson in Tokyo during the 'Bad' world tour. Robert Thompson, professor of popular culture at Syracuse United, has written that "This is when the weirdness began to reach mythic proportions."

Bubbles generated almost as many headlines as Jackson himself. Bubbles had his own agent, learned to moonwalk and featured in Michael's video for 'Liberian Girl', as well as attending after show parties during the 'Bad' tour.

He and Michael would spend hours watching movies in the private theatre at the Neverland ranch and eat together at the dining table.

Bubbles joined Jackson and Elizabeth Taylor at the opening of the Whitman-Walker Clinic's Elizabeth Taylor Medical Centre. It was even reported that Bubbles acted as the ring bearer to her eighth wedding, hosted at Neverland.

The story was probably untrue but typical of the "Wacko Jacko" publicity that surrounded Michael and his monkey.

Rumours spread in 1990 that Bubbles had died. Jackson's press agent Lee Solters drily told the press: "When Bubbles heard about his demise he went bananas."

Bubbles was the star of 'Michael's Pets', a range of soft toys based on the animals owned by Jackson and launched in November 1986. The toys consisted of a frog, dog, rabbit, snake, ostrich, giraffe, llama and Bubbles the chimp.

The toys also included a bear wearing sunglasses and a fedora, which was supposed to represent Jackson.

Bob Michaelson designed the toys. He said: "He (Jackson) was very instrumental in designing the toys. He was very instrumental in how it should be programmed... he's got tremendous intuition."

Bubbles was also featured in a sculpture by Jeff Koons that would eventually be sold at auction for a staggering $5.6 million to an anonymous bidder.

Bubbles was said to have his own personal assistant. He sat in on production sessions for *Bad*. He acquired his own fleet of miniature sports cars. His expenses for one tour were rumoured to be $20,000.

But as Bubbles grew older, and almost certainly due to the cruel abnormality of his existence, he began to become aggressive. When Prince Michael II was born Michael Jackson was presented with the hardest decision of his life.

The safety of his son was paramount and so Bubbles was forced to leave Neverland, being relocated to a ranch in Sylmar, California. He then moved to the Centre for Great Apes in Wauchula, Florida where he was living at the time of Michael's death in June 2009.

Animal trainer Bob Dunn, said: "Bubbles is an adult chimp and a wild animal. We don't let him out to play."

Bubbles struggled to cope with his new lifestyle after the pampered luxury and incessant attentions of Neverland but the singer and his family did visit regularly until his death in July 2009.

In an interview after Michael's death, Dunn added: "Bubbles definitely missed him when they parted and will miss him now. Chimpanzees are intelligent. They remember people and stuff. Bubbles and Michael were close friends and playmates. The last time Michael visited, Bubbles definitely recognized and remembered him."

There was speculation that Bubbles was not a lone animal. Media sources suggested there had actually been a number of Bubbleses. It was claimed the chimp had actually died and been replaced.

These rumours appeared to have been unfounded, although Michael did apparently have another chimp in his life.

He introduced a monkey called "Max" to his Neverland home after Bubbles had been removed but he didn't stay long and was moved on to Florida.

In the aftermath of Michael's death in July 2009 there were moves to invite Bubbles to the star's funeral but it was to prove impractical.

Bubbles remained in his new home at the Centre for Great Apes in Wauchula, Florida, a retirement home for former apes that have worked in the entertainment business.

Patti Ragan runs the sanctuary. It is designed as a safe haven for animals that have lived in a "human environment" and are unable to be returned to the wild.

She was staggered by the interest in Bubbles after Jackson's death. Stories were circulating in the media about his reaction to Michael's death including claims he was so stunned he fell out of a tree.

She said: "They've been incredible. Bubbles can teach the public valuable lessons about the need to protect chimpanzees. He came to the sanctuary in better psychological shape than many other entertainment chimps."

Since Michael Jackson's death there have even been rumours that the monkey will release an autobiography.

Bubbles' trainer Bob Dunn incredibly claimed the chimp had been approached about a documentary and a book.

"There's a lot of interest," he said. "Bubbles has led an interesting life."

APPENDIX I

The Declaration of J. Chandler

I, J. Chandler, declare:

1. I am the plaintiff in this lawsuit against Michael Jackson. I was born on January 11, 1980 and am 13 years old. I am currently in the eighth grade. I first met Michael Jackson when I was five years old at a restaurant that my mother, stepfather and I often went to.

2. In about May of 1992 I met Michael Jackson again at my stepfather's car rental business, Rent-a-Wreck. My stepfather called me and told me that Michael Jackson was at Rent-a-Wreck and that I should come down and see him. Later I learned from my stepfather that Michael Jackson's car had broken down and that he was at Rent-a-Wreck to get another car while his was being repaired.

3. After I met Michael Jackson at Rent-a-Wreck he began calling me on the telephone. From about May of 1992 until about February 1993 (when I first spent the weekend with Michael Jackson at Neverland), I received many telephone calls from Michael Jackson. For at least part of this time Michael Jackson was on tour and he would be calling me from various places throughout the world. On occasion these telephone conversations lasted as long as three hours. Michael Jackson and I talked about video games, the Neverland Ranch, water fights, and famous people that he knew.

4. In about February 1993, my mother, Lily (my half-sister), and I went to Neverland at the invitation of Michael Jackson. The three of us stayed together in the guest area. I did not spend the nights with Michael Jackson. This was a weekend trip.

5. I spent the entire weekend with Michael Jackson. We went on jet skis in a small lake he had, saw the animals that he kept at Neverland, played video games and went on golf cart rides. One evening he took Lily and me to Toys 'R Us and we were allowed to get anything we wanted. Although the store was closed, it was opened just for our visit.

6. In late March 1993, my mother, Lily and I went to Las Vegas as a guest of Michael Jackson. We flew on a private airplane. We stayed at a large suite at the Mirage hotel. My mother and Lily shared a bedroom. We stayed at the Mirage hotel about a week. One night Michael Jackson and I watched the Exorcist in Michael Jackson's bedroom. When the movie was over, I was scared. Michael Jackson suggested that I spend the night with him, which I did. Although we slept in the same bed there was no physical contact.

7. From that time, whenever Michael Jackson and I were together, we slept in the same bed. We spent two or three additional nights in the same bed at Las Vegas. Again, there was no physical contact.

8. After I returned from the Las Vegas trip, my friendship with Michael Jackson became much closer. My mother Lily and I started making frequent trips to Neverland. At Neverland I would always sleep in bed with Michael Jackson. I also slept in bed with Michael Jackson at my house and at hotels in New York, Florida and Europe. We were together until our relationship ended in July 1993. During our relationship Michael Jackson had sexual contact with me on many occasions.

9. Physical contact between Michael Jackson and myself increased gradually. The first step was simply Michael Jackson hugging me. The next step was for him to give me a brief kiss on the cheek. He then started kissing me on the lips, first briefly and then for a longer period of time. He would kiss me while we were in bed together.

10. The next step was when Michael Jackson put his tongue in my mouth. I told him I did not like that. Michael Jackson started crying. He said there was nothing wrong with it. He said that just because most people believe something is wrong, doesn't make it so.

11. Michael Jackson told me that another of his young friends would kiss him with an open mouth. Michael Jackson said that I did not love him as much as this other friend.

12. The next step was when Michael Jackson rubbed up against me in bed. The next step was when we would lie on top of each other with erections.

13. During May of 1993, my mother, Lily and I went with Michael Jackson to Monaco in Europe. Michael Jackson and I both had colds so we stayed in the

room all day while my mother and Lily were out. That's when the whole thing really got out of hand. We took a bath together. This was the first time that we had seen each other naked. Michael Jackson named certain of his children friends that masturbated in front of him.

14. Michael Jackson then masturbated in front of me. He told me that when I was ready, he would do it for me. While we were in bed, Michael Jackson put his hand underneath my underpants. He then masturbated me to a climax. After that Michael Jackson masturbated me many times both with his hand and with his mouth.

15. Michael Jackson had me suck one nipple and twist the other nipple while Michael Jackson masturbated. On one occasion when Michael Jackson and I were in bed together Michael Jackson grabbed my buttock and kissed me while he put his tongue in my ear. I told him I didn't like that. Michael Jackson started to cry.

16. Michael Jackson told me that I should not tell anyone what had happened. He said that this was a secret.

17. My relationship with Michael Jackson ended when my father obtained custody of me in July 1993 and I started living permanently at my father's house.

I declare under penalty of perjury that the foregoing is true and correct. Executed on December 28, 1993, at Santa Monica, California.

J. Chandler

APPENDIX II

Michael Jackson, Philanthropist

Michael Jackson's work as a philanthropist rivalled his work as a musician.

As well as setting up his burns unit and establishing the Heal The World Foundation, Jackson wrote 'We Are The World' with Lionel Richie and helped organize the 'United We Stand: What More Can I Give' benefit concert in the wake of September 11.

He often donated items to charity auctions and reportedly planned to donate some profits from London's 'This Is It' tour to charity.

But it was only the tip of the iceberg.

He visited sick children in hospital, funded under-privileged black students and gave money to youngsters caught in disaster zones or hit by HIV Aids.

Jackson's full list of charity work is listed by "Jackson Action", a website which describes itself as a comprehensive source of news on the singer for over a decade.

It begins in January 1984 and lasts for several pages...

January 10, 1984: Michael visits the unit for burn victims at Brotman-Memorial Hospital in Los Angeles.

April 9, 1984: David Smithee, a 14-year-old boy who suffers from cystic fibroses is invited to Michael's home. It was David's last wish to meet Michael. He dies 7 weeks later.

April 14, 1984: Michael equips a 19-bed-unit at Mount Senai New York Medical Center. This center is part of the T.J. Martell-Foundation for leukemia and cancer research.

July 5, 1984: During the Jackson's press conference at Tavern On The Green, Michael announces that his part of the earnings from the 'Victory' tour will be donated to three charitable organizations: The United Negro College Fund, Camp Good Times, and the T.J. Martell-Foundation.

July 14, 1984: After the first concert of the 'Victory' tour, Michael meets 8 terminally ill children backstage.

December 13, 1984: Michael visits the Brotman Memorial Hospital, where he had been treated when he was burned very badly during the producing of a Pepsi commercial. He donates all the money he receives from Pepsi, $1.5 million, to the Michael Jackson Burn Center for Children.

January 28, 1985: Michael and 44 other artists meet to record 'We Are The World', written by Michael and Lionel Ritchie. The proceeds of this record are donated to the starving people in Africa.

1986: Michael set up the "Michael Jackson UNCF Endowed Scholarship Fund". This $1.5 million fund is aimed towards students majoring in performance art and communications, with money given each year to students attending a UNCF member college or university.

February 28, 1986: After having had a heart-transplant, 14-year-old Donna Ashlock from California gets a call from Michael Jackson. He had heard that she is a big fan of his. Michael invites her to his home as soon as she is feeling better. This visit takes place on March 8. Donna stays for dinner and watches a movie together with Michael.

September 13, 1987: Michael supports a campaign against racism. He supports efforts of the NAACP, to fight prejudices against black artists.

October 1987: At the end of his 'Bad' tour, Michael donates some personal items to the UNESCO for a charitable auction. The proceeds will be for the education of children in developing countries.

February 1, 1988: The Song "Man In the Mirror' enters the charts. The proceeds from the sales of this record goes to Camp Ronald McDonald for Good Times, a camp for children who suffer from cancer.

March 1, 1988: At a press conference held by his sponsor Pepsi, Michael presents a $600,000 cheque to the United Negro College Fund.

April 1988: Free tickets are given away for three concerts in Atlanta, Georgia to the Make A Wish Foundation.

May 22, 1988: Michael visits children who suffer from cancer in the Bambini-Gesu Children's Hospital in Rome. He signs autographs and gives away sweets and records to the little patients. He promises a cheque of 100,000 pounds to the hospital.

July 16, 1988: Before a concert at Wembley Stadium Michael meets the Prince of Wales and his wife Diana. He hands over a cheque of £150,000 for the Prince's Trust, and a cheque of £100,000 for the children's hospital at Great Ormond Street.

July 20, 1988: Michael visits terminally ill children at Great Ormond Street Hospital. At a unit for less critical patients he stays a little bit longer and tells a story.

August 29, 1988: At his 30th birthday Michael performs a concert in Leeds, England for the English charity-organization "Give For Life". The goal of this organization is the immunization of children. Michael presents a cheque for £65,000.

December 1988: Michael visits 12-year-old David Rothenburg. His father had five years earlier burned him very badly in an act of revenge against his former wife.

January 1989: The proceeds of one of Michael's shows in Los Angeles are donated to Childhelp USA, the biggest charity-organization against child-abuse. In appreciation of the contributions of Michael, Childhelp of Southern California is founding the "Michael Jackson International Institute for Research On Child Abuse".

January 10, 1989: The 'Bad' tour comes to an end. Under-privileged children are donated tickets for each concert and Michael donates money to hospitals, orphanages and charity-organizations.

February 7, 1989: Michael visits the Cleveland Elementary School in Stockton, California. Some weeks earlier a 25-year-old man had fired at the school's playground. Five children had been killed and 39 had been wounded.

March 5, 1989: Michael invites 200 deprived children of the St. Vincent Institute for handicapped children and of the organization Big Brothers and Big Sisters to the Circus Vargas in Santa Barbara. After this event he invites them to his ranch to introduce his private zoo at his Neverland Ranch to them.

November 13, 1989: The organization "Wishes Granted" helps 4-year-old Darian Pagan, who suffers from leukemia to meet Michael. Michael invites the little boy to a performance of Canadian acrobats.

December 28, 1989: Young Ryan White, who suffers from haemophilia, spends his holidays on Michael's ranch. Ryan had been infected with AIDS by contaminated blood transfusions in 1984. After he was excluded from his school in Kokomo, Ryan fought against the discrimination of AIDS victims.

January 6, 1990: Michael invites 82 abused and neglected children through Childhelp to his Neverland Ranch. There are games, a Barbeque and a movie show provided for them.

July 1990: 45 children from the Project Dream Street, Los Angeles, for children with life-threatening illness are invited to Neverland Valley.

August 18, 1990: Michael invites 130 children of the YMCA summer program of Los Angeles and Santa Barbara to his Neverland Ranch.

May 6, 1991: Michael is invited to the Jane Goodall Charity event. Michael supports her, an advocate of behavioral research concerning chimpanzees in Gombe, Nigeria for more than 30 years.

July 26, 1991: Michael pays a visit to the Youth Sports & Art Foundation in Los Angeles. This Foundation supports families of gang members, and helps dealing with drug-abuse. Michael talks to the kids and presents them with a wide-screen TV set and a financial gift.

December 1991: Michael's office MJJ Productions treats needy families in Los Angeles with more than 200 turkey dinners.

February 1992: Within 11 days Michael covers 30,000 miles in Africa, to visit hospitals, orphanages, schools, churches, and institutions for mentally handicapped children.

February 3, 1992: At a press conference at the New York Radio City Music Hall, Michael announces that he is planning a new world tour, to raise funds for his new Heal The World Foundation. This Foundation will support the fight against AIDS, Juvenile Diabetes and will support the Camp Ronald McDonald and the Make A Wish Foundation.

May 6, 1992: Michael defrays the funeral-expenses for Ramon Sanchez, who was killed during the Los Angeles riots.

June 23, 1992: At a press conference in London, Michael makes an announcement about his Heal The World Foundation.

June 26, 1992: Michael presents the Mayor of Munich, Mr. Kronawitter, with a 40,000 DM-cheque for the needy people of the city.

June 29, 1992: Michael visits the Sophia Children's Hospital in Rotterdam and presents a cheque for £100,000.

July 1992: Michael donated L. 821,477,296 to La Partita del Cuore (The Heart Match) in Rome and donated 120,000 DM to children's charities in Estonia and Latvia.

July 25, 1992: On the occasion of a concert in Dublin, Ireland, Michael announces that he will give £400,000 of the tour earnings to various charities.

July 29, 1992: Michael visits the Queen Elizabeth Children's Hospital in London. To the surprise the children, he brings Mickey Mouse and Minnie Mouse from Euro-Disney to the hospital.

July 31, 1992: On the Eve of his second concert at Wembley Stadium, Michael presents Prince Charles with a cheque of £200,000 for the Prince's Trust.

August 16, 1992: six-year-old Nicholas Killen, who lost his eyesight caused by a life aiding cancer surgery, meets Michael backstage in Leeds, England.

September 1992: Michael donated 1 million pesetas to charity headed by the Queen of Spain.

September 30, 1992: President Iliescu of Romania inaugurates a playground for 500 orphans which Michael has financed. Michael discusses his Heal The World Foundation.

October 1, 1992: Michael chooses a concert in Bucharest, Romania for worldwide television broadcast. Bucharest is a logical choice due to the numerous orphanages the country is known for.

November 24, 1992: At Kennedy Airport in New York, Michael supervises the loading of 43 tons of medication, blankets, and winter clothes destined for Sarajevo. The Heal The World Foundation collaborates with AmeriCares to bring resources totaling $2.1 million to Sarajevo. They will be allocated under the supervision of the United Nations.

December 10, 1992: During a press conference at the American Embassy in Tokyo Michael is presented with a cheque for $100,000 for the Heal The World Foundation by tour Sponsor Pepsi.

December 26, 1992: During a broadcast request for donations to the United Negro College Fund, Michael declares: "Black Colleges and Universities are breeding some of the leading personalities of our time. They are on top in business, justice, science and technologies, politics and religion. I am proud, that the Michael Jackson Scholarship Program enabled more than 200 young men and women to get a qualified education."

January 19, 1993: Michael is one of the stars to perform at the Presidential Inauguration of Bill Clinton. Before he sings "Gone Too Soon" he draws the attention to the plights of the victims of AIDS and mentions his friend Ryan White.

January 26, 1993: At a press conference held at Century Plaza hotel in Century City, Los Angeles, Michael is presented with a $200,000 donation from the National Football League and the Sponsors of the Super Bowl. He gets another $500,000 from the BEST Foundation for his Heal The World Foundation. At this occasion the foundation of "Heal L.A." is officially announced.

February 1993: In association with Sega, launched an initiative to distribute more than $108,000 of computer games and equipment to children's hospitals, children's homes, and children's charities throughout the U.K.

March 1993: The foundation of an independent film company is announced. They will produce family-oriented movies. A part of the earnings will go to the Heal The World Foundation.

March 27, 1993: At a meeting at Century Plaza hotel in Los Angeles, Michael gives a 5-minute speech to 1,200 teachers and politicians.

April 26, 1993: Within his "Heal LA" tour, Michael visits the Watta Health Foundation, and two schools in Los Angeles South Central.

May 5, 1993: Former President Jimmy Carter and Michael, who are chairmen of the "Heal Our Children/Heal The World" initiative, are in Atlanta to promote their "Atlanta Project Immunization Drive".

June 1993: Michael has announced that he will donate $1.25 million for children who have suffered from the riots in Los Angeles.

June 1993: 100 children from the Challengers Boys and Girls Club visit Neverland.

June 10, 1993: Michael promotes the new DARE-program. The purpose of the program is to inform children about the dangers of drug abuse.

June 18, 1993: Michael pays a visit to a hospital in Washington. He spends several hours with the young patients and plays chess with some of them.

August 1993: With Pepsi-Cola Thailand, donated $40,000 to Crown

Princess Maha Chakri Sirindhorn's charity, the Rural School Children and Youth Development Fund, in support of school lunch programs in rural villages in Thailand.

August 1993: In conjunction with Pepsi-Cola International, donated new ambulances to the Contacts One Independent Living Center for Children in Moscow, Russia and the Hospital de Ninos Dr. Ricardo Gutierrez in Buenos Aires, Argentina.

October 1993: Donated $100,000 to the Children's Defense Fund, the Children's Diabetes Foundation, the Atlanta Project, and the Boys and Girl Clubs of Newark, New Jersey.

October 22, 1993: Michael visits a hospital in Santiago.

October 28, 1993: Michael makes it possible for 5000 underprivileged children to visit the Reino Aventura Park, where the whale Keiko ("Free Willy") is living.

November 5, 1993: Michael is guest at a children's party at the Hard Rock Cafe in Mexico City.

December 1993: With the Gorbachev Foundation airlifted 60,000 doses of children's vaccines to Tblisi, Georgia.

December 16, 1993: The Heal The World Foundation UK supports "Operation Christmas Child" delivering toys, sweets, gifts and food to children in former Yugoslavia.

1994: Michael donates $500,000 to Elizabeth Taylor's AIDS Foundation.

January 7, 1994: On the weekend of Martin Luther King Jr.'s birthday, Michael gives a party for more than 100 underprivileged children at his Neverland Ranch.

February 22, 1994: "The Jackson Family Honors" is televised. The earnings of the show are given to their own newly formed charity, "Family Caring for Families".

August 6, 1994: Michael and his wife Lisa Marie are visiting two children's hospitals in Budapest. They distribute toys to the ill children.

1995: Michael wants to free dolphins that have been locked up for years. He believes there should be legal guidelines about the way dolphins have to live in zoos and parks.

March 1995: Little Bela Farkas received a new liver. Michael and Lisa Marie met this 4-year-old boy during their trip to Hungary in 1994. Michael did everything to help Bela, whose only chance to live was getting a new liver. The Heal The World Foundation covered the surgery and the cost for caring.

June 21, 1996: Michael donated a four-times platinum disc of HIStory in aid of the Dunblane appeal at the Royal Oak hotel, Sevenoaks in England.

July 18, 1996: In Soweto, South Africa Michael is laying down a wreath of flowers for youngsters who have been killed during the fights involving Apartheid.

September 1996: The first Sports Festival "Hope" was held for orphans and disadvantaged children. 3000 children and 600 volunteers took part in the Sports Festival and Michael Jackson was a special guest.

September 6, 1996: Michael visits the children's unit of a hospital in Prague.

October 1996: Michael visited a hospital for mentally challenged children in Kaoshiung, Taiwan and offered 2,000 free tickets to the sold out performance in Kaoshiung.

October 1, 1996: Michael donated the proceeds of his Tunisia concert to "The National Solidarity Fund", a charity dedicated to fighting poverty.

October 3, 1996: Michael visits a children's hospital and brings small gifts for the patients during a 'HIStory' tour visit in Amsterdam. A room in the hospital (for parents who want to be with their children) is named after Michael.

November 1, 1996: Michael donates most of the earnings from a HIStory concert in Bombay, India to the poor people of the country.

November 7, 1996: Before his first concert in Auckland, New Zealand, Michael fulfills the wish of little Emely Smith, who is suffering from cancer, who wants to meet Michael.

November 25, 1996: Michael visited the Royal Children's Hospital in Melbourne, delivering toys, signing autographs, and visiting with children.

December 9, 1996: During a 'HIStory' tour visit in Manila, Michael visits a children's hospital. He announces that a part of his concert earnings will be donated to the renovation of the hospital.

January 25, 1997: Michael waved his personal fee for his Bombay appearance and donated $1.1 million to a local charity helping to educate children living in slums.

April 4, 1997: British magazine OK! is publishing exclusive photos of Michael's son Prince. The magazine pays about £1 million for the photos. Michael donates the money to charity.

June 18, 1997: Michael signed the Children in Need book auctioned by the charity UNESCO.

September 1998: Michael meets 5-year-old Aza Woods, who suffers from cancer, at the Hilton hotel in Las Vegas. Michael introduces Aza to the attraction "Star Trek: The Experience" and spends the rest of the afternoon with the little boy. Finally Michael invites Aza to spend some time with him at his Neverland Ranch.

November 16, 1998: Michael arrives in Harare, Zimbabwe. He is a member of the American Delegation invited by the Minister of Defense. The delegation thanks the government of Zimbabwe for helping to keep the peace in this area.

September 4, 1999: Michael presented Nelson Mandela with a cheque for 1,000,000 South African rand for the "Nelson Mandela Children's Fund."

January 22, 2000: During Christmas last year a violent storm ravaged the park of the Chateau de Versailles and destroyed 10,000 trees in the park. The estimated cost for rebuilding the park is around $20 million. Some celebrities are supporting the restoration of the park. French officials are reporting that Michael Jackson is one of them. He was one of the first people to donate money to this cause.

October 28, 2000: Michael painted a plate to be auctioned for the "Carousel of Hope Ball" benefiting childhood diabetes research.

March 6, 2001: Michael donated a black hat, a birthday phone-call and a jacket worn at the Monaco Music Awards in 2000 to the Movie Action for Children auction, an event being given by UNICEF with all proceeds will going to UNICEF's efforts to prevent mother-to-child HIV transmission in Africa.

March 26, 2001: Michael handed out books to young people at a Newark, NJ theater. The event, which helped to launch the Michael Jackson International Book Club, part of his new Heal the Kids charity, aims to promote childhood reading and encourage parents to return to reading bedtime stories.

September 15, 2002: Michael donated 16 exclusively autographed items consisting of CD's, videos and 2 cotton napkins to aid in the support of the victims of a severe flood in Germany. These items were auctioned off for charity and managed to raise 3935 Euro (US$ 3,814).

October 12, 2002: Michael Jackson invited more than 200 Team Vandenberg members, who recently returned from overseas deployments, and their families to his Neverland Ranch. This was to show his appreciation for the sacrifices the military in his community make.

November 19-29, 2002: Michael donated an autographed teddy bear dressed in his likeness to Siegfried & Roy's celebrity teddy bear auction. This auction benefits Opportunity Village, which is a non-profit organization, based in Las Vegas (USA) that enhances the lives of individuals with intellectual disabilities and their families. Michael's autographed teddy bear raised $5,000 for the charity.

November 21, 2002: Michael donated a jacket to The Bambi Charity Event in Berlin, which raised $16,000.

April 25, 2002: Michael Jackson performed at a fundraiser for the Democratic National Committee at the Apollo Theater in Harlem helping to raise nearly $3 million towards voter registration.

June 2003: The Wolf family, who experienced serious damages to their belongings during the flood in Saxony, Germany last August, was invited to Berlin by Michael Jackson when he was at the Bambi Awards. On that occasion Michael invited them to Neverland. In June, they spent three days at Neverland, meeting Michael and his children.

Charity Awards

May 14, 1984: At a ceremony in the White House President Reagan presents Michael an award for special efforts; he is honoured for his participation in a national ad campaign against drunk driving.

January 1989: The "Say Yes To A Youngsters Future" program honours Michael in recognition of his efforts to encourage children to natural sciences and award him with the "National Urban Coalition Artist/Humanitarian Of The Year Award".

March 1989: At the Universal Amphitheater in Universal City, California, Michael receives the Black Radio Special Award for his humanitarian efforts.

September 22, 1989: The Capital Children's Museum awards Michael with the Best Of Washington 1989 Humanitarian Award in recognition of his efforts to raise money for the museum, and for his never-ending support of children.

February 3, 1990: From Japan Michael receives a Role Model Award.

April 5, 1990: During a ceremony, where Michael is awarded as "Entertainer Of The Decade", Michael meets President George Bush, who honors him with the "Point Of Light" award. Michael receives this award for his philanthropic activities. President Bush explains Michael's humanitarian commitments to the press.

September 14, 1990: The Council of the American Scouts honours Michael with the first "Good Scout Humanitarian Award". Michael receives this award for his humanitarian activities by supporting the Make A Wish Foundation, the Prince's Trust, the United Negro College Fund and Childhelp USA.

October 23, 1990: Michael Jackson and Elton John will be the first recipients of the award in memory of Ryan White, which will be handed over in 1991.

May 1, 1992: President George Bush presents Michael with the "Point of Light" award for his continuing support of deprived children. During his stay, Michael visits little Raynal Pope, who had been injured very badly by dogs.

June 3, 1992: The organization "One To One", who is caring for better living conditions of young people, honors Michael with an award for his commitment to deprived youngsters.

July 1993: The American Friends of Hebrew University honours Michael with the Scopus Award 1993.

August 1993: The Jack The Rapper Awards are presented and Michael is honoured with the "Our Children, Our Hope Of Tomorrow" award.

November 17, 1993: Michael rejects the Scopus Award. He was nominated for this award, which was planned to be given him on January 29th, 1994.

April 12, 1994: On occasion of the 2nd Children's Choice Award ceremony at Cit Center in New York, Michael is presented with the "Caring For Kids" award. This award is to honor celebrities, who take time for young people. 100,000 children and young people from 8 to 18 years old gave Michael their vote of confidence. Body Sculpt, a charity organisation that offers drug-prevention programs for young people, sponsors the Children's Choice Awards.

November 2, 1995: Michael receives the award "Diamont of Africa".

March, 30, 1996: The Ark Trust-Foundation, who wants to draw the attention of the public eye on animal's problems, presents the 10th Genesis Award. Michael is presented with the 1995 Doris Day Award. He gets this award for the "Earth Song" video, which draws attention to the plight of the animals.

May 1, 1999: At the Bollywood awards in New York, Michael is presented with an award for his humanitarian activities. The award is signed: "Though he comes from the young American tradition, Michael is the embodiment of an old Indian soul. His actions are an expression of the philosophy of Weda, which asked to work for the people – not for one's own interests."

The Millennium-Issue of the *Guinness Book Of Records* names Michael as the Pop Star who supports the most charity organizations. The following projects are among those supported by him:

AIDS Project L.A.; American Cancer Society; Angel Food; Big Brothers of Greater Los Angeles; BMI Foundation; Brotherhood Crusade; Brothman Burn Center; Camp Ronald McDonald; Childhelp U.S.A.; Children's Institute; InternationalCities and Schools Scholarship Fund; Community Youth Sports & Arts Foundation; Congressional Black Caucus Dakar Foundation; Dreamstreet Kids; Dreams Come True Charity; Elizabeth Taylor Aids Foundation; Heal The World Foundation; Juvenile Diabetes Foundation; Love Match; Make A Wish Foundation; Minority Aids Project Motown Museum; NAACP; National Rainbow Coalition; Rotary Club of Australia; Society of Singers; Starlight Foundation; The Carter Center's Atlanta Project; The Sickle Cell Research Foundation; Transafrica; United Negro College Fund; United Negro College Fund Ladder's of Hope; Volunteers of America; Watts Summer Festival; Wish Granting; YMCA – 28th Street/Crenshaw

ACKNOWLEDGEMENTS

Michael Jackson: The Magic & The Madness, by J. Randy Taraborelli. Updated edition [Pan books, 2004]

Moonwalk by Michael Jackson [Doubleday, 1988]

A *Paper Life* by Tatum O'Neal [Harper Entertainment, 2004]

Unmasked: The Final Years of Michael Jackson by Ian Halperin [Simon, 2009]

The *Daily Mirror* newspaper archive.

The Sunday Mirror archive

The Sunday People archive

Jordie Chandler's affidavit to court 1993 [Appendix I]

"Living with Michael Jackson" – TV interview with Martin Bashir [Granada TV, 2003]

GMTV Interview with Debbie Rowe [ITV, February 2003]

Ebony Magazine, Interview with Michael Jackson [December 2007]

With thanks to the archives of the BBC, CNN and SKY news

Motown 25 TV Special [NBC, May 1983]

Oprah Winfrey Interview [ABC, February 1993]

CBS *60 Minutes* Interview [December, 2003]

Diane Sawyer Interview with Lisa Marie Presley [Prime Time Live, ABC, 2003]

Diane Sawyer Interview with Michael and Lisa Marie [Prime Time Live, ABC, 1995]

Interview with Barbara Walters

South Park episode "The Jeffersons" [Comedy Central, April 2004]

Jesse Jackson Interview with Michael Jackson [Jesse Jackson Radio Show, Premiere Radio Network, March, 2005]

At Large with Geraldo Rivero [Fox News, 2005]

TV Guide Interview: The Once and Future King [Dec, 1999]

James Fletcher is a journalist with more than 17 years' experience with national and regional newspapers working across news and sport. He has written extensively for the *News of the World* (Chief Northern Football Writer), the *Daily Mirror* (Sports Writer, News Reporter and Night News Editor/Deputy Night News Editor) and is a regular correspondent for SKY TV, the BBC, ITV, Radio Five, ITV Granada, BBC North West, MUTV and BBC GMR.

He has spent the past nine years specializing in sport – and football in particular – working closely with Manchester United, Liverpool, Manchester City and the England National Team.

He now works as a PR and media consultant, working most recently with the Professional Footballers Association, *Mirror* Group Newspapers and News International and as an advisor to Trimedia UK, Europe's leading PR and Communications Consultancy. He can be contacted at www.onsidepr.com

Jan Disley is a journalist with more than 25 years' experience on national and regional newspapers. She was a reporter for the *Daily Mirror* for 18 years, writing news and features, and has also written for the *Daily Express* and *The Mail on Sunday*. She now runs her own communications and media training company and lives in Cheshire with her husband and two sons.

Ros Wynne-Jones is an award-winning journalist and novelist, covering subjects as diverse as celebrity interviews to war-reporting in conflict zones from Kosovo and dispatches from the African continent.

The *Daily Mirror's* senior feature writer from January 2001 to December 2008, she has also been a staff writer on the *Independent on Sunday*, *Independent*, *Daily Express* and *Sunday Mirror*.

She is now freelance, and recently published her first novel, *Something is Going to Fall Like Rain*, set in famine-stricken South Sudan. She may be contacted at www.roswynnejones.com